RADICAL INTERPRETATION
IN RELIGION

This landmark interdisciplinary volume presents new methodological options for the study of religion in the twenty-first century. Ten distinguished scholars offer radical interpretations of religious belief and language from a variety of perspectives: anthropology of religion, ritual studies, cognitive psychology, semantics, post-analytic philosophy, history of religions, and philosophy of religion. For the first time, a collection of original essays explores the significance of Donald Davidson's "radical interpretation," Robert Brandom's "inferentialism," and Richard Rorty's pragmatism for issues in the study of religion. Related topics include cultural variations in belief from Madagascar to China, experimental research from cognitive science, and the semantics of myth, metaphor, mana, and manna. *Radical Interpretation in Religion* will be of interest to both general readers and specialists seeking a deeper understanding of new directions in the study of religion.

NANCY K. FRANKENBERRY is John Phillips Professor of Religion at Dartmouth College, Hanover, New Hampshire, USA. She is the author of *Religion and Radical Empiricism* (1987), and co-editor of *Language, Truth, and Religious Belief* (1999) and *Interpreting Neville* (1999).

RADICAL INTERPRETATION
IN RELIGION

EDITED BY

NANCY K. FRANKENBERRY

Dartmouth College, New Hampshire

PUBLISHED BY THE PRESS SYNDICATE OF THE UNIVERSITY OF CAMBRIDGE
The Pitt Building, Trumpington Street, Cambridge, United Kingdom

CAMBRIDGE UNIVERSITY PRESS
The Edinburgh Building, Cambridge CB2 2RU, UK
40 West 20th Street, New York, NY 10011-4211, USA
477 Williamstown Road, Port Melbourne, VIC 3207, Australia
Ruiz de Alarcón 13, 28014 Madrid, Spain
Dock House, The Waterfront, Cape Town 8001, South Africa

http://www.cambridge.org

First published 2002

Printed in the United Kingdom at the University Press, Cambridge

Typeface Baskerville Monotype 11/12.5 pt   *System* LATEX 2ε   [TB]

A catalogue record for this book is available from the British Library

Library of Congress Cataloguing in Publication data

Radical Interpretation in Religion / edited by Nancy K. Frankenberry.
p.   cm.
Includes bibliographical references and index.
ISBN 0 521 81686 6 (hardback), 0 521 01705 X (paperback)
1. Religion – Congresses. I. Frankenberry, Nancy, 1947–
BL21 .R33 2002
200'.7 – dc21   2002024644

ISBN 0 521 81686 6 hardback
ISBN 0 521 01705 X paperback

*This book is dedicated to Hans H. Penner,
in gratitude for his work in the
study of religion*

Contents

vii

PART III   SEMANTICS

Contributors

CATHERINE M. BELL holds the Bernard J. Hanley chair at Santa Clara University where she is Professor of Religious Studies and Director of the Asian Studies Program. In addition to numerous articles and book chapters on methodology in the study of religion and Chinese popular religion, she is the author of *Ritual Theory, Ritual Practice* and *Ritual: Perspectives and Dimensions*. She is currently completing a work on Chinese morality books.

MAURICE BLOCH is Professor of Social Anthropology at the London School of Economics and Research Fellow at the Centre D'épistémologie Appliquée Ecole Polytechnique in Paris. He is the author of a number of books, including *From Blessing to Violence; Prey into Hunter: The Politics of Religious Experience; How We Think They Think: Anthropological Studies in Cognition, Memory and Literacy*, as well as recent articles on "Internal and External Memory" and "La Psychoanalyse au secours de colonialise."

NANCY K. FRANKENBERRY is the John Phillips Professor of Religion at Dartmouth College. The author of *Religion and Radical Empiricism*, she specializes in philosophy of religion, the modern critique of religion, and American religious thought. Her next book is tentatively titled *Pragmatism and the End of Religion*.

TERRY F. GODLOVE Jr. is Professor of Philosophy and Religion at Hofstra University. In addition to articles on Durkheim, Kant, Freud, and leading figures in the study of religion, he is the author of *Religion, Interpretation, and Diversity of Belief: The Framework Model from Kant to Durkheim to Davidson*. He is currently completing a book with the working title *Radical Interpretations of Religion*.

E. THOMAS LAWSON is Professor of Comparative Religions at Western Michigan University. His areas of interest include the Religions of

Africa, particularly Zulu and Yoruba Religion; philosophical issues in theory and method, particularly issues in interpretation and explanation; and cognitive science and its application to the scientific study of religion. In addition to numerous scholarly articles, he is co-author with Robert McCauley of *Rethinking Religion: Connecting Cognition and Culture* and most recently of *Bringing Ritual to Mind: Psychological Foundations of Cultural Forms*.

HANS H. PENNER retired in 2001 as the Kelsey Professor of Religion at Dartmouth College. His areas of expertise include the history of religions, with special interest in the religions of India, as well as methodological and theoretical questions in the academic study of religion. He is the author of many articles on topics in the study of religion, as well as *Impasse and Resolution: A Critique of the Study of Religion*. He is the editor of *Teaching Levi-Strauss* and co-editor of *Language, Truth, and Religious Belief*.

WAYNE L. PROUDFOOT is Professor of Religion at Columbia University. A philosopher of religion, he has published articles on Edwards, James, and Peirce, among others. He is the author of *Religious Experience*, and is working on a book on pragmatism and American religious thought.

RICHARD RORTY is currently Professor of Comparative Literature at Stanford University. He is the author of *Philosophy and the Mirror of Nature*; *Contingency, Irony, and Solidarity*; *Objectivity, Relativism, and Truth*; *Essays on Heidegger and Others*; *Achieving Our Country*; and *Philosophy and Social Hope*. His major papers during the 1990s are collected in *Truth and Progress: Philosophical Papers, Volume 3*, and his recent replies to leading philosophers' assessments of his work appear in *Rorty and His Critics* (ed. Robert Brandom).

JONATHAN Z. SMITH is the Robert O. Anderson Distinguished Service Professor of the Humanities at the University of Chicago. His published works include *Map Is Not Territory: Studies in the History of Religions*; *Imagining Religion*; *To Take Place: Toward Theory in Ritual*; *Drudgery Divine: On the Comparison of Early Christianity and the Religions of Late Antiquity*.

JEFFREY STOUT is Professor of Religion at Princeton University and co-editor of Cambridge Studies in Religion and Critical Thought. He is the author of *Flight from Authority: Religion, Morality, and the Quest for Autonomy* and *Ethics after Babel: The Languages of Morals and Their Discontents*, along with numerous papers on pragmatism, religion in America, and religious ethics. His forthcoming book is tentatively entitled *Democracy and Tradition*.

Preface

To many investigators, the phenomenon of religion resembles a petri dish brimming with exotic specimens and puzzling data. Viewed under the microscope, it teems with strange cultures. Even to a trained eye, the study of religion – its structure, persistence, and meaning – poses acute interpretative challenges. Until recently, students of religion usually regarded their work as a matter of uncovering beliefs and worldviews that issue in religious behavior. Interpretation followed representationalist models, of one kind or another, that presumed realist correspondences between language and reality. Currently, however, both the category of "belief" and the act of "interpretation" are receiving critical attention by scholars in such areas as anthropology of religion, ritual studies, cognitive psychology, semantics, post-analytic philosophy, history of religions, and philosophy of religion. *Radical Interpretation in Religion* consists of original chapters by ten prominent authors in these fields who propose a variety of new ways of interpreting believers.

As a collection, these studies focus primarily on religion as a form of linguistic behavior. In Part I, Terry Godlove, Jeffrey Stout, Richard Rorty, and Wayne Proudfoot assess the pragmatics of radical interpretation in religion in light of recent developments in Anglo-American philosophy of language. The chapters in Part II by Catherine Bell, Thomas Lawson, and Maurice Bloch consider related questions of belief and interpretation in the context of cultural variations from Madagascar to China and experimental research from cognitive science. In Part III, Hans Penner, Nancy Frankenberry, and Jonathan Z. Smith explore the semantics of myth, metaphor, "mana" and "manna."

These interpretations are radical in the broad sense and the narrow sense. In the broad sense, each chapter critiques root assumptions in the study of religion or presents a fundamental thesis or reinterpretation. The theoretical scope thus ranges over issues of belief, meaning, truth, interpretation, explanation, and comparison, and focuses on very basic ways religion has been thought about in the modern and late-modern West. In the narrower sense of radical interpretation, these chapters can be read in light of the philosopher Donald Davidson's theory of "radical interpretation" which concerns the conditions of correct attribution of beliefs and other propositional attitudes. Some chapters present data that pose problems for Davidson's theory, or express doubts about the utility of "belief" as an ethnological or analytic category; other essays illustrate that theory at work in the study of religion, or suggest a specific applica-tion of it; still others trace a dialectic beyond Davidsonian semantics to Robert Brandom's inferentialism and Richard Rorty's pragmatism.

Despite the variety of viewpoints and subject matter, all of the authors share at least three things. First, they move away from older models of representation and symbolic expression to holistic ways of thinking about the interrelations of language, meaning, beliefs, desires, and ac-tion. If beliefs have inferential relations to other beliefs, an interpreter can ascribe a single belief to a person only against the background of a very large number of other beliefs. On this view, the meaning of a sentence depends on the meaning of other sentences in the semantic structure of a language as a whole. Some authors would even general-ize this principle to religions as such, understood as holistic systems in which, to take one example, Hindu caste has meaning only in relation to Buddhist renouncer/ascetic. Second, they stand in a critical tradi-tion that explains religion in entirely naturalist terms, rather than on supernatural or faith-based premises. For the most part, these authors are and have been long-standing critics of the approach to the study of religion that begins and ends with cosmology and the category of "The Sacred." Far from treating religion as a *sui generis* phenomenon, they as-sume that whatever explains how language and minds work generally explains how religious language and religious minds work. Third, all recognize that, to be descriptively adequate, a definition of religion must include "superhuman agent" or one of its variants as characteristic of what makes ritual action or belief specifically "religious" for believers and interpreters alike. All the authors thus adopt an externalist view of the subject matter and do not offer much to please religious realists or those who hanker after Radical Orthodoxy in theology.

In place of theological and metaphysical preoccupations, then, these chapters offer pragmatic, semantic, or cognitive accounts. In theory and in method, *Radical Interpretation in Religion* represents new departures for thinking about religion, myth, and ritual, but makes no pretense to com-prehensiveness or uniformity, still less to a methodology that would rule the increasingly multidisciplinary and multicultural study of religion. It is intended for readers who are seeking a more critical analysis of the current study of religion, rather than of the contemporary significance of "religion." In brief introductions to the three parts of this book, I have tried to indicate the scope of each author's contributions to an understanding of religion's place in culture, or to particular problems in the study of religion. Readers interested in further work by these authors are invited to consult the Select bibliography at the end of this book.

Acknowledgments

This book originated with a select conference on "Radical Interpretation in Religion" in honor of Hans H. Penner, sponsored by Dartmouth College and held in October 2000 at the Minary Center on Squam Lake, New Hampshire. For funding of that memorable event, grateful acknowledgment is made to the following sources at Dartmouth College: The Department of Religion; the James and David T. Orr Fund; the Dickinson Fund; Edward Berger for the Dean of the Faculty office; and Michael Mastanduno for the Dickey Foundation. I also wish to express my appreciation to the following Religion Department colleagues who join in saluting Hans Penner as he concludes thirty-six years of teaching at Dartmouth: Fred Berthold (emeritus), Charles Stinson, Ron Green, Bob Henricks, Kevin Reinhart, Susan Ackerman, Ehud Benor, Amy Hollywood, Ifi Amadiume, Chris Jocks, and Susannah Heschel.

I would like to thank all the contributors not only for writing such stimulating and original chapters, but also for being consistently gracious and cooperative with this project. I am especially grateful to Jeff Stout for excellent suggestions along the way and only sorry I could not take all of his advice.

Thanks are owed to Gail Vernazza for preparation of the manuscript; to Sandy Curtis and Stephanie Nelson for office assistance; to Laura and Drew Hinman for overseeing the weekend at the Minary Center; to Tom West for giving me helpful advice; and to Kevin Taylor at Cambridge University Press for his receptivity to the idea of this book. Gillian Maude was astute in her editing of the manuscript, and Rick Furtak was meticulous in his preparation of the index.

Finally, this book is for Hans. He has been a standard-bearer for the importance of the academic study of religion throughout four decades in which various fideisms and passing gurus have flourished. Although he would be the last to allow that any one of us here has "got it right," all the chapters in this volume address questions that have been central to his career.

PART I

Pragmatics

Introduction

The following chapters by Terry Godlove, Jeffrey Stout, Richard Rorty, and Wayne Proudfoot draw their inspiration from three variations on the theme of holism: Donald Davidson's radical interpretation, Robert Brandom's semantic inferentialism, and the pragmatism of Richard Rorty and William James. Godlove argues that there are good Davidsonian reasons for scholars of religion to keep the category of "belief" even though it has come under suspicion. Stout replies that, when interpreting belief, as well as "meaning," "intention," and "truth," the Sellarsian model developed by Brandom, rather than the Davidsonian model, is a better alternative for pragmatists. Making further explicit use of Brandom, Rorty complements Stout's account by showing why the unavailability of norms to regulate discussion of topics such as "the existence of God" throws it open to cultural politics, and invites the privatization of religious beliefs along the lines of William James's "right to believe." Taking up where Rorty leaves off, Proudfoot contends that beliefs about non-natural, superhuman religious objects, as supposed in William James's "right to believe" argument, cannot qualify for the private sphere where Rortyan pragmatism locates religious beliefs.

Readers will find each of these chapters significant for interpreting believers. Readers not familiar with Davidson's philosophy will gain from Terry Godlove a deft introduction to his most important ideas. Godlove pioneered with the publication in 1989 of the first book-length study of the relevance of Donald Davidson's work to interpretation in religion. Much-cited, his *Religion, Interpretation and Diversity of Belief* situated Davidson in relation to the work of Kant, Durkheim, and advocates of what he criticized as the "framework theory" in religious studies. If divergence of belief in general must be relatively limited, and this carries over into religion, then divergence over religious matters will also be comparatively limited, concerning highly theoretical discourse. Thus religious beliefs may have what Godlove calls an "interpretive priority"

3

for believers, in the sense that their religious beliefs can come to bear on their interpretation of all (or most) of the objects and events in their lives. But religious beliefs should not be thought of as having an epistemic priority, in the sense that they limn the structure of objectivity for their adherents or provide a framework or conceptual scheme through which a believer's "world" or "experience" is organized. Godlove concluded that the Davidsonian arguments against conceptual schemes find a ready target in the flawed framework model of religious belief employed by a wide variety of theorists, including Durkheim, Geertz, Mitchell, Winch, Kaufman, and Horton.

In his chapter here, Godlove introduces the three most useful features of Davidsonian radical interpretation for scholars of religion: "content holism;" the argument from "natural history" or causation; and the argument from an agent's overall rationality. Distilling the methodological import of these principles, he shows how the effort of "saving belief" as an analytic category in the study of religion can benefit from these principles. Is belief in danger of disappearing from scholarly agendas? Godlove finds recent evidence of neglect of this category in the widespread shift of interpretive attention to the materiality of "the body," particularly in ritual studies (compare the chapters by Bell and Penner, this volume.) The current trend tends to decouple bodily movement from the agent's beliefs. This produces an emphasis that Godlove regards, on the one hand, as compatible with the argument from causation that looks to the material circumstances of action and speech, but, on the other hand, as in tension with the principle of holism that weaves together action and belief. If anything is to be understood as "religious," he suggests, the interpreter must see the action through the agent's religious beliefs and desires, that is, "by taking the agent herself to be taking herself to be pursuing religious ends." What exactly is "religious" about religious practices? Godlove's frank, pithy answer to this question delivers a clear and powerful punchline in conclusion.

Jeffrey Stout's chapter provides the first major introduction for a religious studies audience to Robert Brandon's achievement in *Making It Explicit* (1994), a work that philosopher John McDowell rightly hailed as "huge, cohesive, quirky, and brilliant."[1] Stout has been a leading interpreter of Davidson's and Rorty's work, and an astute social critic of the standpoints of Alasdair MacIntyre, Stanley Hauerwas, and others. He has been at the forefront of connecting religious ethics and moral

---

[1] John McDowell, "Brandom on Representation and Inference," *Philosophy and Phenomenological Research* 57:1 (March 1997): 157.

philosophy with social and political criticism. In this chapter, Stout interprets Brandom's work within the ongoing debates about the notion of truth and pragmatism. He performs a Herculean labor of expository analysis that will be helpful to all readers interested in the conversation enjoined by Davidson, Rorty, and Brandom. Arguing for Brandom's approach, Stout calls it "ideally suited for application in religious studies" because, with religion and ethics as our subject matter, "what we are examining . . . is precisely what Brandom's . . . theory directs us to: the inferences being made by the people we are studying, the transitions they make into discourse when they perceive something, and the discursive exits they execute by acting intentionally in the world."

Brandom's work continues a line of thought that derives from Wittgenstein and Wilfrid Sellars and shares much with Davidson. Because Stout's chapter, and the one by Rorty that follows, together offer masterly treatments of Brandom's method, I will not attempt a summary here. Some background may be helpful, however, for readers not acquainted with the new directions in post-analytic philosophy. To put it simply, Brandom has engineered a conceptual sea change by arguing that what distinguishes knowers and agents – that is, creatures that can apply concepts, and have minds – from merely natural beings, is not their possession of some special mental stuff, but rather their capacity to take responsibility for what they do, to undertake commitments, and to have entitlements. Judgments and actions are, in the first instance, things we are in a distinctive sense responsible for. They express commitments we have as participants in the essentially social and linguistic game of giving and asking for reasons. This is not an ontological matter, but a deontological, or normative one. The issues are not descriptive, but prescriptive. Normative statuses (such as being responsible or authoritative, committed or entitled) are, according to Brandom, social statuses. At the bottom of everything we talk about are our social practices, all the way down. Social practices are not the same as conventions, however, and here Stout's work has been most valuable in refuting the parody of pragmatism as appealing only to utility and consensus, as though social practices amount to the same thing as group consensus. Rather, contemporary pragmatists like Stout in the field of religion and ethics seek ideals of objectivity and justification that make explicit those norms that are implicit in practices of inquiry and reason-exchange.

This cluster of fundamental insights has obvious relevance to Stout's ongoing interest in what he has called "the languages of morals and their discontents." In previous work, especially *The Flight From Authority* (1981) and *Ethics After Babel* (1988, 2001), Stout has richly elaborated his own pragmatist accounts of justification as a social practice and of religious ethics without foundations. In his forthcoming work, from which his chapter here is excerpted, he explores the intertwining of democracy and tradition.

The extent to which Richard Rorty's radical interpretations of the history of philosophy are bound up with an original reading of the place of religion in culture has only lately become apparent. His philosophy of religion emerges in such papers as "Religion as Conversation-stopper" (1994), "Religious Faith, Intellectual Responsibility, and Romance" (1997), and "Pragmatism as Romantic Polytheism" (1998). But it also forms the deep background for a larger narrative about the de-divinization of the world and the hope for completing the Enlightenment project of liberation and freedom from authority. As language has replaced God as the *locus* of rationality, the language–world relation has taken over many of the roles formerly played by the God–world relation. In the anti-authoritarian spirit of all Rorty's writing, he presents pragmatism as opposing a whole slew of religious and quasi-religious authorities, including "representations," "reality," and the "way things are." Any non-human altar at which humans are supposed to bow down, worship, and obey only blocks the road to full maturity.

In this account, Donald Davidson's philosophy has often provided an important point of departure for Rorty's critique of the transcending ambitions of epistemology in underwriting word–world relations. Indeed, much of Rorty's vision for a post-metaphysical, post-epistemological, thoroughly naturalistic culture makes vivid applications of Davidson's repudiation of the appearance–reality distinction, the "third dogma of empiricism." He has welcomed Davidson's project especially for showing how we can understand belief, justification, and truth without appeal to representations, and, as an ultimate gesture of respect, he has positioned Davidson within the pragmatist tradition.

Here, in his chapter for this volume, Rorty links Robert Brandom's inferentialism to his own project for the transformation of human culture and extols Brandom's treatment of the "priority of the social" as it bears on the question "does God exist?" This chapter not only amplifies our understanding of Brandom's inferentialism, but also advances Rorty's own agenda of depicting parallels between theism's dependence on an all-powerful god and epistemological realism's dependence on "external" reality. "Cultural Politics and the Question of the Existence of God" thus forms another absorbing chapter in Rorty's philosophy of religion. One effect of both Davidson's and Brandom's philosophies is to dispel the dubious philosophical quests to "get in touch with" reality that replaced earlier religious quests to get in tune with a God.

"Cultural Politics and the Question of the Existence of God" should also dispel any impression that Rorty thinks there is no objective standard against which to measure the correctness of a view except its acceptance. For here he makes plain his view, in agreement with Brandom, that norms can be derived inferentially without being imposed transcendentally, that solidarity based on shared social practices can be shown to be rational, and that we can talk about getting it right with the Trinity, or with numbers, or with a host of other things about which we have discursive practices. What we cannot possibly "get it right" about, however, is "the world" or capital-R Reality, according to Rorty. This is because, whereas there are norms for engaging in snow-talk and Zeus-talk, and even Trinity-talk, there are none at all for engaging in Reality-talk. And that is because, as Brandom explains, there are no "background canonical designators" to such discourse. Davidson's way of making basically the same point has been to say, "A community of minds . . . provides the measure of all things. It makes no sense to question the adequacy of this measure, or to seek a more ultimate standard."[2] In the formulation Rorty gives here, ingeniously comparing the God of monotheists and "consciousness" as used by Cartesians, "the coherence of talk about X does not guarantee the discussability of the existence of X." Rorty concludes by invoking a distinction between private matters, where individuals have a Jamesian "right to believe," and public matters, where individuals have responsibilities to their fellow-citizens.

Wayne Proudfoot's chapter picks up where Richard Rorty leaves off with an analysis of the pragmatist William James and the "right-to-believe" argument. But Proudfoot and Rorty offer two different views of what that argument comes to for interpreting believers today. The juxtaposition of Rorty's and Proudfoot's chapters should alert readers to some of the unresolved questions in the pragmatics of religious belief. What does holism's principle that beliefs have content only by virtue of inferential relations to other beliefs entail? Removing anomalous and idiosyncratic beliefs from the web of justifying reasons while keeping the attribution of intentional states to explain believers' actions (Rorty)? Or

[2] Donald Davidson, "Three Varieties of Knowledge," in A. Phillips Griffiths (ed.), *A. J. Ayer: Memorial Essays* (Cambridge University Press, 1991), 164.

accepting holism as involved in understanding both the attribution of beliefs and their justifications (Proudfoot)?

Proudfoot's chapter pinpoints these questions with the compelling clarity and analytic rigor he has brought to the interpretation of religious experience. His landmark work *Religious Experience* (1985) remains state of the art today. Distinguishing between "descriptive reduction" and "explanatory reduction," Proudfoot has proposed that religious studies scholarship avoid the first and practice the second. In place of descriptive reduction, which fails to identify an emotion, practice, or experience under the description used by the subject, the scholar offers a phenomenological interpretation, which is an empathetic description that can be endorsed by the subject. The scholar's second step is explanatory description, which augments the description with comparative or contextual information and selected theoretical perspectives. It turns description into data, and subjects the data to interpretive translation and recontextualization. According to Proudfoot, "failure to distinguish between these two kinds of reduction leads to the claim that any account of religious emotions, practices, or experience must be restricted to the perspective of the subject," a move that precludes legitimate explanatory reduction and becomes an illegitimate protective strategy.[3]

What sort of explanation of religious experience is best? In "Religious Belief and Naturalism," Proudfoot endorses a naturalistic explanation that is congruent with the holism favored by other authors in this volume. His chapter also relates to what others in this volume refer to as "superhuman agents" and regard as the defining characteristic of "religion." Advancing an overall interpretation of William James's philosophy of religion, he shows that the belief James takes as paradigmatically religious has to do with the conviction that there is a moral order in the universe, one that is shaped to human thought and action, but is not put there by humans. The *more* that James thinks is continuous with the higher part of the self is therefore also independent of human thought and action, operating in the cosmos outside of, and in addition to, human life. But this belief in a *more*, Proudfoot says forthrightly, is no longer plausible. Therefore, such a descriptive characterization makes trouble for Richard Rorty's original reading of James's religious belief as a private option, and complicates Rorty's own attempt to redescribe the place of religion in culture as a free and personal preference for beliefs that stand

---

[3] Wayne Proudfoot, *Religious Experience* (Berkeley: University of California Press, 1985), 196–97.

in no justification to others, because they are private and not public.[4] For what could be more pertinent to the public realm than naturalistic accounts that seek to explain an "unseen moral order" as a product of human thought and action, that is, of the very "social practices" whose normative force Rorty highlights in his chapter on Brandom?

To avoid descriptive reduction in the study of religion, scholars need to employ a *definition* of the religious hypothesis that makes reference to something superhuman. At the same time, if they believe that anything shaped to the moral life of humans is something that we humans have put there ourselves, the *explanatory* account of religion will inquire into entirely natural causes. The radical feature of "Religious Belief and Naturalism" is Proudfoot's compelling way of making these two interpretive strategies consistent. Readers should also attend to his carefully formulated reflections on the nature of holism, of explanation, and of religion's origin in imagination.

[4] Richard Rorty, *Philosophy and the Mirror of Nature* (Princeton University Press, 1979); *Essays on Heidegger and Others* (Cambridge University Press, 1991); *Objectivity, Relativism, And Truth: Philosophical Papers* (Cambridge University Press, 1991); "Religion as Conversation-stopper," in *Common Knowledge* 3:1 (Spring 1994): 1–6, reprint, Rorty, *Philosophy and Social Hope*; "Religious Faith, Intellectual Responsibility, and Romance," in Ruth Ann Putnam (ed.), *The Cambridge Companion to William James* (Cambridge, 1997), 84–102; "Pragmatism as Romantic Polytheism," in Morris Dickstein (ed.), *The Revival of Pragmatism: New Essays on Social Thought, Law, and Culture* (Durham and London: Duke University Press, 1998), 21–36.

Saving belief: on the new materialism in religious studies

Terry F. Godlove Jr.

One of my enduring memories from graduate school has me shuffling back and forth between the classrooms of Mircea Eliade and Donald Davidson, trying to shake a persistent headache. Though at the time I did not see it in such antiseptic terms, it now strikes me that the general problem was the status of attributions of intentionality – in particular, how to respect the dizzying variety of religious belief and practice while recognizing that all of us share pretty much the same set of concepts. I was impressed early on with the principle of charity – roughly, the claim that broad agreement is a condition of linguistic interpretation, a claim defended, of course, by Davidson, but also endorsed in one form or another by Baker, Bennett, Brandom, Dennett, Putnam, Rorty, and Stich, to name only a few. While it is not a miracle cure, I have continued to urge its application to several of the outstanding methodological problems that arise in the study of religion, including reductionism, rationality, and relativism.

In the present chapter I turn from application to defense. I would like to address an important doubt about just how relevant this literature is to religious studies, after all. When the above-named philosophers discuss action and interpretation, they typically give pride of place to the notion of belief.[1] Indeed, belief seems to lie at the heart of many other propositional attitudes, and at the heart of our ordinary notion of intentional action – action undertaken on the basis of what we believe. But it seems clear that belief, as an analytical category, is now

---

[1] For example, in Davidson's work the primacy of belief is already clear in the 1974 essay, "Thought and Talk" (in *Inquiries into Truth and Interpretation* [New York and Oxford, 1984], 156–57): "Belief is central to all kinds of thought. If someone is glad that, or notices that, or remembers that, the gun is loaded, then he must believe that the gun is loaded. Even to wonder whether the gun is loaded, or to speculate on the possibility that the gun is loaded, requires the belief, for example, that a gun is a weapon, that it is a more or less enduring physical object, and so on."

coming under unprecedented criticism from scholars of religion. Not that religious belief itself is in decline – there seems no immediate danger on that score – but the concept of belief itself does appear to be in some difficulty; conversely, materiality and embodiment seem everywhere to be in ascension. The view seems to be – to paraphrase Putnam on linguistic meaning – religion just ain't in the head.

As symptoms of this decline, consider two recent, much cited works in theory and method: Talal Asad's *Genealogies of Religion: Disciplines and Reasons of Power in Christianity and Islam*, and Mark Taylor's *Critical Terms for Religious Studies*. Asad argues against the belief-oriented conception of religion, tracing it to "the triumphant rise of modern science, modern production, and the modern state."[2] Fully half of the essays in Taylor's collection take explicit aim at belief and urge its subordination, and even, as we will see, its elimination. Donald Lopez's contribution to the Taylor anthology is representative. Admonishing the stragglers, Lopez writes that, "even though we may no longer believe in God, we still believe in belief."[3]

Again, here is the doubt: the approach to interpretation I favor emphasizes the centrality of belief in understanding human speech and action. At the same time, an increasing number of scholars of religion are apparently finding the notion of belief of decreasing analytical value. The invited conclusion is that any point of view that puts so much weight on belief may not be so helpful after all. My response will come in three steps. First, I give an informal account of Davidson's work on interpretation, and say where I think its value lies for the study of religion. Second, I examine the apparent decline of belief in the recent literature. And, third, I suggest why it is important for scholars of religion to clarify the role of belief in their inquiries. I am confining myself to Davidson for reasons of space. Even so, my portrayals of his positions will be skeletal; for those already familiar with his work, they will serve as reminders of his arguments; for those new to the literature, they may serve as an impetus for further inquiry. While I do want to recommend a broadly Davidsonian picture of interpretation, I have reserved detailed treatment for my main interests, namely, the decline of belief and its associated costs.

[2] Talal Asad, *Genealogies of Religion: Disciplines and Reasons of Power in Christianity and Islam* (Baltimore: Johns Hopkins University Press, 1993), 39.
[3] Donald S. Lopez, Jr., "Belief," in Mark Taylor (ed.), *Critical Terms for Religious Studies* (University of Chicago Press, 1998), 34.

RADICAL INTERPRETATION AND RELIGIOUS STUDIES: THREE POINTS OF CONTACT

The argument from content holism

Davidson is, of course, well known for his argument against "the very idea" of a conceptual framework. I think of the argument [4] as proceeding from two compelling premises: first, that concepts and thoughts with propositional content stand in logical and evidential relations to one another. And, second, that, in order competently to use a given concept, a speaker must have a fair idea of what these relations are. Taken together, they place a rather striking constraint on interpretation. If, for example, I am going to interpret someone as asserting that the cow is sacred, I am going to have to presume that he appreciates many of these or closely related truths: that a cow is a living animal, self-locomoting, has four legs, must eat to live, and so on without definite limit. For Quinean reasons, apparently we should not insist or rely upon any particular list of agreed upon facts. Still, when suitably generalized, the doctrine of content holism suggests that we must share vastly more belief than not with anyone whose words and actions we are able to interpret than that over which we differ. [5]

In what sense might the argument from content holism be important for those who study religion? I am glad to be counted with those who think that it requires us to reject the notion that religions are alternative conceptual frameworks. [6] That is, that it requires us to reject conceptual relativism in any interesting form – say, the imputation of divergent epistemes, paradigms, worldviews, forms of life, radical alterity, and so on. Since scholars of religion study whole systems of belief and practice, the argument from content holism stands as a particularly apt reminder that, however systematic they may be, our objects of study by necessity emerge from a much broader background of agreement and commonality.

[4] More precisely, the argument which occupies Davidson in the second half of "On the Very Idea of a Conceptual Scheme," *Inquiries*, 195ff.

[5] For a defense of this and the other results listed in this section, see my *Religion, Interpretation and Diversity of Belief: The Framework Model from Kant to Durkheim to Davidson* (New York: Cambridge University Press, 1989), ch. 4.

[6] See, for example, Nancy Frankenberry, "Religion as a 'Mobile Army of Metaphors,'" this volume; Warren Frisina, "Response to J. Wesley Robbins' 'Donald Davidson and Religious Belief,'" *American Journal of Theology and Philosophy* 17:2 (May 1996): 157–66; Hans Penner, "Why Does Semantics Matter to the Study of Religion?" *Method and Theory in the Study of Religion* 7:3 (1995): 221–49; J. Wesley Robbins, "Donald Davidson and Religious Belief," *American Journal of Theology and Philosophy* 17:2 (May 1996): 141–56; Kevin Schilbrack, "The Study of Religious Belief after Davidson," *Method and Theory in the Study of Religion* 14:2 (2002).

The argument from natural history

Davidson has argued in many places that many basic sentences must be true at those times when they are held true by a speaker.[7] This is not much more than the simple thought that "we catch on to the interpretation of basic predicates in ostensive situations . . . We notice the situations in which [a speaker] is prompted to accede or dissent from a sentence of the form 'This is red,' 'That is a dog,' etc." Davidson calls this, "a form of 'charity' in the sense that it assumes meanings are more or less the same when relevant verbal behaviors are the same."[8] With this assumption in place, causation stands ready to do the heavy interpretive lifting. As Davidson puts it: "We must, in the plainest and methodologically most basic cases, take the objects of a belief to be the causes of that belief. And what we, as interpreters, must take them to be is what they in fact are. Communication begins where causes converge: your utterance means what mine does if belief in its truth is systematically caused by the same events and objects."[9]

How is the argument from natural history relevant to religious studies? While it is too large a claim to defend here, I believe the argument plays a crucial, if subterranean role in many of our most important theories of twentieth-century religion – many of them can be viewed as turning on the "natural history" of religious belief and practice. For example, Durkheim found so strong a causal connection between the periodic gathering of society and the generation of religious belief that he suggested we try thinking of belief in God as belief in society.[10] A vexed question for Weber's *Protestant Ethic* is whether, by the late nineteenth century, the meaning-giving connections between the material world and such abstract, dogmatic theological constructions as predestination had, over time, been weakened to the point where they could no longer influence the piety of ordinary people.[11] Again, Wittgenstein faults Frazer for not taking seriously the causal context of the rain dance; they dance,

[7] See, for example, Donald Davidson, "Radical Interpretation Interpreted," in James E. Tomberlin (ed.), *Philosophical Perspectives 8: Logic and Language* (Atascadero, CA: Ridgeview Publishing Co., 1994), 123.

[8] Davidson, "Reply to Kirk Ludwig," in Ursula M. Zeglen (ed.), *Donald Davidson: Truth, Meaning and Knowledge* (New York: Routledge, 1999), 46–47.

[9] Davidson, "A Coherence Theory of Truth and Knowledge," in Ernest Lepore (ed.), *Truth and Interpretation: Perspectives on the Philosophy of Donald Davidson* (New York: Blackwell, 1986), 317–18.

[10] I explore this claim in greater detail in, "Interpretation, Reductionism, and Belief in God," *The Journal of Religion* 69:2 (1989): 184–98.

[11] For discussion, see Friedrich W. Graf, "The German Theological Sources and Protestant Church Politics," in H. Lehmann and G. Roth (eds.), *Weber's Protestant Ethic: Origins, Evidence, Contexts* (NY: Cambridge University Press, 1993), 38ff.

after all, only in the rainy season.[12] Finally, the contemporary work of Colleen McDannell and others in the "material culture" approach to religion vividly illustrates Davidson's point that causal ties between speech, action, and ordinary objects in the world must be methodologically basic.[13]

The argument from rationality

Davidson has long claimed that we must find a large degree of rationality on the part of speakers and agents. We can see how rationality fits into Davidson's picture by reflecting on his theory of meaning. Davidson is sometimes read as identifying meaning with truth-conditions, as holding that meanings just are truth-conditions. But this is misleading. Rather, I think Davidson is best understood as favoring an account that delivers or specifies meanings in truth-conditional form. To get at Davidson's views on meaning, we have to focus on, as Michael Williams has recently put it, "those constraints that particular theories of meaning must satisfy in order to be judged acceptable"[14] – just the sort of thing we have been doing in these last few pages. Having said what we can about the methodology of interpretation, there is no more to be said about what meaning is. It is not as though linguistic meaning could somehow serve as an independent standard by which to judge the adequacy of our best interpretive practices. Rather, meaning is constituted partly out of the logical and evidential relationships that interpreters take speakers to appreciate, and partly out of the causal regularities they observe between occasions of use and the world (and by much else). Meanings are not independently existing entities – rather, they are the distillate of the interpreter's attempt to make sense of speakers.[15]

---

[12] Ludwig Wittgenstein, *Remarks on Frazer's Golden Bough*, ed. Rush Rhees, trans. A. C. Miles, rev. Rhees (Atlantic Highlands, NJ: Humanities Press, Inc, 1979), 12.

[13] Colleen McDannell, *Material Christianity: Religion and Popular Culture in America* (New Haven: Yale University Press, 1995). Of course I am not claiming that McDannell has Davidson's point in mind, only that the comparison is suggestive: "The material world of landscapes, tools, buildings, household goods, clothing, and art is not neutral and passive; people interact with the material world thus permitting it to communicate specific messages," 2. J. Wesley Robbins discusses the importance of the argument from natural history for philosophy of religion in, "Donald Davidson and Religious Belief," 152–54.

[14] Michael Williams, "Meaning and Deflationary Truth," *Journal of Philosophy* 96:11 (November 1999): 553. I have benefited in this and the next paragraph from Williams' illuminating discussion.

[15] For a recent statement of these views, see, Davidson, "Interpretation: Hard in Theory, Easy in Practice," in Mario de Caro (ed.), *Interpretations and Causes: New Perspectives on Donald Davidson's Philosophy* (Dordrecht: Kluwer, 1999), 31–44.

On this picture, rationality is best viewed as governing the process of constituting meaning. As interpreters, we have no choice but to see speakers as appreciating the basic logical and evidential relationships between their sentences and concepts. And we must see them as accurately cognizing the basic features of their environment. Further, as Dagfinn Føllesdal has emphasized, these achievements must exhibit a fair degree of consistency, both at a time and over time. For lack of space, I am leaving out of my breathless discussion of belief and meaning the rationality of action and normative value – except to note, again with Føllesdal, that this street is emphatically two-way: "observation of action is a major source of evidence for our hypotheses concerning a person's beliefs and values, since both beliefs and values play a role in explaining a person's actions."[16] But then, just as it guarantees a large degree of logical, evidential, and perceptual competence, our basic methodology of interpretation guarantees the underlying rationality of action and value. Rationality, in this encompassing sense, is constitutive of the human sciences, including the study of religion.

Of course, this is not to say that our theories of religion (or of any circumscribed sphere of human activity) must always or ever portray religious speech and practices as rationally motivated. Indeed, much good work in recent years in religious studies appeals to non-rational causes, ones that are not at the same time reasons. Among many others, one thinks of Catherine Bell on ritual,[17] of Stuart Guthrie on anthropomorphism,[18] Walter Burkert on evolutionary biology.[19] But Davidson's writings remind us that these theories – *if they are to be theories of speakers and agents* – must be set within a context of encompassing rationality.

In practice, the fun and the frustration in coming to understand one another involves mixing and matching considerations of holism, natural history, rationality of value, together with all we know of our interlocutor's capacities and education, together with our knowledge of the causal, non-rational forces we suspect are in play – group pressure, raging hormones, wishful thinking, and cognitive predispositions might all be candidates. This process of mixing and matching Davidson calls radical

---

[16] Dagfinn Føllesdal, "Intentionality and Rationality," in J. Margolis, M. Krausz, and R. M. Burian (eds.), *Rationality, Relativism and the Human Sciences* (Boston: Martinus Nijhoff, 1986), 117.

[17] Catherine Bell, *Ritual Theory, Ritual Practice* (NY: Oxford University Press, 1992), esp. ch. 8, challenging "the traditional association of belief and ritual," 183ff.

[18] Stewart Elliot Guthrie, *Faces in the Clouds: A New Theory of Religion* (New York: Oxford University Press, 1993).

[19] Walter Burkert, *Creation of the Sacred: Tracks of Biology in Early Religions* (Cambridge, MA: Harvard University Press, 1996).

interpretation, and it is one of his most characteristic theses that: "All understanding of the speech of another involves radical interpretation."[20] When we consider the great theoretical contributions to the study of religion, we see illustrated there the universality that Davidson alleges. Hume, Marx, Durkheim, Weber, Freud, James, Wittgenstein, Douglas – they, among many others, are constantly checking what religious persons are doing against what they are saying; constantly triangulating speech against non-verbal action against causes from the environment. We may, if we like, view all this theorizing as exercises in the hypothetico-deductive method, so long as we recognize that they are unavoidably constrained by the requirements of holism, natural history and rationality.[21]

So much for my survey of the Davidsonian landscape. I turn now to Lopez's and others' doubts about belief.

DOUBTS ABOUT BELIEF

In his contribution to the Taylor anthology, Jonathan Z. Smith documents fundamental shifts in our understanding of the term "religion." For my purposes, the crucial move comes in the time of Zwingli and Calvin when the prevailing tendency to see religion in terms of ritual gave way to, as Smith puts it, "belief as the defining characteristic."[22]

---

[20] Davidson, "Radical Interpretation," in *Inquiries into Truth and Interpretation*, 125. Much ink has been spilt over the question of whether Davidson's radical interpreter is too far removed from real interpretation, domestic or foreign, to be of any real interest (see, for example, Jerry Fodor and Ernest LePore, "Is Radical Interpretation Possible?" in Tomberlin (ed.), *Philosophical Perspectives 8*, 101–19). Davidson has replied that his concern has never been to show how people do understand one another but how they could (see, for example, "Radical Interpretation Interpreted," 125). But this response undersells the point, for, abstracted from the context of real interpretation, we would then not know what to make of Davidson's bedrock claim that, "all understanding of the speech of another involves radical interpretation." The point that needs to be kept in view, I think, is that the arguments supporting the unavoidable constraints on interpretation discussed in this section (holism, the matching up of distal causes, and the appreciation of basic logical and evidential relationships) do not depend on the possibility of an interpreter understanding a speaker "from scratch." In fact, radical interpretation (in the sense of interpretation of an unknown language without the aid of a bilingual or a dictionary) might be impossible – and yet the arguments for the unavoidable constraints on real interpretation still stand. The thought-project of radical interpretation (still taken as interpretation "from scratch") depends on the constraints having already been established; its own possibility neither supports nor undermines them. Thus, I take Davidson's slogan, "all understanding of the speech of another involves radical interpretation," as no more than fallout from the basic claim that the constraints on real or imagined interpretation that interest him are, indeed, unavoidable.

[21] As far as I am aware, the most sustained, detailed discussion of this triangulation as applied to cases of real interpretation is James Hopkins, "Wittgenstein, Davidson and Radical Interpretation," in Lewis Edwin Hahn (ed.), *The Philosophy of Donald Davidson* (Chicago: Open Court, 1999), 255–85.

[22] Jonathan Z. Smith, "Religion, Religions, Religious," in Mark Taylor (ed.), *Critical Terms for Religious Studies* (University of Chicago Press, 2000), 271.

It is useful, I think, to view the contemporary offensive against belief as continuous with older attempts to take back the ground lost to the Protestant Reformation.

I detect two lines of attack. First, there is the common, modest claim that our efforts to understand religious activity are seldom aided by insight into the agent's doctrinal commitment. Second, and more ambitious, is the claim by Lopez and others that the very notion of belief is methodologically suspect.

The modest thesis – the explanatory impotence of doctrinal commitment – is, of course, very old. It is prosecuted with unmatched subtlety and comedic flair in Hume's *Natural History of Religion* (1757), where Hume records the reaction of the unfortunate soul to whom the priest has accidentally given a wood chip rather than a wafer: "I wish . . . you had not given me God the Father: He is so hard and tough there is no swallowing him."[23] We may imagine that this fellow's doctrinal commitment meets the minimal Quinean test of empirical significance – when prompted by the doctors of theology he has learned to assent in such a way as to promote smooth conversation, successful prediction of verbal and non-verbal reactions, and so on. But his understanding is so limited as not to impinge on any other behavior outside that of prompted assent. Freud picks up this theme in his early essay, "Obsessive Actions and Religious Practices" (1907). It is no use, says Freud, trying to see the ordinary person's religious practices in light of his or her supposed doctrinal beliefs, because it is only the professionals, the leisured, educated functionaries who have a tolerably clear idea what the ritual or practice is supposed to mean.[24] The modest thesis is neatly captured in Gregory Schopen's remark (again in Taylor) that "we need to learn to distinguish formal doctrine from belief."[25] Schopen thinks that students of religion may indeed need to attend to the agent's beliefs, just not ones having to do with formal doctrine. Hume, Freud, and Schopen may not believe in God, but they believe in belief.

The more ambitious thesis presses deeper doubts about belief. Thus, among others and in very different ways, Walter Burkert, Stewart Guthrie, Fritz Staal, and E. O. Wilson have each brought to the religious studies table the resources of evolutionary biology. They do not dispute talk of beliefs as such, but they do find such talk beside the

---

[23] David Hume, *The Natural History of Religion*, ed. H. E. Root (Stanford University Press, 1957), 55–56.
[24] Sigmund Freud, "Obsessive Actions and Religious Practices," *Standard Edition*, IX, 122–23.
[25] Gregory Schopen, "Relic," in Taylor (ed.), *Critical Terms*, 266.

point in understanding a broad range of religious practices. I understand Catherine Bell's work on ritual in the same light – she, too, has
no trouble with belief per se, and urges (in Taylor) what I am calling the
modest thesis: we should go beyond viewing ritual "as a simple reflection
of religious beliefs."[26] But then she raises a deeper doubt. Bell endorses
Barbara Meyeroff's claim that "ritualization . . . is capable of constructing meaningful events out of the raw happenings of life." The key here is
the absence of intentional action – for the agents involved see themselves
as doing no such thing. The creation of meaningful events out of raw
happenings is not something the participant intends. Rather, it results
from the performance itself, from "the movements of the body in space
and time."

One of the harshest critics of belief is Lopez. He raises questions even
about Freud's intellectual elite, adducing a representative case – that of
the thirteenth-century Dominican saint Peter of Verona (Peter Martyr).
On the received story, Peter was martyred by the Manicheans for his
tenacious, expressed belief in one God. But, in fact, says Lopez, "belief
served as a substitute, an elusive interior state that masked a host of far
more material circumstances," the latter centering on Peter's role in the
confiscation of Cathar property.[27] Indeed, Lopez wonders whether there
is even any such thing as belief – it is, he says, "difficult to determine."
I take it that Lopez is attracted here to the view that there really are
no such allegedly contentful mental states as belief, hope, and doubt,
that, really, these are names for enormously complex, ill-understood
bits of matter interacting with one another in enormously complex, ill-
understood ways. It is the view that Paul and Patricia Churchland and
others have long championed in cognitive science and the philosophy of
mind, namely, the doctrine of eliminative materialism. In fact, at least one
reviewer considers not only Lopez's contribution but the entire Taylor
anthology in just this light: writing in the *Journal of the American Academy
of Religion*, David Chidester says that, "the best essays in this collection
suggest an emergent horizon for the study of religion that might be called
a new materialism."[28]

---

[26] Catherine Bell, "Performance," in Taylor (ed.), *Critical Terms*, 214; next quotations, 212, 216. For
Barbara Meyeroff, see, "A Death in Due Time: Construction of the Self and Culture in Ritual
Drama," in John J. MacAloon (ed.), *Rite, Drama, Festival, Spectacle* (Philadelphia: Institute for the
Study of Human Issues, 1984), 167.

[27] Lopez, "Belief," 21; next quotation, 34. "Peter was murdered not for his beliefs but for his deeds,
specifically for the confiscation of the property of two Cathar noblemen," 26.

[28] David Chidester, "Material Terms for the Study of Religion," *Journal of the American Academy of
Religion* 68:2 (June 2000): 374.

Now, in philosophy of mind, eliminative materialism is no doubt a serious contender in the marketplace of ideas. I shall return in closing to the question of its place in religious studies. For now, I merely note the distance we have come from Zwingli and Calvin. I take the leading theme of this story to be the progressive decoupling of the bodily movements in view from what we had once seen as the agent's motivating beliefs and desires. The interpreter learns to see the practices apart from, not only the agent's putative religious beliefs, but also any discursive context whatever. Put differently, on the story I am now telling, the interpreter brings his or her theoretical resources to bear on the putatively religious activity in question without regard for detailed knowledge of the agent's associated beliefs and attitudes, if, indeed, there are any to be known.

If, now, we ask what connection this story has to the Davidsonian one about radical interpretation, I am afraid my rather transparent strategy will be fully exposed. For, of course, the impoverished evidential position I have just described *is* very nearly the position Davidson contemplates in his famous thought experiment. That is, Davidson has tried to show how an interpreter could come to understand someone's words and actions without relying on any prior understanding of either.[29] We have, then, an ironic confluence: all parties joining in a methodologically driven decoupling of action – movement, really – from belief. Of course, the parties have arrived by somewhat different means and with somewhat different agendas. As I read them, Bell, Chidester, and Schopen (among others) are reacting against a tradition in religious studies which prizes ideas over artifacts and mentality over materiality – hence their suspicion of the propositional attitudes. Lopez's suspicion, as I have noted, appears to cut somewhat deeper. For his part, Davidson denies himself knowledge of the agent's discursive practices as a way of more fully illuminating the semantic concepts that interest him. Davidson's self-denial is in the service of illumination, Lopez's in elimination.

Let us return to our motivating tension, namely, that between an emphasis on the centrality of belief in understanding human speech and action and recent doubts about its place in the study of religion.

To some extent, the tension dissolves under closer inspection. Consider, first, that the Davidsonian interpreter has no interest in explaining all human behavior, or any particular piece of behavior, by

---

[29] For Davidson's fullest discussion of radical interpretation, see, "Structure and Content of Truth," *Journal of Philosophy* (1990): 279–328.

appeal to the agent's reasons. Whether this or that ritual or practice can be best understood by appeal to the agent's beliefs, desires, and attitudes is – as Tom Lawson and Robert McCauley have emphasized – an empirical question, subject to the usual standards of theory confirmation, and not something about which philosophers should have any views.[30] We want the deepest possible understanding, and we cannot say beforehand whether in advancing that cause we will want to implicate the agent's attitudes and discursive practices. But we *can* say in advance that, if we want to see the movements at stake as intentional actions, or even if we simply want to put the movements in the context of other intentional actions – in short, unless we want our theories of religion to abandon the notion of intentional agency altogether – we will have to rely on the unavoidable interpretive constraints on which Davidson and others have cast so much light. Second, as we have seen, there simply is no room in Davidson's theory of interpretation for the dualism of the material and the discursive. Shoulder to shoulder with the new materialists, the radical interpreter also embraces the causal, material circumstances of speech and action; indeed, the argument from natural history requires her to weave them into the very fabric of meaning. Those in religious studies looking for an interpretive stance from which to integrate the material and the mental will find one in Davidson's account of radical interpretation.

PERCEPTUAL JUDGMENT

In conclusion, I want to argue that we must be confident in our assignments of specifically religious beliefs in order to see a given practice as religious. I intend the present strategy as a generalization of Wayne Proudfoot's in *Religious Experience*, where he argues that an experience is religious only if the interpreter understands it in those terms or if the agent does so herself.[31]

Suppose that, for whatever reason, we have come to doubt that the apparently religious practices before us are in fact motivated by what we had once taken to be the agents' religious beliefs, desires, and the like. We are able to describe the movements we see before us in great

---

[30] E. Thomas Lawson and Robert N. McCauley, *Rethinking Religion: Connecting Cognition and Culture* (New York: Cambridge University Press, 1990), 22ff.

[31] Wayne Proudfoot, *Religious Experience* (Berkeley: University of California Press, 1985). I have benefited in this section from Proudfoot's comments. I do not mean to imply that Proudfoot sees the present argument as a legitimate extension of his.

detail, but none of this detail rests on the religious self-understanding of the agents themselves. Under these conditions, are we still viewing the movements as religious?

If our description is purely physical (say, Bell's "movements of the body in space and time"), and if we detect no informative connections between the movements and their surroundings, whether religious, economic, ecological, sociological, biological, psychological, or other – then I would answer, no. Describing our change of heart, we might say that what we receive has not changed, but that what we perceive has. Certainly we may find it convenient to continue to label these movements "religious"; that is, we might (with, for example, Freud), want to continue to use the term "religious ritual" to pick out these movements even as newly perceived (for Freud, as acts of displacement). We might do this just in order to make clear that we intend continuity of reference (as a similar tagging device, compare the newscaster's continued use, years after its dissolution, of "the former Soviet Union"). But that would be merely to attach a label to movements viewed physically. Since there is nothing plausibly religious about this merely physical context, it makes no sense to say that we are seeing the practice in question as religious.

A second case: again we eschew belief, but this time we uncover informative material connections – for example, we might have a Marxist or evolutionary theory that we think explains the given practice purely in economic or biological terms. Lopez's discussion of Peter Martyr might fit here.[32] Here again "religious" merely tags and does not license seeing. We may usefully include these explanations under the heading of "theories of religion," and in textbooks on "approaches to the study of religion," so long as we recognize that the context in which we are now seeing the behavior is no longer recognizably religious, but rather economic or biological. Their inclusion is justified solely by the (quite legitimate) desire to announce that they are theories of the same movements that we used to see, or that others see or have seen, as religious. Many of the entries in the Taylor anthology seem to be offered in this spirit.

The point is that in none of these cases have we put the practices in view in a religious context so that they can be seen as such. I do

---

[32] Except that, even in Lopez's quite plausible retelling, belief is still very much in play. If Peter was murdered because he had ordered the confiscation of Cathar property, then it is natural to think that he believed that, by giving the order, the property would be confiscated, that, all things considered, giving the order was best, and so on without end. Of course, other reconstructions are possible (perhaps he was weak-willed: he did not think it best but gave the order anyway), but all seem to rely on Peter's beliefs.

not see how – except by taking the agent herself to be taking herself to be pursuing religious ends – to situate her movements in a specifically religious context, and so to see her movements as religious.

Someone might object that, by requiring the interpreter to see the action through the agent's religious beliefs and desires (if she is to see it as religious), I am setting up a standard that is routinely and productively ignored in neighboring disciplines. For example, the study of politics as such clearly survives the political scientist's inability to assign recognizably political beliefs to the persons she has in view. Indeed, these persons may be inarticulate at all levels about their politics. Yet their movements may well have unintended political consequences (say, for governance), or be describable in political terms (as, say, helping to undermine a political party's power base). That is, as a matter of fact and quite apart from anyone's intentional attitudes, people are governed and there are political parties. Thus, we can place a person's movements in a political context, and so can view them as political, in ignorance of that person's political attitudes (if any). Plausibly, we could make parallel cases for many other cultural phenomena, including art, athletics, economics, and education. Why not for religion?

But in order for the parallel to go through we would have to say that, even absent rationalizing religious beliefs, desires, and the like, the practices we have in view have religious consequences, or are describable in religious terms. But that would commit the inquirer to seeing the practices in question as in some way involved in commerce with – here I favor Hume's happy phrase – invisible, intelligent powers. That is, unlike the example from politics, the consequences are not themselves religious in nature; short of requiring religious commitment from the interpreter, they cannot be described as involving the actions of or commerce with gods, goddesses, revered ancestors, and their kind. Certainly the given practices may have consequences for some religious group – expansion, perhaps, or contraction. But that is to place them in a sociological rather than in a religious context.

If this is right – if we are justified in seeing a piece of behavior as religious only when we can situate it in the right kind of discursive context – then we have hit on a fundamental distinction between ritual activity and such religious artifacts as, for example, paintings and statuary. These latter may be religious by content, by the religious themes and characters they represent, quite apart from the artist's intentions and beliefs. But not so in the case of human activity. Indeed, ordinary language marks the relevant distinction with some precision: the clever government informant

or boorish tourist may, in a ritual context, be observationally indistin-
guishable from the genuine participant, but of such persons we would
say that they are merely mimicking and not engaging in the ritual. They
would be engaging in the ritual only if they possessed the right sort of
self-understanding, and, in fact, can only mimic it because those around
them do possess it. If no one did, then we would have no reason to speak
of religion.

Based on these considerations, I offer the following tentative conclusion: when we detach a range of bodily movements from what we had
formerly taken to be rationalizing religious beliefs, desires, hopes, fears,
and the like – more generally, from a context of discursivity – we thereby
let lapse a necessary condition for seeing them as religious practices.
Apparently, we view a practice as religious when and only when we
place it in a specifically religious context. Otherwise "religious" merely
tags, and does not license seeing. There seem to be only two ways to effect
this placing. Either we may find that the agent believes her practices to
be so situated (or hopes or unreflectively assumes or has faith, etc., that
they are), or we may find that they *are* so situated. But, if we disallow
belief, the first way is not open to us. And the second, for me anyway, is
neither lively, nor forced, nor momentous. Under these circumstances,
we students of religion are effecting the disappearance of our object of
study.

The analogy with the debate in philosophy of mind over eliminative
materialism is instructive. Defenders of "folk" or "belief–desire" psychology sometimes argue that eliminative materialists are, in effect, proposing
that we give up being persons, that to give up the discursivity in (what we
had seen as) our discursive practices is to give up a condition of ethics,
value, and culture. The suggestion is that to give up belief is to perform
a kind of "cognitive suicide."[33] Whatever its fate in philosophy of mind,
the suicide argument finds only partial application in the present context.
True, the argument I have sketched in this section does suggest that we
give up religious belief on pain of giving up the study of religion, in the
sense that we would lose the ability to see any given practice as religious.
But the study of what we had seen as religious would of course live on; it
would become a matter of tagging what had been seen as religious and
learning to see it differently. (By contrast, it is not clear that "tagging" and
"learning" have any application under eliminative materialism.) I have

---

[33] For discussion, see, for example, Lynne Rudder Baker (from whom I have taken my title), *Saving
Belief: A Critique of Physicalism* (Princeton University Press, 1987), esp. chs. 6 and 7.

already expressed my admiration for several recent studies that take precisely this line. Nor am I alleging reductionism: in any given case, the only question can be whether we are justified in seeing the practice in light of the agent's religious beliefs and attitudes; in any given case we might not be.

Insofar as it redresses a long-standing bias favoring mentality, I applaud the recent drift toward the material. One hopes that scholars of religion can agree that, taken together, their subject matter includes both discursive and non-discursive elements, and that inquiry into them ought to go forward together.[34] But perhaps it is well to be reminded that, because belief is central to other kinds of thought, we cannot both neglect it and still take seriously the hopes and fears, purposes and strivings, errors and insights of religious persons through the ages, inquiry into which must be important both for scholars and – why not? – believers.[35] While students of religion need not believe in God, we do need to believe in belief.[36]

[34] In this connection, Taylor's *Critical Terms* might usefully be paired with Willi Braun and Russell McCutcheon's (eds.) *Guide to the Study of Religion* (New York: Cassell, 2000), which seems to give materiality and discursivity more nearly equal play. In the Prologue, Braun writes that, "the object of the scholar's study is not the gods but the complex social operations by which, and the conditions under which, people discursively bring the gods to life" (11). In his essay, "Rationality," Rodney Stark, in apparent counterpoint to what I have called the impotence of doctrinal commitment, gives examples of "doctrinal causation," urging that "one can utilize religious doctrine as a causal factor vis-à-vis other religious phenomena, both individual and organizational" (255). See also Daniel Pals, "Intellect," and E. Thomas Lawson, "Cognition," among others.

[35] See, Wayne Proudfoot, "William James on an Unseen Order," *Harvard Theological Review* 93:1 (2000), 66.

[36] I am grateful to my fellow contributors to this volume for discussion and comments; special thanks to Tony Dardis, Warren Frisina, Nancy Frankenberry, Jack Hanson, Hans Penner, Wayne Proudfoot, Walter Sinnott-Armstrong, Roy Sorenson, Jeff Stout, and Ann Taves.

2

Radical interpretation and pragmatism: Davidson, Rorty, and Brandom on truth

Jeffrey Stout

A central question for this volume is what difference Donald Davidson's account of radical interpretation might make for the study of religion. But as compared with what? We are apt to focus initially on Davidson's break from familiar versions of realism and relativism that have strongly influenced religious studies. In thus emphasizing his opposition to a received philosophical tradition, we highlight his similarities to the pragmatists. It is plausible to group these philosophers together, for they are opposing many of the same ideas, and they often echo or borrow each other's arguments. Richard Rorty has made every effort to persuade Davidson, the living philosopher he most admires, to join him behind the banner of pragmatism.[1] The best book on Davidson, Bjorn Ramberg's, places him in close proximity to Rorty's pragmatism.[2] But Davidson has never embraced pragmatism openly, and over the years he and Rorty have criticized one another repeatedly on particular issues. Evidently, there are differences between them that are worth attending to. What they are is less clear.

Perhaps it will help to broaden the range of figures to be compared. In this chapter, I focus primarily on the work of Rorty's former student, Robert Brandom. Part of my purpose is simply to introduce Brandom's work to a religious studies audience. The massiveness and theoretical intricacy of his 1994 book, *Making It Explicit*, have kept it from having the influence it deserves to have on neighboring fields.[3] But Brandom must now be counted as the most important American philosopher in my generation to describe himself as a pragmatist. If we want to have an adequate understanding of the relationship between contemporary

---

[1] See especially, Richard Rorty, "Pragmatism, Davidson, and Truth," in *Objectivity, Relativism, and Truth* (Cambridge University Press, 1991), 126–50.

[2] Bjorn Ramberg, *Donald Davidson's Philosophy of Language* (Oxford: Blackwell, 1989).

[3] See especially Robert B. Brandom, *Making It Explicit: Reasoning, Representing, and Discursive Commitment* (Cambridge, MA: Harvard University Press, 1994). Cited hereafter as "*MIE*."

pragmatism and Davidson's views on radical interpretation, we will have to take Brandom's work into account. What, if anything, is at stake here for students of religion? What difference do the differences between Davidson and the pragmatists make? I will focus mainly on differences concerning the concept of truth.

To situate this topic properly in relation to our discipline's interest in interpretation, one needs to keep in mind an aspect of Davidson's theory of interpretation that Brandom accepts – namely, that interpretation is an inherently normative affair. We cannot ascribe meaning to the utterances or inscriptions of our fellow human beings without (implicitly or explicitly) committing ourselves to judgments about how well they are doing at avoiding error. And that involves applying our own norms to the people we are studying.[4] Davidson's well-known principle of charity is an attempt to make explicit what we are taking for granted when interpreting our fellow language-users. It places limits on how much error one can attribute to a speaker. The attribution of beliefs (and desires) goes hand in hand with the interpretation of sentences. Because it is always possible to make a trade-off between the former and the latter, we cannot get the project of interpretation off the ground without limiting the attribution of error to the minimum required for explanation of the behavioral evidence. In charity the interpreter therefore imputes as little error to a speaker as possible while still accounting for what the speaker says and does. Davidsonian charity is, however, only one idiom in which the normative dimension of interpretation has been discussed in contemporary philosophy. Another, as we shall see, is Brandom's talk of normative scorekeeping.

TRUTH AND JUSTIFICATION

Brandom repeatedly calls attention to a familiar distinction between two species of error that believers can incur. There is a difference between believing something that is false and being unjustified in believing something. Being justified or unjustified in believing something, in Brandom's idiom, is a matter of entitlement, a normative status. One can believe something with or without being entitled to believe it. What one believes can be either true or false. When we, as interpreters, attribute knowledge to someone, we take that person to believe something that is true

---

[4] For one of Davidson's most explicit statements of this point, see "Could There Be a Science of Rationality?" *International Journal of Philosophical Studies* 3 (1995): 1–16. Brandom discusses this matter in *MIE*, 623–50.

and we take him or her to be epistemically entitled to that belief. But one can believe something that turns out to have been true even though one lacks epistemic entitlement to believe it. And one can be entitled to believe something that turns out to have been false. Despite being joined together in our concept of knowledge, the notions of truth and justification swing free of each other.

In the *Summa Theologiae*, Thomas Aquinas claimed that sodomy is second only to bestiality among the unnatural sins of lechery. Because I take Aquinas at his word, I attribute to him the belief that sodomy is sinful. To make sense of this belief, I also attribute to him certain other commitments, which I take to be his reasons for deeming sodomy sinful – beliefs about natural law, for example, and about what God intended sexual organs to be used for. It so happens, however, that I consider sodomy morally innocuous. My belief that sodomy is morally innocuous conflicts with the belief that sodomy is sinful. This means that one of my beliefs and a belief I attribute to Aquinas cannot both be true. So I attribute (what I take to be) a false belief to Aquinas. What about the reasons Aquinas had for reaching his negative verdict? They do not persuade me, and I do not see why they should have persuaded him. As far as I can see, his reasons for his belief about the sinfulness of sodomy fail to cohere with the account of natural law he offers and applies in various other passages in the *Summa*. According to my interpretation of Aquinas, then, he not only held a false belief about sodomy, he was also unjustified in holding that belief.

Needless to say, this interpretation of Aquinas puts me at odds with others in my field. Vatican theologians, for example, agree that Aquinas considered sodomy sinful, but they endorse the belief they thus ascribe to him. On their account, Aquinas held (what they take to be) a true belief about sodomy. Was he justified in holding that belief? Yes, they say, because he inferred the sinfulness of sodomy from a coherent doctrine of natural law that is consistently defended and applied throughout the ethical sections of the *Summa*. This is where the trouble comes, however, for Aquinas' defenders have not shown, at least to my satisfaction, that his various sentences about the natural law mean what they want them to mean. Nor have they shown that the commitments he expresses when discussing the natural law succeed in justifying his conclusion about sodomy.

Our respective interpretations of Aquinas appear to involve not only (1) mapping his sentences onto our own, but also (2) attributing commitments to him, (3) deciding whether to count those commitments as true or false, and (4) determining whether to count him as justified in holding those commitments. If we tried to confine ourselves to (1), while bracketing (2), (3), and (4), we would get nowhere, because (2), (3), and (4) are needed to impose the constraint of interpretive charity on the mapping undertaken in (1). Charity places a limit on how much falsehood we can attribute to the people we are interpreting and also on the extent to which we can make those people out to be unjustified in believing what they believe (if we want to attribute beliefs to them at all).

Davidson and Brandom both emphasize the need to distinguish between (3) and (4), between claiming that someone is justified in believing something and claiming that what someone believes is true. Being justified in believing something (that is, being entitled to believe it) is what Brandom calls a normative status. This status has to do with how people comport themselves in relation to the patterns of reasoning and evidence available in their context. People who behave in a fully responsible way, epistemically speaking, with respect to some subject matter are justified in believing what they believe even if what they believe turns out to be false.

Aquinas held that the earth is the center of the created world. To say that he was not justified in believing this seems too harsh because it blames him for not knowing something he could not have known, something we are privileged to know only because of our different epistemic circumstances. This and various other similar considerations show that the concept of being justified in believing something is closely related to the activities of blaming, praising, and excusing people for the use they make of the epistemic resources available in their contexts. When I say of Aquinas that he believed something false about the earth's relation to the sun but that he was nonetheless justified in believing it, I am excusing him for accepting a falsehood. The standard for attributing this normative status to him is rather permissive. One is ordinarily excused for believing falsehoods when one's epistemic context makes available little or no conclusive evidence against those falsehoods. That the belief is false does not imply that the person who held it was unjustified. By the same token, if you say that the medieval village blacksmith's belief that the earth revolves around the sun is true, you need not imply that he was justified in holding the belief he held. People who believed such a thing in the medieval period would not have been justified in doing so, given the evidence and conceptual tools available to them. And no blacksmith was in a position to change his epistemic circumstances enough through disciplined scientific inquiry to achieve such a breakthrough by rational means. Justification and truth are distinct notions.

You and I claim that the earth revolves around the sun. To put the same point in terms of semantic ascent, we claim that the sentence, "The earth revolves around the sun," is true. Once we translate Aquinas' cosmology into contemporary English, it becomes clear that he held a cosmological belief that is false if our claim is true. But if we say that he held a false belief about the earth's relation to the sun, we are not necessarily blaming him for misapplying the norms of reasoning and items of evidence available in his context – as I was doing in interpreting his views on sodomy. So "true" and "false" clearly behave differently from "justified" and "unjustified" in the discourse of interpretation. When I say that Aquinas was committed to a false cosmology, I am saying something directly about the content of what he believed, not about his normative status as a believer in a context. What belief am I referring to? *That the earth is the center of the created world.* The propositional content expressed in this clause is all I am talking about when I say that his belief is false. If it is true now that the earth revolves around the sun, it was also true several centuries ago, when Aquinas believed otherwise. The earth has not changed its relative position in the solar system since the Middle Ages. What is true now about the earth's relation to the sun was true then.

When I say of the sentence, "The earth revolves around the sun," that it is true, I commit myself to the content of the claim that the quoted sentence expresses. I also commit myself to denial of anything incompatible with the content of that claim, such as Aquinas' contrary belief. This does not mean that I am casting aspersions on Aquinas, because it is the content of his belief that my cosmological commitment conflicts with, not his normative status as a responsible believer. If I say of Aquinas only that he was justified in believing that the earth is the center of the created world, I have not yet committed myself to the content of his belief. I have only committed myself to a normative stance with respect to the normative epistemic relations he stood in. Talk of being justified in believing something, then, is about epistemic responsibility, and is sensitive to context in the way all talk of responsibility is. Talk of truth, in Brandom's view, takes the correctness of conceptual contents as its subject matter, not the epistemic responsibilities of believers and asserters. It is this difference in subject matter that accounts for the differences between the concepts of truth and justification with respect to contextual relativity. But both of these concepts belong, according to Brandom, to the vocabulary of ordinary interpretive discourse – the language game we play when engaging in normative scorekeeping with respect to one another's attitudes.

Davidson agrees with Brandom about the importance of distinguishing truth from justification. Indeed, he criticizes Rorty for playing down
the distinction.[5] Whether he reads Rorty with sufficient charity is unclear, however. The passage Davidson refers to can be found in *Truth and
Progress*, where Rorty says, somewhat too casually, that pragmatists are
"suspicious of the distinction between justification and truth."[6] I take
Rorty's point in that passage to be that there is no practical difference –
from the first-person, present-tense perspective of the inquirer – between
aiming to hold true beliefs and aiming to hold beliefs that one is entitled to. This point bears on whether it makes sense to think of truth
as a (distinct) goal of inquiry, a question both Rorty and Davidson answer in the negative. If there is no practical difference for the inquiring
agent between aiming to hold true beliefs and aiming to hold beliefs that
one is entitled to, then the distinction between truth and justification is
irrelevant to the question of what the inquiring agent's goal should be.
If this is all Rorty meant to say, he should have expressed suspicion of
appealing to the distinction between truth and justification *in the context
of answering this question*. His arguments do not show that there is something suspicious about the distinction itself. Rorty has long since given
up the old pragmatic habit of running truth and justification together
by saying such things as: "Truth is whatever your peers will let you get
away with saying." As Rorty now often puts it, the term "true" has a
(perfectly legitimate) *cautionary* use that invokes a contrast between truth
and justification, as in the sentence: "You may be justified in believing what Professor Jones just predicted about global warming, but his
prediction might not be true."[7] In acknowledging the legitimacy of the
cautionary use of "true," Rorty is granting two things. First, he is granting that "true" and "justification" behave differently in some contexts.
Second, he is granting that one can use these terms as most of us do
in those contexts without committing oneself to a dubious metaphysical
picture (according to which truth-makers of some kind explain the truth
of true representations). Rorty, Brandom, and Davidson agree on both
of these points.

These philosophers do not speak with one voice, however, on the
question of what one ought to say about truth beyond pointing out
how it differs from justification. Davidson's responses to this question, in

[5] Donald Davidson, "Truth Rehabilitated," in Robert B. Brandom (ed.), *Rorty and His Critics*
(Oxford: Blackwell, 2000): 65–74. See especially 74, note 3.
[6] *Truth and Progress* (Cambridge University Press, 1998), 19.
[7] "Pragmatism, Davidson, and Truth," 128.

particular, have generated a great deal of puzzlement. Despite an early flirtation with the label, "correspondence theory," he now grants that:

Truth as correspondence with reality may be an idea we are better off without ... The trouble lies in the claim that the formula has explanatory power. The notion of correspondence would be a help if we were able to say, in an *instructive* way, which fact or slice of reality it is that makes a particular sentence true. No-one has succeeded in doing this.[8]

He has also described the attempt to define truth as "folly."[9] These moves seem to put him in close proximity to Brandom's pragmatism, which includes a deflationary account of truth. Yet Davidson remains reluctant to call himself a pragmatist, and he charges that deflationary accounts of truth fail to recognize the importance of the concept.[10] Davidson appears to feel that a great deal is at stake in the debate between his own position, which takes "true" as an undefined primitive term, and that of deflationary pragmatism, but it is not easy to determine what it is.

BRANDOM'S THEORY IN OUTLINE

Assuming, then, that truth and justification are distinct concepts, both of which have roles to play in interpretive discourse, what else needs to be said about truth? Brandom agrees with philosophers like Arthur Fine that truth is not a substantial something, so he sees no point in theoretically defining the substantial something that truth is. In this sense, then, he holds that defining truth is folly. But there is a fairly strong sense in which he offers a theory of (the concept of) truth, and his theory is deflationary in a sense that would concern Davidson. To grasp the significance of this theory, one needs to understand its position within the larger theoretical structure of Brandom's pragmatic philosophy of language. This structure differs enormously from the one within which the standard forms of realism and anti-realism carry out their debate over how to define truth. The most direct way to show that "realism" and "anti-realism," as typically understood, do not exhaust the available options for truth-theory is to show that there is an alternative to the theoretical structure that these "isms" have been fighting over (and, in that sense, taking for granted).

---

[8] "Truth Rehabilitated," 66, italics in original.
[9] "The Folly of Trying to Define Truth," *Journal of Philosophy* 94 (1997): 263–78.
[10] In addition to "Truth Rehabilitated," 68–73 and "The Folly of Trying to Define Truth," see "The Structure and Content of Truth," *Journal of Philosophy* 87 (1990): 281–328.

Brandom refers to the theoretical structure he is trying to replace as representationalist and to his alternative structure as inferentialist. Representationalism, as he understands it, is a two-part explanatory strategy in which *representational* notions, principally truth and reference, are taken to be the most basic concepts in which explanations of linguistic affairs will be given. The first part of the representationalist strategy is therefore to provide a semantics. The semantics has two components: one in which the basic concepts of truth and reference are explicated and another in which the remaining semantic concepts (such as meaning or conceptual content, implication, and incompatibility) are accounted for in terms of the basic concepts. The second part of the strategy is to provide a pragmatics in which the varied uses of various linguistic units (in the making of assertions, the asking of questions, the giving of commands, and so on) are accounted for against the background already provided in the semantics. The second part of the explanatory strategy presupposes the first, because the pragmatics takes for granted that the conceptual content involved in the varied uses of various linguistic units (words, sentences) has already been explicated in terms of the basic concepts of truth and reference. The structure of the representationalist strategy can therefore be represented as follows:

1   a semantics, including

    1.1 an account of truth and reference as basic semantic concepts and

    1.2 an account of other semantic concepts in terms of truth and reference; and

2   a pragmatics that presupposes the semantics.

The strengths of representationalism lie mainly in the explanatory power of the accounts belonging to (1.2), the second component of the first part. This power has been achieved, Brandom says, "primarily by employing a variety of set-theoretic methods to show how proprieties of inference can be determined by representational properties of the claims that serve as their premises and conclusions" (*MIE*, xvi). Representationalist pragmatics, though underdeveloped by comparison, has also produced some powerful results. The major weaknesses in representationalism, however, have to do with (1.1), the first component of the first part. "The explanatory challenge" for representationalism, according to Brandom, lies "in saying what it is for something to have representational content, and in what the grasp or uptake of that content by speakers and thinkers consists" (*MIE*, xvi). The reason that so much anxiety arises when realistic theories of truth are charged with being unhelpful, vacuous, or incoherent as explanations is that everything else in the long-dominant explanatory strategy of representationalism depends on the theory of truth essential to (1.1).

The familiar varieties of anti-realism, aside from having trouble accounting for the behavior of the term "true" in ordinary language, seem ill-equipped to theorize truth in a way that would allow it to function as a basic concept of representationalist semantics. So opposition to realism, construed strictly in relation to the representationalist explanatory structure, seems both implausible and a threat to the whole enterprise. Anti-realism's tendency is to reduce truth to an enriched version of some epistemic concept – a concept like justification, which has to do with the responsibilities of believers and asserters in a context. This move not only makes it hard to account for the cautionary use of "true," but also appears to place in jeopardy all the crucial concepts relating to inference, for these are treated in a representationalist explanatory strategy in terms of the more basic notions of truth and reference. What anti-realists say about truth appears to deprive inference, and thus reasoning and rationality, of their conceptual underpinnings. So anti-realists are typically portrayed in representationalist rhetoric as irrationalists, whether they want to admit it or not. They are said to be nihilists because they are thought to deprive us of the very concept of truth on which our inferential concepts – and thus our image of ourselves as rational animals – depend.[11]

Some critics of realism, many of them specialists in literary theory or cultural studies, revel in the role here attributed to them. They are eager to draw the conclusion that the concept of truth and the ideals of rationality that depend on it should simply be dropped in favor of a "marching army of metaphors." Wittgenstein's response was the more modest one of holding that his philosophical doubts about realist theory leave ordinary language, including all non-philosophical uses of the term "true," as it is. His way of showing this was to perform thought experiments designed to make the representationalist explanatory structure seem inessential from the vantage point of life. Each thought experiment aimed to wean his students and readers as well as himself away from spiritual and intellectual dependence on that structure. He did not propose an alternative to that structure because he worried that any theory

---

[11] This, if I read him correctly, is the line Edmund Santurri is arguing against my version of pragmatism in "Nihilism Revisited," *Journal of Religion* (January 1991): 67–78. Santurri concludes that I am a moral nihilist despite my efforts to resist. Timothy Jackson has expressed similar doubts about my position on more than one occasion. See, for example, *Love Disconsoled* (Cambridge University Press, 1999), 137, n. 23.

of comparable explanatory ambition with respect to the same cluster of concepts was likely to partake in the obsessiveness and other spiritual vices he associated with representationalism. His objective was not to live in terms of an anti-representationalist theory, but to live in a way not dominated by the theoretical obsessions, pro or con, that have been generated by representationalism. Wittgenstein's philosophy is an ascetic therapy of desire intended to return himself and others to a form of life that neither is, nor takes itself to be, dependent on an essentially explanatory approach to topics like truth and meaning. It is a form of pragmatism in part because it recommends seeing a life of sound understanding as prior to philosophy.[12]

To see what Brandom is doing and why, it is helpful to distinguish him from Wittgenstein and Rorty, as well as from Davidson. While he is always respectful of Wittgenstein and makes ample use of his arguments, Brandom sidesteps Wittgenstein's theoretical asceticism. He seems not to be preoccupied in the ways Wittgenstein was with the spiritual consequences of representationalism. He is not trying to secure his ethical well-being by practicing asceticism in the theory of language. Brandom, like Davidson, proposes to develop a full-scale theoretical alternative to representationalism. His point of departure, however, is neither Tarski on truth nor Quine on radical translation but Sellars's realization in the 1930s that: "What was needed was a functional theory of concepts which would make their role in reasoning, rather than [their] supposed origin in experience, their primary feature" (quoted in *MIE*, 93). The theory's emphasis on reasoning makes it a variety of inferentialism. Its interpretation of reasoning as a social practice qualifies it as a form of pragmatism.

Brandom differs from Rorty in holding steadily to the goal of articulating an alternative theory. He distances himself consistently both from proposals to junk the vocabulary of ordinary objectivity-talk and from Wittgenstein's ascetic refusal of theory. Rorty, in contrast, presents himself in some passages as a revolutionary striving for a transvaluation of values that would slough off all references to objectivity, the attempt to "get things right." These are the passages that lead people to interpret him as an anti-realist. In other passages, Rorty sounds like a Wittgensteinian

[12] For useful accounts of Wittgenstein's attitudes on the spiritual dangers of representationalism, see James C. Edwards, *Ethics without Philosophy: Wittgenstein and the Moral Life* (Tampa: University of South Florida, 1982) and *The Authority of Language: Heidegger, Wittgenstein, and the Threat of Philosophical Nihilism* (Tampa: University of South Florida, 1990). For an account of Wittgenstein's spiritual preoccupations, see Ray Monk's wonderful biography, *Ludwig Wittgenstein: The Duty of Genius* (London: Penguin, 1990).

offering therapy for philosophical obsessiveness and adopting a stance, like Fine's, conceptually distinct from both realist and anti-realist theories of truth. In yet other passages he appears to be proposing that Davidson has succeeded in providing a full-scale theoretical alternative to representationalism and that Davidson's theory is best understood, *pace* Davidson, as a form of pragmatism. Brandom, however, clearly rejects the Nietzschean and Wittgensteinian styles, and confines himself rigorously to the provision of a full-scale theoretical alternative to representationalism, but with Sellars in Davidson's place as the chief provider of theoretical tools.

What, then, is the inferentialist alternative he proposes? Like representationalism it accepts the burden of explicating the concepts it takes as basic and then accounting for other concepts successfully in terms of those, but here the primitive concepts are normative ones that are implicit in the *activities* performed within our discursive practices. Those practices are understood as belonging to language games that essentially involve the self-committing behavior and social interactions in which we do all of the following things:

- observe or perceive what is going on in our environs,
- make inferences from one bit of acquired information to another,
- make inferences from beliefs to practical conclusions and then act intentionally,
- exchange reasons and requests for reasons with one another,
- issue inferential licenses to one another by asserting things,
- ascribe commitments to ourselves and each other, and
- hold one another responsible for the commitments we adopt by declaring ourselves and others entitled or not entitled to those commitments.

The essential role of inference in such practices is what justifies using the label "inferentialist" as a name for this explanatory strategy. For it is in terms of *social practices that essentially involve inference* that Brandom proposes to work out the most important details of his theoretical structure.

There is a danger in using this label, however, because it does not bring out that the practices being called upon to play crucial explanatory roles here also essentially involve activities that are not strictly speaking inferential, such as observation and acting. In Brandom's Sellarsian model, these activities are designated as discursive entry and discursive departure moves and not as inferential moves within the language game. It is important to stress that these two types of non-inferential moves engage the player of the language game in physical, causal interaction with physical objects. Because the language game includes non-inferential moves of these kinds, it is not insulated from the world of non-linguistic entities, as idealistic forms of inferentialism are. It is also important to stress that, while these moves are not to be understood as forms of inference, they are not moves that anyone unskilled in making inferential moves could make. The reason a pre-linguistic infant cannot *perceive that* a pie just fell off the table (in the epistemically relevant sense), even though she just watched while a pie fell off the table, is that she has not yet acquired the inferential and linguistic capacities associated with the concept of a pie.[13] This point distinguishes a Sellarsian theory from what Sellars called empiricism, according to which non-inferential perception secures epistemic access to the immediately given without any assistance from inferential capacities. Non-inferential moves are not themselves inferences, but they have the significance they have because they are moves in a game that essentially includes inferential moves with which they share terms and to which they are related inferentially. So they are not disconnected from inferential capacities in the way that empiricist references to the immediacy of perception implied.[14] Hence the (slightly misleading) moniker for Brandom's position, "inferentialism."

The pragmatics is a theory of what goes on, normatively speaking, within the self-committing activities in which players of the language

[13] This point deserves further explanation, but only a small fraction of the story can be given here. Suppose a pre-linguistic infant sees a pie fall off the table. She does not thereby acquire the epistemic status of having perceived that a pie fell off the table, because such a status confers a license in the language game to make inferences from the perception. The infant lacks the conceptual know-how to make the inferences this status would entitle her to make. The line between *seeing* a pie fall off the table and *perceiving that* a pie is falling off the table is crossed only when the child acquires the conceptual–inferential know-how needed to do the sorts of things that the relevant epistemic status licenses her to do. This know-how involves mastery of the inferential significance of a conceptually contentful that-clause. No infant who lacks the concepts of pie and table has the conceptual know-how required to use the relevant inferential license. It does not make sense to say of such a pre-linguistic infant that she has the epistemic status of having perceived something. When she acquires a language, however, seeing the pie fall off the table can constitute a move on her part into the normative space of reasoning – a language-entry transition into a game that confers epistemic status on the position she occupies in it. The technical term for this kind of seeing is perception.

[14] Sellars's great breakthrough was precisely to notice that we are not faced with an exclusive choice between seeing perception as completely unshaped by inferential capacities – "the myth of the given" – and seeing it as a variety of inference. The Sellarsian alternative is to see perception, in the epistemically relevant sense of the term, as non-inferential but also as something only a concept-using reason-exchanger can engage in. An analogous reinterpretation of intentional action is also required by Sellars's approach. Once these ideas are incorporated into inferentialism, perception and action can be factored into a broadly inferentialist account of conceptual content along with the contribution of strictly inferential relations. This is the revision in inferentialism that is required to avoid idealistic inferentialism's loss of contact with the world. See Wilfrid Sellars, *Empiricism and the Philosophy of Mind*, with an introduction by Richard Rorty and a study guide by Robert Brandom (Cambridge, MA: Harvard University Press, 1997).

game exchange reasons with one another. The basic terms of the theory are the normative terms, "commitment" and "entitlement." The theory is pragmatic in the deeper sense that the norms or proprieties it theorizes are held in the first instance to be implicit in the practice itself. Logic and related reflective activities play the expressive role of making proprieties explicit in the form of claims, so that they can be offered discursively as reasons and so that reasons can be requested for accepting them. But the most basic level of language use, according to Brandom's pragmatic view, is that in which all proprieties are implicit. They are not to be thought of as rules, because proprieties do not take the form of rules until they are made explicit as such. A rule is an explicitly stated propriety. This element of Brandom's approach is a consequence of the discussion of "following a rule" in the *Philosophical Investigations*, where Wittgenstein shows that a rule-centered view of normativity generates an unacceptable regress.

Brandom's approach is pragmatic in two senses. First, it is pragmatic in the sense that it assigns discursive *practices* a more basic role in the order of explanation than it assigns to the categories of semantics.

Pragmatism in this sense is the view that what attributions of semantic content-fulness are *for* is explaining the normative significance of intentional states such as beliefs and of speech acts such as assertions. Thus the criteria of adequacy to which semantic theory's concept of content must answer are to be set by the pragmatic theory, which deals with contentful intentional states and the sentences used to express them in speech acts. (*MIE*, 143, his italics)

Second, Brandom's approach is pragmatic in the sense that he takes the normative know-how of unreflective language-users to be more basic than the reflective expression of norms in rules. This is what Brandom dubs "a *pragmatist* conception of norms – a notion of primitive correct-nesses of performance *implicit* in *practice* that precede and are presupposed by their *explicit* formulation in *rules* and *principles*" (*MIE*, 21, his italics). The proprieties are instituted at the most basic level by what people *do* in taking claims or claimers to be proper or improper. The major challenge Brandom faces in setting out the first part of his theory is to vindicate the possibility that proprieties can be instituted in this way, without making illicit use of notions that will later need to be explained in terms of them.

The second part of the theory is, then, a semantic theory of meaning as use. Brandom's task here is that of showing how a pragmatics-based approach can generate an account of the conceptual content of linguistic items. He accounts for them in terms of their role in observation, infer-ence, and action, in the mutual scorekeeping that language-users use to keep track of each other's commitments and entitlements, and in the social exchange of reasons. The principal challenge he faces is to demonstrate that he can explain what he calls the representational dimension of semantic content. This is where his account of the concept of truth comes in, for truth and reference are the two main representational concepts that need to be accounted for. The question is whether a semantic theory that takes a normative pragmatics and inferential practices as its starting points can generate the tools needed to do the job.

Brandom rejects the account of truth as warranted assertibility associated with classical pragmatism. It is, he says,

flawed in its exclusive attention to taking-true as a variety of *force* or pragmatic significance – as a doing, specifically an asserting of something. For "true" is used in other contexts, for instance, embedded in the antecedent of a conditional; the semantic content that it expresses is accordingly not exhausted by its freestanding assertional uses. (*MIE*, 322)

Brandom does not, however, simply catalogue other uses of "is true" and note that they behave differently from terms like "is justified." He offers an account of "refers" according to which it functions as a pronoun-forming operator. This puts him in a position to argue that pronouns are paradigmatic instances of a broader class of linguistic expressions he calls "proforms." Among these are prosentences. The expression "is true" he takes to be a prosentence-forming operator. Each of these accounts, he says:

explains the use of a bit of traditional *semantic* vocabulary in terms of the formation of *anaphoric* proforms. Indirect descriptions formed from "refer" both *mention* a term expression (in picking out anaphoric antecedents) and *use* that expression. The effect of applying an indirect description-forming operator to a mentioned term is that of turning the mentioned occurrence into a used occurrence. (*MIE*, 322f.)

The technical tools that Brandom places at the center of this theory include the concept of proforms, Frege's concept of substitution, and Charles Chastain's concept of anaphora. To get an initial grasp of what "anaphora" means, consider the case of pronouns. If I utter the sentence, "Aquinas proposed a just-war theory, whereas Hauerwas, having read the theory, rejects it," you will know without thinking about it that the pronoun "it" with which the sentence concludes refers to Aquinas' just-war theory. What pronouns refer to depends on something Chastain calls an *anaphoric chain* that links them to other referring expressions already introduced in a discursive context. To see what "it" refers to in this case, we follow the chain back to the subject matter identified and referred to at the beginning of the sentence. Anaphora involves the use of a substitute expression to refer to something the reference of which has already been fixed by an antecedently used expression.

Brandom's account of "refers" extends the anaphoric analysis of pronouns to pronoun-forming operators. His account of "is true" offers a parallel analysis of prosentence-forming operators. I will not try to explain the details of the theory here. All that matters for present purposes is that the theory, if successful, explains the conceptual work done by "is true" in non-philosophical contexts entirely in terms of anaphoric chains analogous to the ones everyone relies on when using and interpreting pronouns in relation to their antecedents. The anaphoric account operates entirely, that is, in terms of relationships among tokens of words. This does not make it a coherence theory like those traditionally associated with anti-realism. One of the advantages of Brandom's theory is that it keeps truth nicely distinct from justification, and yet it does so without construing truth as a property. For this reason it does not invite either realist or idealist metaphysical pictures to resolve the mystery of what such a property might consist in. It also accounts for both the embedded use of "is true" in the antecedents of conditionals and what Rorty calls the cautionary use of the term, as acceptance-based theories do not.

The anaphoric account of truth does not, by itself, explain why truth and justification are connected. They are connected because talk of truth and talk of justification both have roles to play in social practices of objective evaluation. Brandom's model for such practices is one of deontic scorekeeping. The reason that truth is not a property – despite appearances to the contrary at the level of surface grammar – is that it is a propriety, a deontic status. As a propriety, it is not reducible to a property. That is why "correspondence to reality," construed as a relational property, gets us on the wrong track in truth-theory. Being justified in believing something is also a propriety, but a different one, having to do with the responsibilities of a believer. Truth is a propriety that has to do with the correctness of propositional contents. Objective inquiry is a game in which all the players make epistemic commitments – roughly speaking, they adopt beliefs – while also attributing both commitments and entitlements to one another. Being entitled to one's commitments is a normative status one earns by playing the game well. But, entitlements aside, a player necessarily counts all of his or her own beliefs, at any given moment, as true. These epistemic commitments have implications with respect to the truth or falsity of the commitments a player attributes to other players. If I attribute a belief to you that conflicts with one of my epistemic commitments, I am bound to score your belief as "false" until or unless I either withdraw the attribution or withdraw my own belief. Each player keeps score on the commitments and entitlements of other players from his or her own point of view, and the game ends only when all inquirers die out.

In sandlot baseball there are no umpires. In street soccer there are no referees. The players keep track of runs or goals and of how well everyone played. In the game of objective inquiry, players make commitments and attribute commitments to one another. They give credit to one another for being entitled to commitments and occasionally blame one another for commitments undertaken irresponsibly. They also award points, so to speak, for commitments they deem correct. Any scorekeeper can withdraw a point once awarded if he or she thinks that subsequent developments in the practice of inquiry warrant such a change in the awarding of endorsement status to propositional contents. The way to withdraw a point once awarded is to say something like: "I thought Euclid's belief about X was true, but it isn't." When this happens, no aspersions need be cast on how Euclid played the game, on his entitlement to his commitment. He may still count as a responsible inquirer or even be ranked among the best. A scorekeeper who thinks so will be inclined to excuse Euclid for failing to commit himself to some post-Euclidean theory about X. The way to excuse him is to say something like: "What Euclid believed about X wasn't true, but he was justified in believing it."

It would not improve the rules of baseball if we appended to them a chapter on the nature of scoring runs, explaining that a player who touches home plate after rounding the bases has scored only if he or she has *really* touched it. We would be no more enlightened if we were told that scoring a run within the game *corresponds* to the physical state of affairs in which the player actually touches home plate. But sandlot baseball would be a much different game if players did not feel constrained to award runs by conforming their scorekeeping to a sort of discipline. At a minimum this discipline involves attentiveness to evidence and an attempt to avoid being influenced by wishful thinking. These features of scorekeeping discipline contribute to the objective dimension of baseball as a practice. Objective inquiry includes similar features, and endeavors to extend and perfect them. Its objectivity is a matter of the constraints the practice imposes on its players when they make commitments and when they keep track of normative statuses involving other players and the propositions they commit themselves to. The constraints are object-directed in the sense that they involve attentiveness to something being investigated as well as disciplined avoidance of wishful thinking, rationalization, and related intrusions of "merely subjective" factors.

Ethical and religious discursive practices have an objective dimension insofar as they involve constraints of this kind. Why does it make sense to say that there are moral or religious truths and falsehoods? Because the deontic scorekeeping by means of which we keep track of one another's commitments and entitlements pertaining to ethical and religious topics includes the same implicit distinction between the "how you play the epistemic game" factor and the correctness of commitments. The fact that ethical topics are themselves often normative statuses does not diminish the need to earn entitlement to one's commitments about them by attending to matters other than one's own subjective states. Whether one's commitments, attributions of commitments, and attributions of entitlements in ethical discourse are correct is not a matter of willing or wanting them to be so.

A divine command theorist might want to insist that the appropriate model for deontic scorekeeping in ethical discourse would include an umpire or a referee. The rules of major-league baseball and major-league soccer designate the head umpire or the referee as the only scorekeeper. A run or a goal can then be defined as having been scored when and only when the officially designated scorekeeper says so. Brandom's theory shows that a discursive practice can be objective in the sense at issue here without being construed on an authoritarian model of scorekeeping. If Brandom is right, in a pluralistic society, where no single scorekeeper is recognized by all ethical discoursers, it should still be possible in principle to make sense of being entitled to commitments and of making commitments that are correct in content. For the same reasons that baseball can be played on the sandlots and soccer can be played on the streets, ethical discourse can retain an objective dimension without prior agreement on a single scorekeeper. In ethics, as in most other forms of objective discourse, we are all keeping score.[15]

Brandom is not the first to develop a prosentential account of truth or to stress the concept's role in expressing endorsement of claims within social practices oriented toward objective inquiry, but he has combined these two elements impressively in a single theory of language. More important, he has set it within a larger theoretical structure that drastically

---

[15] The social–perspectival dimension of scorekeeping turns out to be essential to Brandom's account of propositional contents themselves. See *Making It Explicit*, ch. 8.

diminishes the temptation to require something more or essentially different from truth-theory. That structure, as we have seen, is as follows:

1 a *normative* pragmatics centered on the notions of commitment and entitlement; and
2 a semantics that calls upon *inferential practices* to explain conceptual content.

Unlike representationalism, which gives truth and reference primacy in the order of explanation, Brandom's inferentialism saves them for last. He does not dispense with them by any means, and considers it highly important to account for them successfully, but he does not assign them the important explanatory role that representationalism does. The concept of truth turns out to be *expressively* valuable as a device that allows us to move back and forth between used expressions and mentioned expressions while keeping track of cognitive commitments, but it is not needed to *explain* the essential operations of language. This means that, by the time he begins his consideration of truth, Brandom has already secured the exchange of reasons and broadly inferential practices as basic human activities. The concept of truth is not the point on which everything else teeters, as theorists anxiously try to dispel its mysteries. It enriches the expressive resources of our semantic vocabulary immensely, but it is not the explanatory basis of everything else – the without-which-not of discourse itself.

Furthermore, by describing perception of objects and action in the world as aspects of the broadly inferential activities he has in mind, Brandom has already avoided the idealist implications of a view that focuses solely on mental or linguistic entities and moves when accounting for conceptual content. It therefore does not fall to the theory of truth to break out of what Nietzsche called the "prison-house of language" to secure contact with real objects and their properties, for the prison-house-of-language picture has been obviated beforehand in the pragmatic account of our broadly inferential practices. This means that one does not need a so-called realist theory of truth as correspondence to make the overall theory of language-use offered under the heading of inferentialism a realist one in a perfectly intelligible (non-metaphysical) sense. The traditional realist theory of truth as correspondence is a phony explanation, and its metaphysical emendations and elaborations only make it worse. But in Brandom's view, truth-theory turns out to be the wrong place to begin theorizing about language and also the wrong place to overcome what is wrong with Berkelean idealism and its linguistic descendants. If Brandom's explanatory strategy is correct, then truth-theory shrinks to manageable proportions, but only when it is no longer given a starring role in the drama of civilization and only when it is given a surprisingly late entrance on the stage in technical philosophy. This is the main sense in which Brandom's theory of truth is deflationary: it drains the concept of its purportedly explanatory significance in philosophy.

In short, Brandom is arguing that representationalists have been asking truth-theory to do too much. It is a mistake to assume that denial of the standard form of realism in truth-theory places much of what we care about as reason-exchangers in jeopardy. That would only be so if representationalists were right about the order of explanation most likely to give us what we need in this area of philosophical reflection. But it may be that they are not right. And it is simply a lack of imagination for representationalists to assume that the options open to truth-theorists are confined to the realism of the correspondence theory and the anti-realism of linguistic idealism. When they think in this way, they are neglecting the possibility of approaching the concept of truth in pragmatically rectified inferentialist terms. (They are implicitly deferring to the representationalist mainstream in philosophy since Descartes, while ignoring the existence of inferentialist alternatives that go back to equally profound philosophers like Leibniz and the early Frege.) A principal disadvantage of the representationalist strategy, when viewed in light of Brandom's alternative strategy, is that, because it tries to make sense of truth so early in the explanatory project, it goes at the topic essentially empty-handed. So when honest doubts are raised about the adequacy of its accounts of truth, representationalism is quick, on the one hand, to invoke a mysterious metaphysical property that does nothing to dispel the doubts and, on the other hand, to accuse the doubters of threatening the basis of rationality. Brandom implies that both of these responses result from the explanatory primacy accorded to truth-theory – and thus to the concept of truth itself – in representationalism. Such primacy pretty much guarantees both that the theorist is empty-handed and that much of great value appears to depend on not being empty-handed. When the anti-realist then says, "You're empty-handed," the realist tends to reply with hocus-pocus and incrimination.

TRUTH AND THE VOCABULARY OF OBJECTIVITY

Davidson and Brandom agree that interpretation is inherently normative, that truth and justification are distinct, and that defining truth is folly. Yet they appear to differ over truth. Brandom is prepared to retain the idea that truth and reference are "representational" concepts, but he holds that such concepts, being merely expressive in function, cannot explain "what is expressed by the declarative use of sentences" (*MIE*, 496). The source of the trouble, he thinks, is the representationalist order of explanation, which fails to make semantics answer to pragmatics. As Rorty has pointed out, however, Davidson "may seem to resist Brandom's classification."[16] When Brandom identifies representationalism with a particular order of explanation, he appears to imply that Davidson is himself a representationalist, for Davidson obviously gives priority to semantics over pragmatics. Davidson wants the concept of truth to play the pivotal role in semantics, and has no use for "meaning as use," which is the very notion that Brandom's inferentialist semantics intends to explicate. Yet Davidson wants to eliminate the very idea of representations from the theory of interpretation.[17] The truth of a sentence is not, according to his theory, a relation between a representation and something that makes the representation true. Truth is a philosophically important concept, Davidson says – much more important than deflationists make it out to be – but it is not a representational one. This conclusion seems to put Davidson in opposition to Brandom on both points, for Brandom's deflationism takes truth to be a representational concept that has no explanatory work to do. His deflationism consists in saying that truth is a concept whose importance resides solely in the expressive resources it adds to our language when deontic scorekeeping operates at the level of semantic ascent.

It may well be, however, that these differences are mainly verbal. Ramberg rightly says that Davidson's theory "is not a semantic theory of truth as much as a truth-based theory of semantics."[18] This way of summarizing the theory implies that it is misleading to describe Davidson and Brandom as proponents of competing *theories of truth*. Michael Williams has recently argued that the concept of truth Davidson needs for his truth-based semantics is no more robust – no more *explanatory* – than the one accounted for by deflationists like Brandom.[19] Williams and Paul Horwich have both argued that Davidson's theory of radical interpretation implicitly commits him to a theory of meaning as use or conceptual

---

[16] "Representation, Social Practice, and Truth," in *Objectivity, Relativism, and Truth*, 152.
[17] "The Myth of the Subjective," in Michael Krausz (ed.), *Relativism: Interpretation and Confrontation* (University of Notre Dame Press, 1989), 165–66.
[18] Ramberg, *Davidson's Philosophy of Language*, 40.
[19] Michael Williams, "Meaning and Deflationary Truth," *Journal of Philosophy* 96 (1999): 545–64.

role – the same kind of theory Brandom defends.[20] I find both of these arguments persuasive. If they are sound, I see no remaining reason for Davidson to insist that deflationary pragmatism in the theory of interpretation is simply unacceptable. And, if Davidson's theory does boil down, in the end, to a use theory of meaning, I am inclined to favor Brandom's version, in part because it succeeds in making explicit the kind of theory it is and the expressive role it assigns to the concept of truth.

What shall we make of the apparent differences over representationalism? Is this disagreement also largely verbal? Clearly Brandom and Davidson do not mean exactly the same things by representationalism. Suppose we take a paradigmatic representationalist to be someone who holds both that semantics is prior to pragmatics *and* that semantics must explain the truth of true representations by appealing to truth-makers of some kind. Then we can say that Davidson and Brandom both break with the paradigm but do so in quite different ways. Davidson does so by inverting the relationship that representationalism typically envisions between truth and reference within semantics, and then using Tarski's work to provide "a method of defining truth for a language without depending on some property or relation that makes sentences true."[21] Brandom breaks with the paradigm by inverting the relationship that the paradigmatic representationalist envisions between semantics and pragmatics and then reworking semantics in inferentialist terms. As a result, the concept of truth plays very different roles in their respective philosophies of language. The question, however, is not which account of truth one ought to prefer, but rather which philosophy of language holds more promise overall.

On this last point, I have long shared Gilbert Harman's doubts about the notion that a theory of meaning or interpretation ought to take the form of a Davidsonian truth-based semantics.[22] So I am inclined to favor an approach that emphasizes conceptual role. Brandom's version of that approach strikes me not only as the most promising developed so far, but also as ideally suited for application in religious studies. When we take religious and ethical discourse as our subject matter, what we are examining in the course of our work, it seems to me, is precisely what Brandom's Sellarsian theory directs us to: the inferences being made by the people we are studying, the transitions they make into discourse when

---

[20] *Ibid.*, 562–63. Paul Horwich, *Meaning* (New York: Oxford University Press, 1998), 72.

[21] Ramberg, *Davidson's Philosophy of Language*, 49.

[22] See Gilbert Harman, "Meaning and Semantics," in *Reasoning, Meaning, and Mind* (Oxford University Press, 1999), 192–205.

they perceive something, and the discursive exits they execute by acting intentionally in the world. These are the sorts of moves we are trying to interpret when we engage in our own variety of normative score-keeping. In short, I find Brandom's model more useful than Davidson's – more illuminating as an account of what I do in one precinct of the humanities.

In Davidson's philosophy, truth is supposed to play a highly important role as an undefined primitive term in semantics, a role essential to the project of securing connections between words and objects. Truth is im-portant to Davidson mainly because he relies on it to secure such connec-tions. Perhaps he imagines that an inferentialist deflationary pragmatism cannot, in the end, make sense of word–world connections. This would fail to come to grips with the complexity of Brandom's pragmatism, how-ever. As I emphasized in the previous section, Brandom's deflationary account of truth is only one part of his broader project. And his infer-entialist semantics emphasizes discursive entry and exit transitions in a way that avoids the perils of idealism.

Davidson and Brandom both want to distance themselves from meta-physical idealism without ending up committed to some form of meta-physical realism. They both insist on the importance of explicating word–object relations in some way. But Brandom chooses not to place this particular philosophical burden on his account of truth. For this reason, he feels that he can *afford* to accept a deflationary account of this concept. The main point at issue between Davidson and Brandom turns out to be the question of *how* one ought to honor the intuitions that made realism seem attractive to philosophers in the first place. Davidson is closer to traditional realism in one respect, because he still thinks that one ought to honor those intuitions by constructing a semantic theory in which the concept of truth pulls much of the theoretical weight. The trick, he thinks, is to do this without construing truth as a relation between truth-makers and true representations – a relation such that the truth-makers explain the truth of true representations.

Brandom agrees that truth should not be construed as a relation of this sort, but he honors "realistic" intuitions in a different way, a way indebted to both Sellars and Heidegger. His response to the worry that he has failed to distinguish his position from linguistic idealism is to declare it "a misplaced concern":

What must not be lost is an appreciation of the way in which our discursive practice is empirically and practically *constrained*. It is not up to us which claims are true (that is, what the facts are). It is in a sense up to us which noises and marks express which claims, and hence, in a more attenuated sense, which express true claims. But empirical and practical constraint on our arbitrary whim is a pervasive feature of our discursive practice . . . [D]iscursive practices as here conceived do not stand apart from the rest of the world. (*MIE*, 331)

Brandom continues:

For those practices are not things, like words conceived as marks and noises, that are specifiable independently of the objects they deal with and the facts they make it possible to express. Discursive practices essentially involve to-ing and fro-ing with environing objects in perception and action. The conceptual proprieties implicit in those practices incorporate both empirical and practical dimensions. All our concepts are what they are in part because of their inferential links to others that have noninferential circumstances or consequences of application – concepts, that is, whose proper use is not specifiable apart from consideration of the facts and objects that responsively bring about or are brought about by their application. (*MIE*, 331)

What Brandom is saying here applies to religious and ethical concepts as well as to concepts of other kinds. One consequence of his approach, of course, is that his own philosophy of language is itself implicated in the very practices it reflects on. But, while such complicity is something any pragmatist must be prepared to acknowledge, it does not entail loss of contact with the world.

Neither does it entail thinking that what claims are true depends on anyone's claiming of them. Brandom distinguishes between claims in the semantic sense of what is claimed and claims in the pragmatic sense of an act of claiming. The former is "a matter of content," the latter a matter "of force or deontic attitude" (*MIE*, 327). To call something a fact, on Brandom's theory, is to take it to be true – that is, a true claim in the semantic sense. But saying this "does not commit one to treating the facts as somehow dependent on our claimings; it does not, for instance, have the consequence that had there never been any claimers, there would have been no facts" (*MIE*, 328).

This point responds to the heart of Santurri's argument for construing pragmatism as a form of nihilism, but it also brings me into the middle of a dispute between Brandom and Rorty. Rorty's worry seems to be that Brandom is implicitly abandoning his pragmatic commitment to the priority of social practices when he denies that had there never been any claimers, there would have been no facts. Facts, as Brandom has defined them, are merely true claims in the semantic sense of what is claimed. But claims, according to Brandom's Sellarsian theory, are what they are only by virtue of the roles that they play in social practices that involve observation, inference, and action. For it is these social practices that confer conceptual content. These social practices would not exist if there were no claimers, if there were no people to make the various possible assertory moves that the practices involve. So how could there have been conceptually contentful claims, and thus *true* ones, if there had been no claimers? Rorty suspects that Brandom has been tempted, at this late point in his theorizing, to reinstate the metaphysical picture of the world as containing independent demands for our practices. In this case, the picture takes the form of holding that there could have been claims, and thus true claims ("facts"), independently of the very social practices that had previously been said to give claims whatever conceptual content they have.[23]

In responding to this suspicion, it seems to me, Brandom simply needs to reaffirm that, whenever one makes a claim, one is necessarily *relying on* (but not necessarily *referring to*) the social practice within which this and other claims acquire their conceptual content. He can then acknowledge that when, in claiming something, one refers to facts or to true claims in the semantic sense, one is still necessarily relying on the underlying social practice. While keeping this acknowledgment in mind, he can, without implicitly revoking it, go on to use the conceptual resources of a discursive social practice to discuss all sorts of things, including possible states of affairs in which there are no discursive social practices. One of the things he can discuss is what would have been the case if we language-users had not existed and there had therefore been neither discursive social practices nor the conceptual resources they institute. For example, he can discuss what things would have been like in the area now known as New Jersey if, as a result of the climatic catastrophe that killed the dinosaurs, all animals had died out, thus preventing the evolution of claimers. Brandom can discuss such counterfactual circumstances for the same reason that any of us can discuss what *actually* transpired in the history of the universe *before* language-users came along and invented the social practices that confer conceptual content on what is claimed. These are both among the many things that our language equips us to talk about.

We implicitly rely on social practices whenever we make (or consider) claims about anything whatsoever. But some of the coherent claims we can make (thanks to the conceptual richness of our social practices) are

---

[23] For Rorty's worries about Brandom's distinction between two senses of "claim," see *Truth and Progress*, 135ff. and his response to Brandom in *Rorty and His Critics*, 183–90.

about counterfactual states of affairs in which there would have been no claimers. Others are about actual pre-historic states of affairs in which there were not yet any claimers. These two sets of claims, like all claims, have the conceptual content they do because of the roles they play in our social practices. Also, like all coherent claims, they are either true or false. Some such claims, presumably, are true. That they have conceptual content at all "presupposes" the existence of our social practices. But, thanks to the conceptual content they do have, we can, in asserting some of them, affirm *true claims* about states of affairs in which our social practices would not have existed or did not yet exist. Given Brandom's definition of "facts" as true claims and his pragmatic thesis about the dependence of claimers on social practices, it follows (a) that there are *facts* about possible but not actual states of affairs in which there would have been no claimers. It also follows (b) that there are *facts* about actual but past states of affairs in which there were no claimers.

When Brandom denies "that had there never been any claimers, there would have been no facts," I take him to be affirming (a). If that is all he means to be doing, then I see no problem here that ought to be of concern to Rorty. Do any of the facts mentioned in (a) entail that our social practices do not now exist? No, they do not. So there appears to be no logical difficulty in affirming (a) while also affirming the pragmatic thesis that the claims mentioned in (a), like all claims, presuppose the current existence of our social practices. The paradox is further dispelled when we realize that the sense of presupposition at work in the pragmatic thesis is not logical, but causal. The sense in which the claims in question presuppose the existence of our social practices is simply that our social practices are a *material prerequisite* for the institution of all conceptually contentful claims. This causal truth places no logical restriction on what *content* the claims thus instituted can have. In particular, it does not prevent those claims from being about merely possible or long-past states of affairs in which our social practices did not exist. So I see no metaphysical backsliding in Brandom's treatment of this issue.

In his response to Brandom in *Rorty and His Critics*, Rorty appears to recommend abandoning ordinary objectivity-talk in a way that puts him at odds with Davidson as well as with Brandom. Brandom distinguishes his two senses of "claim" in order to make explicit an idea he takes to be implicit in ordinary objectivity talk. This is the idea that whether our claimings get things right is not up to us but a matter of how things are with the objects we are talking about. Neither the idea nor the explication of it need involve a metaphysical commitment, as far as I can tell, provided that Brandom is prepared to accept what I have said in his defense in the preceding paragraphs. Perhaps Rorty sees something here that I do not. The move Rorty finds suspicious belongs to Brandom's larger project of showing how ordinary objectivity-talk can be accounted for as arising out of "the social soup" of norms that are implicit in practices. The crucial question is whether this larger project is plausible, as I believe it is.

Brandom endorses a form of pragmatism according to which our ideals of objectivity are best seen as explicit statements of norms that are, in the first instance, implicit in practices of inquiry and reason-exchange. This is a claim about the normative priority of practices, not a claim about the need to define truth in terms of utility. Brandom, like Wittgenstein, thinks that representationalists have been tempted by such misleading factors as the surface grammar of truth-talk to explicate our ideals of objectivity in a metaphysical way. Brandom helps us to see much of our ordinary talk of truth and objectivity in ethics as untainted by metaphysics in the pejorative sense. His explications of such discourse are meant to be equally untainted, and, as far as I can see, they are.

In this way, Brandom hopes to avoid the either–or imposed on philosophy in the Cartesian era by representationalism's subject–object dualism. Norms are to be understood *either* as objective in the sense of being pictures of the real *or* as subjective in the sense of being projections of human subjects. In rejecting this either–or, Brandom's pragmatism adds the category of social–practical phenomena to the categories of objective and subjective phenomena, thus denying the Cartesian dualism, and it accords the new category priority over the other two in its account of norms. This does not entail elimination of either objectivity or subjectivity. It simply maintains, with Sellars and Heidegger, that objectivity and subjectivity "precipitate" out of social practices, that they are less basic than the social–practical in the best available account of norms. Pragmatism with respect to norms resists reduction of the social–practical to either pole of the Cartesian dualism. Norms are not to be understood ultimately as objects or as properties of objects. Nor are they to be understood as projections of subjects. *Norms are initially proprieties implicit in practices.* It is part of the business of reflective practices to make norms explicit in the form of rules or ideals. Once made explicit, norms can be subjected to criticism and offered as reasons when subjecting other norms to criticism. Ideals of objectivity and our ability to hold ourselves responsible as subjects are implicit in social practices from the start. The social practices we engage in both constitute us as the self-committing, responsibility-oriented subjects we are and make possible the various ways in which we hold one another responsible and aim for correctness when addressing religious topics and deciding what to do.

Brandom's sort of pragmatism does not make religious, ethical, or scientific objectivity out to be any less important than we might have thought it to be. Neither does it prepare the way for eliminating the ordinary talk in which ideals of objectivity are implicit. It simply rejects and replaces a set of bad philosophical accounts of them. The Nietzschean mode of contemporary postmodernism, which Rorty sometimes echoes, combines a pragmatic approach to norms with a desire to eliminate ordinary talk about objectivity and subjectivity as inherently metaphysical. The most extreme postmodernist proposals involve prophecies of the death of the subject and reduction of all truth-talk to assertions of power. Metaphysical realists suspect that any form of deflationary pragmatism stands at the top of a slippery slope leading inevitably to nihilistic abandonment of trying to get things right (ethically and otherwise). Brandom would grant that he is in a bit of terrain that is surrounded by slippery slopes, for that is what all philosophy is like. But he is trying to define a space between the cliffs where it is possible to be neither nihilist in this sense nor representationalist. His way of defining this space is to show in detail that ordinary uses of terms like "true" and "refers" can be accounted for without resort to representationalism.

The debate within the pragmatist camp between Brandom and Rorty serves as a reminder that it can be hard to know where the line is between innocuous uses of terms and uses that are tainted by metaphysics. What gives impetus to the more extreme forms of postmodernism is the view that ordinary talk of truth and of subjects is wholly vitiated by a form of metaphysical philosophy that runs through the entire culture. That this view amounts to an over-intellectualized interpretation of culture is a point Rorty has himself made effectively against Heidegger and Derrida.[24] But pragmatists have always recognized that metaphysics, in the pejorative sense, "is not just a technical discourse within philosophy to which, since Kant, a technical apparatus of philosophical criticism has been opposed. It is endemic to our culture."[25] Otherwise, pragmatism would not have its broader intellectual significance as a tradition of cultural criticism primarily interested in defending democratic practices

[24] See, for example, Richard Rorty, *Essays on Heidegger and Others* (Cambridge University Press, 1991), 27–65.
[25] Mark Johnston, "Objectivity Refigured: Pragmatism without Verificationism," in John Haldane and Crispin Wright (eds.), *Reality, Representation, and Projection* (Oxford University Press, 1993), 85.

honestly – without resort to the thought that either nature or nature's God *demands* that we behave democratically.

In his response to Brandom, Rorty appears to argue that we should simply discard the ordinary vocabulary in which our ideals of objectivity are embedded. In his response to Ramberg in the same volume, however, he dramatically recants his previous denial "that true statements get things right."[26] I do not see how to square the latter response with the former. Ramberg and Brandom appear to be explicating the same pre-philosophical ideal of "getting things right" in the somewhat different philosophical idioms of Davidson and Sellars, neither of which strikes me as inherently tainted by metaphysics. Whether his concession to Ramberg leads Rorty to take a more charitable line in interpreting ordinary objectivity-talk remains to be seen, but it does at least open the door to a form of pragmatism I find congenial.

[26] *Rorty and His Critics*, 370–77.

3

Cultural politics and the question of the existence of God

Richard Rorty

CULTURAL POLITICS

The term "cultural politics" covers, among other things, arguments about what words to use. When we say that Frenchmen should stop referring to Germans as "Boches," or that white people should stop referring to black people as "niggers," we are practicing cultural politics. For our socio-political goals – increasing the degree of tolerance that certain groups of people have for one another – will be promoted by abandoning these linguistic practices.

Cultural politics is not confined to debates about hate speech. It includes projects for getting rid of whole topics of discourse. It is often said, for example, that we should stop using the concepts of "race" and "caste," stop dividing the human community up by genealogical descent. The idea is to lessen the chances that the question "who are his or her ancestors?" will be asked. Many people urge that words like "noble blood," "mixed blood," "outcaste," "intermarriage," "untouchable," and the like should be dropped from the language. For, they argue, this would be a better world if the suitability of people as spouses or employees or public officials were judged entirely on the basis of their behavior, rather than partially by reference to their ancestry.

This line of thinking is sometimes countered by saying "but there really *are* inherited differences – ancestry *does* matter." The rejoinder is: there certainly are inheritable physical characteristics, but these do not, in themselves, correlate with any characteristics that could provide a good reason for breaking up a planned marriage, or voting for or against a candidate. We may need the notion of genetic transmission for medical purposes, but not for any other purposes. So instead of talking about different races, let us just talk about different genes.

In the case of "race," as in that of "noble blood," the question "is there such a thing?" and the question "should we talk about such a thing?" seem pretty well interchangeable. That is why we tend to classify discussion of whether to stop talking about different races as "political" rather than "scientific" or "philosophical." But there are other cases in which it seems odd to identify questions about what exists with questions about what it is desirable to discuss.

The question of whether to talk about neutrons, for example, seems a strictly scientific question. That is why people who regret that physicists ever investigated radioactivity, or speculated about the possibility of splitting the atom, are accused of confusing science with politics. It seems natural to separate the political question of whether it was a good thing for humanity that scientists began to think about the possibility of atomic fission from scientific questions about the existence and properties of elementary particles.

I have sketched this contrast between the case of races and that of neutrons because it raises the question I want to discuss: how do we tell when, if ever, an issue about what exists should be discussed without reference to our socio-political goals? How should we split up culture into areas to which cultural politics is relevant and areas which should be kept free of it? When is it appropriate to say "we had *better* talk about them, because they *exist*" and when is that remark not to the point?

These questions are important for debates about what roles religion should play in contemporary society. Many people think that we should just stop talking about God. They think this for much the same reasons that they believe talk of race and caste to be a bad thing. Lucretius' *Tantum religio potuit suadere malorum* has been quoted for two millennia in order to remind us that religious conviction can easily be used to excuse cruelty. Marx's claim that religion is the opiate of the people sums up the suspicion, widespread since the Enlightenment, that ecclesiastical institutions are among the principal obstacles to the formation of a global cooperative commonwealth. Many people agree with Marx that we should try to create a world in which human beings devote all their energies to increasing human happiness in this world, rather than taking time off to think about the possibility of life after death.

To say that talk about God should be dropped because it impedes the search for human happiness is to take a pragmatic attitude toward religion that many religious believers find offensive and that some theologians think beside the point. The point, they would insist, is that God *exists*, or perhaps that human beings really *do* have immortal souls. Granted that the existence of God or of an immortal soul is controversial, that controversy should be explicitly about what exists, not about whether religious belief conduces to human happiness. First things first: ontology precedes cultural politics.

WILLIAM JAMES'S VIEW OF RELIGION

I want to argue that cultural politics should replace ontology, and also that whether it should or not is *itself* a matter of cultural politics. Before turning to the defense of these theses, however, I want to underline the importance of such issues for philosophers who, like myself, are sympathetic to William James's pragmatism. James agreed with John Stuart Mill that the right thing to do, and a fortiori the right belief to acquire, is always the one that will do most for human happiness. So he advocated a utilitarian ethics of belief. James often comes close to saying that *all* questions, including questions about what exists, boil down to questions about what will help create a better world.

James's willingness to say this sort of thing has made him subject to accusations of intellectual perversity. For his view seems to suggest that, when notions like "race-mixing" and "atomic fission" are brought into the conversation, it is apposite to exclaim: "Let's not talk about that sort of thing! It's too dangerous! Let's not go there!" James seems to countenance doing what Peirce forbade: blocking the road of inquiry, refusing to find out what the world is really like because doing so might have harmful effects on human beings.

To give a concrete example, many people have argued that psychologists should not try to find out whether inheritable physical features are correlated with intelligence, simply because of the social harm that a positive answer to this question might produce. James's view of truth seems to suggest that these people are making a good point. People who are suspicious of pragmatism, on the other hand, argue that preventing scientists from doing experiments to find out whether intelligence is genetically transmissible, or to find out whether a neutron bomb is feasible, is to sin against truth. On their view, we should separate practical questions about whether eugenics or racial discrimination should be practiced, from the straightforwardly empirical question about whether Europeans are, on average, stupider than Asiatics – just as we divide the question of whether we *can* build a neutron bomb from the question of whether we *should*.

James was criticized not only for blocking the road of inquiry, and thus for being too restrictive, but also for being too permissive. That criticism was most frequently directed at "The Will to Believe," an essay which he said should have been titled "The Right to Believe." There he argued that one had a right to believe in the existence of God if that belief contributed to one's happiness, for no reason other than that very contribution.

I think that the best way for those of us who find James's pragmatism sympathetic to restate his position is to say that questions about what is too permissive and what is too restrictive are themselves questions of cultural politics. For example, the question of whether religious believers should be asked for evidence of the truth of their belief, and condemned as uneducated or irrational if they are unable to produce sufficient evidence, is a question about what sort of role we want religion to play in our society. It is on all fours with the question raised by the Inquisition: should scientists be allowed cavalierly to disregard scripture when they formulate hypotheses about the motions of heavenly bodies?

The question of whether we should, for the sake of preserving ancient traditions, allow parents to perpetuate a caste system by dictating choices of marriage partners to their children, is the same sort of question. Such questions arise whenever new social practices are beginning to compete with old ones – when, for example, the New Science of seventeenth-century Europe began to compete with the Christian churches for control of the universities, or when a traditional African culture is exposed to European ways.

The question of whether scientists should have been allowed to find out whether the atom could be split, or should be allowed to investigate the correlation of intelligence with skin color, is not a question that can be answered simply by saying "do not block the road of inquiry!" or "seek the truth, though the heavens fall!" Neither is the question of whether France and Germany are right to criminalize Holocaust-denial. There is much to be said on both sides. The argument for letting scientists investigate whatever they please is that the more ability to predict we can get, the better off we shall be in the long run. The argument for blocking them off from certain topics is that the short-run dangers are so great as to outweigh the chances of long-term benefit. There are no grand philosophical principles that can help us solve such problems of risk-management.

To say that James is basically right in his approach to truth and reality is to say that arguments about relative dangers and benefits are the only ones that matter. That is why the statement "we should be talking about it because it's real" is as useless as "we should believe it because it's true." Attributions of reality or truth are, on the view I share with James, compliments we pay to entities or beliefs that have won their spurs, paid their way, proved themselves useful, and therefore been incorporated into accepted social practices. When these practices are being contested, it is of no use to say that reality or truth is on the side of one of the contestants. For such claims will always be mere table-thumping, not serious contributions to cultural politics.

Another way to put James's point is to say that truth and reality exist for the sake of social practices, rather than vice versa. Like the Sabbath, they are social constructs, made for man. This is a dark saying, but I think that it can be defended by appealing to the work of a contemporary neo-Hegelian, Robert Brandom, whose writings provide the best weapons for defending my version of James's pragmatism. Brandom is not a utilitarian, and his work follows out the line of thought that leads from Kant to Hegel, rather than the one that leads from Mill to James. But his construal of assertions as the assumption of responsibilities to other members of society, rather than to "the world" or "the truth," brings him into alignment with James.

BRANDOM ON THE PRIORITY OF THE SOCIAL

The germ of Brandom's later work can be found in an early article he published on Heidegger. There he treats Heidegger as putting forward a doctrine he calls "the ontological priority of the social." The doctrine of the priority of the social is perhaps not happily thought of as an "ontological" one, but Brandom is using it as a way of explicating the consequences of Heidegger's quasi-pragmatist attempt to make the *Zuhanden* prior to the *Vorhanden*. The priority in question consists in the fact that "all matters of authority or privilege, in particular *epistemic* authority, are matters of social practice, and not objective matters of fact."[1]

Brandom enlarges on this claim by remarking that society divides culture up into three areas. In the first of these the individual's authority is supreme (as when she makes sincere first-person reports of feelings or thoughts). In the second, the non-human world is supreme (as when the litmus paper, or the DNA-analysis apparatus, is allowed to determine whether the accused will be freed or punished, or whether a given scientific theory will be accepted or rejected). But there is a third area in which society does not delegate, but retains the right to decide for itself. This last is the arena of cultural politics. Brandom analogizes this situation to

[1] Robert Brandom, "Heidegger's Categories in *Being and Time*," *The Monist* 66 (1983): 389–90.

the constitutional arrangements of the USA, according to which, as he says, "the judiciary is given the authority and responsibility to interpret the proper region of authority and responsibility of each branch [that is to say, of the executive, the legislative, and the judiciary branches of government], itself included."[2]

The question at issue between James and his opponents boiled down to this: is there an authority beyond that of society which society should ac- knowledge – an authority such as God, or Truth, or Reality? Brandom's account of assertions as assumptions of social responsibilities leaves no room for such an authority, and so he sides with James. Both philosophers can appeal to Occam's Razor. The authority traditionally attributed to the non-human can be explained sociologically, and such a sociological account has no need to invoke the rather mysterious beings that theo- logical or philosophical treatments of authority require. (Such entities include "the divine will," "the intrinsic nature of reality, as it is in itself, apart from human needs and interests," and "the immediately given character of experience.")

Suppose that one accepts the thesis of the ontological primacy of the social. Then one will think that the question of the existence of God is a question of the advantages and disadvantages of using God-talk over against alternative ways of talking. As with "race," so with "God." Instead of taking about races we can, for many purposes, talk about genes. Instead of talking about God the Creator we can (as physicists do) talk about the Big Bang. For other purposes, such as providing foundations for morality, we can talk (as Habermas does) about consensus under ideal communicative conditions rather than about the divine will. When discussing the future of humanity, we can talk (as Marx did) about a secularist social utopia instead of about the Last Judgment. And so on.

Suppose, however, one does not accept the priority of the social, pre- cisely *because* one is a religious believer, and holds that God has authority over human society, as well as over everything else. From Brandom's point of view, this is like holding that human society is subject to the au- thority of "reality" or of "experience" or of "truth." All attempts to name an authority which is superior to that of society are disguised moves in the game of cultural politics. That is what they *must* be, because it is the only game in town. (But in saying that it is the only such game, Brandom is not claiming to have made an empirical discovery, much less to have revealed a "conceptual necessity." He is, I would claim, articulating a

---

[2] *Ibid.*, 389.

cultural–political stance by pointing to the social advantages of his account of authority.)

Brandom's view can be made more plausible by considering what people actually have in mind when they say that God has authority over human society. They do not say this unless they think they know what God wants human beings to do – unless they can cite sacred scriptures, or the words of a guru, or the teachings of an ecclesiastical tradition, or something of the sort, in support of their own position. But, from the point of view of both atheists and people whose scripture or guru or tradition is different, what is purportedly said in the name of God is actually said in the name of some interest group – some sect or church, for example. Two competing religious groups (say the Hindus and the Muslims, or the Mormons and the Catholics) will typically say that the other willfully and blasphemously refuses to submit to God's authority.

The battles between two such groups are analogous to arguments between opposing counsel, presenting appellate briefs to a court. Both sets of lawyers will claim to have the authority of "the law" on their side. Alternatively, it can be analogized to the battle between two scientific theories both of which claim to be true to the "nature of reality." Brandom's point is that the appeal to God, like the appeal to "the law," is always superfluous, since, as long as there is disagreement about what the purported authority says, the idea of "authority" is out of place.[3] Only when the community decides to adopt one faith rather than another, or the court decides in favor of one side rather than another, or the scientific community in favor of one theory rather than another, does the idea of "authority" become applicable. The so-called "authority" of anything other than the community (or some person or thing or expert culture authorized by the community to make decisions in its name) can only be more table-thumping.

THE APPEAL TO EXPERIENCE, RELIGIOUS AND OTHERWISE

The counter-intuitive character of Brandom's claims is due in part to the popularity of empiricism. For empiricists tell us that we can break out from under the authority of the local community by making unmediated contact with reality. This view has encouraged the idea that Europe finally got in touch with reality when scientists like Galileo had

---

[3] This is a point which has been made repeatedly, and very persuasively, by Stanley Fish. See his book *Professional Correctness: Literary Studies and Political Change* (New York: Clarendon Press, 1995).

the courage to believe the evidence of their senses rather than bowing to the authority of Aristotle and the Catholic Church.

Brandom agrees with his teacher Wilfrid Sellars that the idea of getting in direct touch with reality through the senses is a confusion between relations of justification, which hold between propositions, and causal relations, which hold between events. We should not treat the causal ability of certain events to produce non-inferential beliefs in suitably programmed organisms as a justification for their holding those beliefs.

Brandom agrees with Sellars that "all awareness is a linguistic affair." On this view, creatures not programmed to use language, such as dogs and human infants, react to stimuli but are no more aware of the characteristics of things than thermostats are aware of heat and cold. There can be no such thing as by-passing the linguistic practices of the community by using one's senses to find out how things really are, for two reasons. First: all non-inferential perceptual reports ("this is red," "this is disgusting," "this is holy") are made in the language of one or another community, a language adapted to that community's needs. Second: the community grants authority to such reports not because it believes in a special relation between reality and human sense-organs, but because it has empirical evidence that such reports are reliable (in the sense that they will be confirmed by the application of independent criteria).

This means that when somebody reports experiencing an object about which the community has no reason to think her a reliable reporter, her appeal to experience will fall flat. If I say that round squares are, contrary to popular opinion, possible, because I have in fact recently encountered several such squares, nobody takes me seriously. The same goes if I come out of the forest claiming to have spotted a unicorn. If I say that I experienced God, this may or may not be taken seriously, depending on what uses of the term "God" are current in my community. If I explain to a Christian audience that personal observation has shown me that God is, contrary to popular opinion, female, that audience will probably just laugh. But if I say that I have seen the Risen Christ in the disk of the sun on Easter morning, it is possible that I shall be viewed with respect and envy.

In short, God-reports have to live up to previous expectations, just as do reports of physical objects. They cannot, all by themselves, be used to repudiate those expectations. They are useful for this purpose only when they form part of a full-fledged, concerted, cultural–political initiative. This is what happens when a new religion or church replaces an old one. It was not the disciples' reports of an empty tomb, all by themselves, that made Europe believe that God was incarnate in Christ. But, in the context of St. Paul's overall public relations strategy, those reports had their effect. Analogously, it was not Galileo's report of spots moving across the face of the planet Jupiter, possibly caused by the transits of moons, that overthrew the authority of the Aristotelian–Ptolemaic cosmology. But, in the context of the initiative being mounted by his fellow Copernican cultural politicians, that report had considerable importance.

I can sum up what I have been saying about appeals to experience as follows: experience gives us no way to drive a wedge between the cultural–political question of what we should talk about and the question of what really exists. For what counts as an accurate report of experience is a matter of what a community will let you get away with. Empiricism's appeal to experience is as inefficacious as appeals to the Word of God unless backed up with a predisposition on the part of a community to take such appeals seriously. So experience cannot, by itself, adjudicate disputes between warring cultural politicians.

THE EXISTENCE OF GOD AND THE EXISTENCE OF CONSCIOUSNESS

I can make my point about the irrelevance of religious experience to God's existence a bit more vivid by comparing the God of orthodox Western monotheism with consciousness as it is understood by Cartesian dualists. In the unphilosophical sense of the term "conscious," the existence of consciousness is indisputable. People in a coma lack consciousness. People are conscious as long as they are walking and talking. But there is a special philosophical sense of the term "consciousness" in which the very existence of consciousness is in dispute.

In this sense of "consciousness," the word refers to something the absence of which is compatible with walking and talking. It is what zombies lack that the rest of us possess. Zombies behave just like normal people, but have no inner life. The light bulb in their brains, so to speak, never goes on. They do not feel anything, although they can answer questions about how they feel in the conventional ways, ways which have the place they do in the language game by virtue of, for example, correlations between their utterances of "it hurts" and their having recently touched hot stoves, been pricked by pins, and the like. Talking to a zombie is just like talking to anybody else, since the zombie's lack of an inner life never manifests itself by any outward and visible sign. That is why, unless neurology someday discovers the secret of non-zombiehood, we shall never know whether our nearest and dearest share our feelings, or are what James called "automatic sweethearts."

Philosophers have spent decades arguing about whether this sense of "consciousness" and this sense of "zombie" make sense. The question at issue is: can a descriptive term have a sense if its application is regulated by no public criteria? Wittgenstein thought that the answer to this question was "no." That negative answer is the upshot of arguments like this one:

Suppose everyone had a box with something in it: we call it a "beetle." No one can look into anyone else's box, and everyone says he knows what a beetle is only by looking at *his* beetle. – Here it would be possible for everyone to have something different in his box. One might even imagine such a thing constantly changing. – But suppose the word "beetle" had a use in these people's language? – If so, it would not be used as the name of a thing. The thing in the box has no place in the language-game at all; not even as a *something*: for the box might even be empty. – No, one can "divide through" by the thing in the box; it cancels out, whatever it is.[4]

The analogues of these private beetles are what philosophers who believe in the possibility of zombies call "raw feels" or "qualia" – the sort of thing that shows "what it is *like* ... [e.g., to be in pain, to see something red]." We all know what it is like be in pain, these philosophers believe, but (despite their sincere avowals that they do) zombies do not. Wittgenstein would say that the word "pain" has a sense only as long as philosophers do *not* treat it as the name of something whose presence or absence swings free of all differences in environment or behavior. On his view, the philosophers who believe in "qualia" and who deploy expressions like "what it is like to be in pain" are proposing, and commending, a new language game. In this specifically philosophical game, we use expressions whose *only* function is to help us disjoin pain from pain-behavior. We use them to separate off the outer behavior and its neurological correlates from something that is a state neither of the body nor of the nervous system. Wittgenstein, when he is being properly cautious, thinks that anything has a sense if you give it one by playing an appropriate language game with it. But he can see no point in playing the "qualia" game. So he thinks that we are entitled to "divide through" by the qualia just as we do by the beetles – to treat them, as Wittgenstein says in another passage, as "a wheel that turns though nothing else moves with it" and which is therefore "not part of the mechanism."[5]

---

[4] Ludwig Wittgenstein, *Philosophical Investigations*, Part I, section 293 (Oxford: Blackwell, 1953).
[5] *Ibid.*, section 271.

Philosophers of mind like Daniel Dennett and Sellars agree with Wittgenstein about this. But they are criticized by philosophers more sympathetic to Descartes, such as David Chalmers and Thomas Nagel. The latter say that the existence of raw feels, of the experience of "what it is like . . . " is incontestable. They reject Sellars' and Brandom's doctrine that all awareness is a linguistic affair. There is, they say, more aware-ness than we can put into words – language can point to things that it cannot describe. To think otherwise, they say, is to be a verificationist, and verificationists display what Nagel regards as an undesirable lack of "the ambition for transcendence." Nagel writes as follows: "Only a dogmatic verificationist would deny the possibility of forming objective concepts that reach beyond our current capacity to apply them. The aim of reaching *a conception of the world which does not put us at the center in any way* [emphasis added] requires the formation of such concepts."[6]

Brandom's doctrine of the ontological priority of the social would, of course, only be adopted by someone who has little interest in "reach-ing a conception of the world which does not put us at the center." Brandom, Sellars, and Wittgenstein simply lack the "ambition of tran-scendence" that Nagel, resembling in this respect the orthodox the-ologians of Western monotheism, thinks it desirable to have. Those theologians, in their anxiety to make God truly transcendent, separated him from the things of this world by describing him as without parts or passions, non-spatio-temporal, and therefore incomparable to his crea-tures. They went on to insist that the fact of God's incomparability is nonetheless compatible with his making himself known to us in expe-rience. Nagel and those who wish to preserve the special philosophical notion of consciousness (i.e., the thing that zombies lack) are trying to give sense to a descriptive term by a series of negations. But they insist that the fact that consciousness is like nothing else in the universe is com-patible with our being directly and incorrigibly aware that we have it, for we know that *we* are not zombies.

Both those who want to use "God" in the way that orthodox theol-ogy does and those who want to use "consciousness" as Chalmers and Nagel do claim that their opponents, the people who do not want to play any such language game, are denying the obvious. Many ortho-dox theologians have claimed that denial of the existence of God simply flies in the face of the common experience of mankind. Nagel thinks that philosophical views such as Dennett's "stem from an insufficiently robust

---

[6] Thomas Nagel, *The View from Nowhere* (New York: Oxford University Press, 1986), 24.

sense of reality and of its independence of any particular form of human understanding." Many religious believers think that it requires considerable perversity to even imagine being an atheist. Nagel, I imagine, thinks that it requires similar perversity to weaken one's sense of reality to the point at which one takes seriously the doctrine of the ontological priority of the social.

The moral I want to draw from the analogy between God and consciousness is that the existence of either is not a matter which appeals to experience could ever resolve, any more than one can appeal to experience to determine whether or not marriage across caste or racial lines is or is not intrinsically disgusting. Cultural politics can create a society that will find the latter repulsive, and cultural politics of a different sort can create one that finds such marriages unobjectionable. There is no way to show that belief in God or in qualia is more or less "natural" than disbelief, any more than there is a way to figure out whether a sense of caste membership or race membership is more or less "natural" than utter indifference to human blood-lines. What one side of the argument calls "natural," the other is likely to call "primitive," or perhaps "contrived."

Similarly, cultural politics of the sort conducted in Europe since the Enlightenment can alternately diminish or increase the obviousness of God's existence, as well as the frequency of reports to have experienced God's presence. Cultural politics of the sort conducted within philosophy departments can diminish or increase the numbers of philosophy students who find the existence of qualia obvious, and find it equally obvious that some humanoids might be zombies. There are Dennett-leaning departments and Chalmers-leaning departments. The disagreement between them is no more susceptible to neutral adjudication than is the disagreement between atheists and theists.[7]

To say that cultural politics has the last word on these matters is to say, once again, that the questions "should we be talking about God?" "should we be speculating about zombies?" "should we talk about what race people belong to?" are not posterior to the questions "does God exist?" "could some of the humanoids in this room be zombies?" "are

---

[7] In his *The Conscious Mind: In Search of a Fundamental Theory* (Oxford University Press, 1996), Chalmers discusses the analogy between consciousness (in the sense of what zombies lack) and God at 186–89 and again at 249. At 187 he says that the difference is that we can explain God-talk sociologically: God was postulated as an explanation of various phenomena. Consciousness, however, is an explanandum. So the only way to account for talk about it is by saying that its existence is obvious to all (except, mysteriously, a few oddballs like Dennett). I would argue that "consciousness" is an artifact of Cartesian philosophy in the same way that God is an artifact of early cosmology. (That was one of the claims made in my book *Philosophy and the Mirror of Nature* (1979). On the view I share with Sellars and Brandom, there are no such things as "natural" explananda.

there such things as distinct races within the human species?" They are the *same* questions, for any consideration relevant to the cultural–political question is equally relevant to the ontological question, and conversely. But, from the point of view of philosophers like Nagel, who warn against the lures of verificationism, to think them the same questions is itself a confusion.

OBJECTS AS MADE FOR MAN

The view that I have been ascribing to Brandom may make it seem as if acknowledging the ontological priority of the social entails allowing existence to be ascribed to anything society finds it convenient to talk about. This may seem ridiculously counter-intuitive. Even though society might set its face against caste-talk or against God-talk, it can hardly set its face against talk of stars and animals, pains and pleasures, truths and falsehoods – all the uncontroversial matters that people have talked about always and everywhere. There are, critics of the ontological priority of the social will say, limits to society's ability to talk things into or out of existence.

Brandom, James, and Sellars would agree, but they would insist that it is important to specify just which considerations set these limits. There are three sorts of limits: (1) *transcendental* limits set by the need to talk *about* something – to refer to objects, things we can represent well or badly, rather than just making noises which, though they may change behavior, lack intentionality; (2) *practical* limits, set by the transcultural need all human beings have to distinguish between, for example, poisonous and nourishing substances, up and down, humans and beasts, true and false, male and female, pain and pleasure, right and left; (3) *cultural* limits set by our previous social decisions – by a particular society's actually existing norms.

Brandom argues for the existence of the first sort of limit by claiming that no society can make much use of language unless it can wield the notion of a certain locution being about a certain object. To be an object, Brandom argues, is to be something that one can be wrong about. Indeed, it is to be something that everybody might always get wrong in certain respects (though not, obviously, in *all* respects).[8] The notion of "object" is thus derivative from that of social practice, as is that of "truth about an object." This is the point of saying, as I did earlier, that truth and

---

[8] Donald Davidson has famously argued that most of our beliefs must be true, for if most of our beliefs about beavers (for example) were wrong we should not be talking about beavers at all.

reality exist for the sake of social practices. We talk about them because our social practices are improved by doing so.

In contrast, for most of the philosophers who hold to what Brandom calls "representationalism" (as distinguished from his own "inferentialism"), the concept of "object" is primitive and inexplicable. Representationalists think that you must grasp this concept in order to have any idea of what language, or mind, or rationality might be. For all of these notions must be understood in terms of the notion of accurate representation of objects. In contrast, Brandom's argument is that the true primitives are those that make possible the application of social norms – notions like "having done A, or said P, you cannot get away with doing B, or saying Q." The latter notions are the ones that enable us to articulate what he calls "proprieties of inference."

Doing things Brandom's way amounts to dropping the old skeptical question "how can the human mind manage to get accurate representations of reality?" in favor of such questions as "why does the human community need the notion of accurate representation of objects?" "why should the question of getting in touch with reality ever have arisen?" "how did we ever come to see an abyss between subject and object of the sort which the sceptic describes?" "how did we ever get ourselves into a position in which sceptical doubts like Descartes' seemed plausible?"

The main point I want to make in this chapter is that the change Brandom is urging parallels the change from a theistic to a humanistic world-view. In recent centuries, instead of asking whether God exists, people have started asking whether it is a good idea for us to continue talking about Him, and which human purposes might be served by doing so – asking, in short, what use the concept of God might be to human beings. Brandom is suggesting that philosophers, instead of asking whether we really are in touch with objects "outside the mind" – objects that are as they are regardless of what we think about them – should ask what human purposes are served by conceiving of such objects. We should reflect on whether talking about them was a good idea.

In the course of his book he argues that it was not only a good idea but a pragmatically indispensable one. For if we had never talked of such objects, we should never have had much to say. Our language would not have developed beyond an exchange of causally efficacious grunts. Talk about objects independent of the mind was valuable because it helped the anthropoids become human, not because humans awakened to their obligation to represent such objects accurately – their obligation to "the Truth."

The "loss of the world" which idealism seemed helpless to avoid is thus not a problem for Brandom's inferentialism, since "objectivity is a structural aspect of the social–perspectival form of conceptual contents. The permanent distinction between how things are and how they are taken to be by some interlocutor is built into the social–inferential articulation of concepts."[9] Yet Brandom is not exactly a "realist," for that distinction is permanent only as long as we humans behave as we do – namely sapiently. This is why he can say that "the facts about having physical properties" supervene upon "the facts about seeming to have such properties."[10] In the causal order which can be accurately represented once humans have initiated the practice of distinguishing causes from effects, the world comes before the practices. Yet space, time, substance, and causality are what they are because human beings need to talk in certain ways to get certain things done. In the place of Kant's inexplicable transcendental constitution of the mind, Brandom substitutes practices which helped a certain biological species flourish. So the question about the existence of God is: "can we get as good an argument for the utility of God-talk as we can for the utility of talk about time, space, substance, and causality?"

For Brandom, the answer to this question is "no." For a priori philosophical inquiry into what exists is exhausted once such questions as "why do we need to talk about reidentifiable spatio-temporal particulars?" have been answered. Giving a transcendental argument for the existence of objects, and of these particular sorts of objects, exhausts the capacity of philosophy to tell you what there just *has* to be (if we are to make inferences at all). There is no further discipline called "ontology" which can tell you what singular terms we need to have in the language – whether or not we need "God" for example.

Brandom often points to analogies between his inferentialism and Spinoza's. But there are, of course, obvious disanalogies. Brandom and Spinoza are both holists, but Brandom's whole, like Hegel's, is the ongoing conversation of mankind, a conversation always subject to the contingencies that afflict finite existence. Spinoza's whole is an atemporal being that can be the object of what he called *scientia intuitiva*, the sort of direct acquaintance that makes further conversation, further inquiry, and further use of language, superfluous. This difference between Brandom and Spinoza encapsulates the difference between philosophers

---

[9] Robert Brandom, *Making it Explicit* (Cambridge, MA: Harvard University Press, 1994), 597.
[10] *Ibid.*, 292.

who see no end to the process of inquiry, and no court of appeal other than our descendants, and those who think that cultural politics cannot be the last word – that there must be what Plato hoped for, a way to rise above the contingent vagaries of conversation to a vision which transcends politics.

BRANDOM ON THE NATURE OF EXISTENCE

Brandom's explicit discussion of existence is confined to a rather brief excursus.[11] He starts out by agreeing with Kant that existence is not a predicate, but his way of making this point is very different from Kant's. Kant distinguished between "logical" notions such as "thing" and "is identical with," which apply to both the phenomenal and the noumenal, and categories of the understanding such as "substance" and "cause" which apply only to the former. Brandom thinks that Kant (and later Frege) erred by thinking of "thing" and "object" as what he calls "genuine sortals," and by treating identity as a property that can be attributed to things without specification of the sorts to which they belong. These errors make plausible the bad idea that things come in two flavors – existent and non-existent – and thereby suggest that one might be able to explain what all the existent ones have in common. They also encourage the view that the sentence "everything is identical with itself" is more than what Wittgenstein said it was – a splendid example of a completely useless proposition.[12]

To get rid of these bad beliefs, Brandom thinks, we have to take "thing" as always short for "thing of the following kind . . . " and "identical with" as always short for "identical with in the following respect . . . " He thinks that Frege should have seen quantifiers as coming with sortal restrictions on the admissible term "substituends." "For," as he says, "quantifiers quantify, they specify, at least in general terms, *how many*, and how many there are depends (as Frege's remarks about playing cards indicate), on *what* one is counting – on the sortal used to identify and individuate them."[13]

Kant's discussion of existence takes for granted that it comes in two sorts – the generic sort had both by pencils and God and the more specific, phenomenal, sort had only by the pencils and their fellow-inhabitants of space and time. Brandom responds that it comes in many sorts, as

---

[11] *Ibid.*, 440ff.   [12] *Philosophical Investigations*, Part I, section 216.
[13] *Making it Explicit*, 439. Frege remarks that it matters whether it is packs, or cards, or honors that are being counted.

many as there are sets of what he calls canonical designators. For him, an existential commitment – a belief that something of a certain description exists – is "a particular quantificational commitment in which the vindicating commitments that determine its content are restricted to canonical designators."[14]

The best way to understand what Brandom means by "canonical designators" is to consider the paradigm case thereof – "egocentric spatiotemporal coordinate descriptions."[15] These designators are the descriptions of spatio-temporal locations on a grid whose zero point is the place where the speaker is now. To say that a physical object exists is to say that the object in question occupies one of those points – that it occupies an address specified with reference to the coordinates of that grid.

Analogously, to say that an object has existence not physically but "in the Sherlock Holmes stories" is to choose as a set of canonical designators all and only descriptions of persons and things mentioned in those stories, or entailed by what is said in those stories. When we say that Dr. Watson's wife exists but Holmes's does not, we mean that appeal to that list of designators will settle the question. Again, to say that there exists a prime between 21 and 25 but no prime between 48 and 50 is to take the numerals as canonical designators. Any such list of designators acquaints us with an exhaustive (finite or infinite) set of things, things that an entity must be identical with if it is to exist, in the relevant sense of "exist."

The only sort of existence that Kant thought we could discuss intelligibly was physical existence. In this logical space the canonical designators are, indeed, the same ones Kant picks – the niches on the spatio-temporal grid. In Kant's system, God inhabits logical space but not empirical, physical, space. So, Kant thought, the question of the existence of God is beyond our knowledge, for knowledge of existence is co-extensive with knowledge of physical existence. (But, Kant goes on to say, this question can somehow be dealt with by "pure practical reason.")

For Brandom, however, the matter is more complicated. We have lots of logical spaces at our disposal (and doubtless more to come) and we can discuss existence within any of them. We have as many such spaces as we have infinite sequences, or finite lists, of canonical designators. We can, for example, treat the sacred scriptures of a given religious tradition as we treat the Holmes stories – as providing canonical designators that permit us to confirm or disconfirm the existence of objects, albeit not physical

---

[14] *Ibid.*, 443.   [15] *Ibid.*, 445.

objects. Kant was right to think that there is no reason why existence has to be physical (for neither that of prime numbers nor that of the Baker Street Irregulars is), but he was wrong in thinking that knowledge of existence is limited to knowledge of physical existence.

This is because the question of whether or not to talk about the existence of immaterial and infinite beings is not one for transcendental philosophy but rather one to be turned over to cultural politics. A representationalist like Nagel or Kant can picture us as surrounded by possibly unknowable facts – objects for which we shall never have words entering into relations we may never understand. But, for an inferentialist, what counts as an object is determined by what a culture has definite descriptions of, and argument about what exists is determined by what canonical designators are in place. Yet any culture may be surpassed by another, since the human imagination may dream up many more definite descriptions and equally many lists of canonical designators. There are no "natural," transcultural, limits to this process of self-transcendence, nor does it have any predetermined goal.

When a culture wants to erect a logical space that includes, say, the gods and goddesses of the Olympian pantheon, nothing stands in its way, any more than anything stood in Conan Doyle's way when he created the list of Holmesian canonical designators. But to ask, after such a culture has become entrenched, "are there *really* gods and goddesses?" is like asking "are there *really* numbers?" or "are there *really* physical objects?" The person asking such a question has to have a good reason for raising it. "Intellectual curiosity" is not such a reason. If one is going to challenge an ongoing cultural practice, one must both explain what practice might be put in its place, and how this substitute will tie in with surrounding practices. That is why to turn a question over to cultural politics is not to turn it over to "unreason." Arguments within cultural politics are usually just as rational, though typically not as conclusive, as those within natural science. To give good reasons for raising skeptical questions about a set of entities, one will have to at least sketch reasons for thinking that the culture would be in better shape if the sort of thing in question were no longer discussed.

TWO BAD DISTINCTIONS: LITERAL–SYMBOLIC AND SENSE–NONSENSE

Brandom's point can be clarified by comparing it with the quasi-Heideggerian claim, made by Tillich and other Christian theologians, that, since God is Being-as-such, and not a being among other beings, the attempt to characterize him – or, in Brandomian language, the attempt to identify him with the help of an already available list of canonical designators – is hopeless. Tillich concluded that "does God exist?" is a bad question – as bad as "is there *really* something it is like to be conscious?" or "are numbers *really* real? Do the numerals *really* refer to entities?"

There is no problem about giving either "what it is like to be conscious" or "God, a being without parts or passions" a place in a language game. We know how the trick is done, and we have had lots of experience watching both games being played. But in neither case is there any point in raising questions about existence, because there is no neutral logical space within which discussion can proceed between people inclined to deny and people inclined to affirm existence of the relevant entity. Metaphysical questions like "does God exist?" and "is the spatio-temporal world real?" are undiscussable because there is no list of "neutral" canonical designators by reference to which they might be answered.

That is why "existent thing," a universal as opposed to a local sortal, is only a pseudo-sortal. The very idea of a universal sortal is incoherent, for to be a sortal is to come with a set of canonical designators in tow. If discussion of God's existence or the reality of the world of common sense were to be discussable (in a way that does *not* boil down to cultural politics), we should have to have somehow transcended both God and the world so as to see them against a "neutral" background.

The fact that "does God exist?" is a bad question suggests that a better question would be: "do we want to weave one or more of the various religious traditions (with their accompanying pantheons) together with our deliberation over moral dilemmas, our deepest hopes, and our need to be rescued from despair?" Alternatively: "does one or more of these religious traditions provide language we wish to use when putting together our self-image, determining what is most important to us?" If none of them do, we shall treat all such traditions, and their pantheons, as offering mere "mythologies." Nevertheless, within each such mythology, as within the Holmes stories, there will be truth and falsity – *literal* truth and falsity – about existence claims. It will be true, for example, that there exists a child of Zeus and Semele but false that there is a child of Uranus and Aphrodite, true that there is a Third Person of the Godhead but false that there is a Thirteenth.

Our decision about whether to treat the religious tradition in which we were brought up as offering literal truths or as telling stories for which we no longer have any use will depend on many things – for example, whether we continue to think that prayer and worship will make a difference to what happens to us. But there are no criteria for when it is rational and when irrational to switch from adhesion to a tradition to a skeptical "mere myth" view of it. Decisions about what language games to play, what to talk about and what not to talk about, and for what purposes, are not made on the basis of agreed-upon criteria. Cultural politics is the least norm-governed human activity. It is the site of generational revolt, and thus the growing point of culture – the place where traditions and norms are all up for grabs at once. (Compare, as Brandom suggests, the decisions of the US Supreme Court in such cases as *Plessy* and *Brown*.)

Paul Tillich remarked that, in a post-Enlightenment Western culture, the vision of a social democratic utopia has begun to play the role of God. This vision has become the symbol of ultimate concern for many intellectuals whose ancestors' symbol was Jesus Christ. Tillich offered various arguments to the effect that that vision was an inadequate symbol, but his arguments are all of the non-criteria-governed sort that I have been putting under the heading "cultural politics." Like most recommendations of religious belief in the West since the Enlightenment, they were arguments that we shall eventually be driven to despair without specifically *religious* symbols of ultimate concern – the sort that Paine and Shelley thought we could perfectly well do without. Such arguments claim, for example, that a person whose sense of what is ultimately important is framed in purely secular terms will be less successful in achieving what Tillich called "the courage to be" than those who use Christian terms.

Tillich's term "finding an adequate symbol of ultimate concern" is, however, not an improvement on such old-fashioned phrases as "finding meaning in life," "formulating a satisfactory self-image," or "discovering what the Good is." Indeed, it is slightly worse than those, because it relies upon a distinction between the symbolic and the literal that is a relic of representationalist philosophy. Tillich thought that scientific and common-sense beliefs could have literal truth, but religious truths could have only "symbolic" truth. He thought this because he believed that the former could be considered accurate representations of reality, whereas the notion of "accuracy" was inappropriate to the latter. A Brandomian inferentialist, however, has no use for the literal-vs.-symbolic distinction. The only relevant distinction she can countenance is one between logical spaces constructed for certain purposes (e.g., those of physical science, of mathematics, or of chess) and other logical spaces constructed for other purposes (e.g., those provided by the Platonic dialogues, the Jataka, the Holmes stories, the New Testament, etc.).

Debate about the utility of such logical spaces and about the desirability or undesirability of uniting them with, or disjoining them from, one another is the substance of cultural politics. From the point of view common to Brandom and Hegel, there is nothing special about natural science (or, better, to the discourse constituted by the union of the logical space of everyday transcultural common sense with that of modern natural science) which entitles it to the term "literal truth." That term harks back to the bad Kantian idea that discourse about physical objects is the paradigm case of making truth claims, and that all other areas of discourse must be thought of as "non-cognitive." If we drop this idea, we shall have no use for what Nancy Frankenberry has called "the theology of symbolic forms" – no use of the attempt (which goes back at least to Schleiermacher) to make room for God by saying that there is something like "symbolic truth" or "imaginative truth" or "emotional truth" or "metaphorical truth" as well as "literal" truth.

Dropping these notions will lead us to drop the idea that God requires to be talked about in a special way because he is a special kind of being. For Brandom, there is no such thing as a certain kind of object demanding to be spoken of in a certain kind of language. To say that God requires to be talked about in a certain way is no more illuminating than to say that transfinite cardinal numbers, or neutrinos, demand to be talked about in a certain way. Since we would not know what any of these entities were if we did not know that they were the entities talked about in these ways, the idea that they "demand" this treatment is unhelpful. It is as if we praised a poet's choice of metaphor for fitting our otherwise indescribable experience perfectly. Such praise rings hollow, simply because we cannot identify the experience without the help of the metaphor. It as if, to paraphase Wittgenstein, we were to exclaim with delight over the fact that a plane figure fits perfectly into its surroundings.

Like Wittgenstein, Brandom thinks that anything has a sense if you give it a sense. More consistently than Wittgenstein, he can follow up on this by saying that whatever philosophy is, it is not the detection of nonsense (*pace* Kant, the *Tractatus*, Carnap, and some misbegotten passages in *Philosophical Investigations*). The language game played by theologians with the transcendental terms, or with Heideggerese, and the one played by philosophers of mind who talk about the independence of qualia from behavior and environment, is as coherent as that played with numbers or physical objects. *But the coherence of talk about X does not guarantee the discussability of the existence of X.* Talk about numbers is ideally coherent, but this coherence does not help us discuss the question of whether the numerals are names of real things. Nor does the coherence of Christian theology help us discuss the existence of God. This is not because of an ontological fact about numbers or God, but because of sociological facts about the unavailability of norms to regulate discussion.

Brandom's favorite philosopher is Hegel, and in this area the most salient difference between Kant and Hegel is that Hegel does not think philosophy can rise above the social practices of its time and judge their desirability by reference to something that is not itself an alternative social practice (past or future, real or imagined). For Hegel as for Brandom, there are no norms which are not the norms of some social practice. So, when asked "are these desirable norms?" or "is this a good social practice?" all either can do is ask "by reference to what encompassing social practice are we supposed to judge desirability?" or, more usefully, "by comparison to the norms of what proposed alternative social practice?"

Early in the Introduction to *The Phenomenology of Spirit*, there is a passage that anticipates what James said in "The Will to Believe" about W. K. Clifford, a philosopher who held that we have no right to believe in the existence of God, given the lack of relevant evidence. Clifford, James said, was too willing to sacrifice truth in order to be certain that he would never fall into error. Hegel criticized the Cliffords of his own day as follows:

if the fear of falling into error sets up a mistrust of Science, which in the absence of such scruples gets on with the work itself, and actually cognizes something, it is hard to see why we should not turn round and mistrust this very mistrust. This fear takes something – a great deal in fact – for granted as truth, supporting its scruples and inferences on what is itself in need of prior scrutiny to see if it is true. To be specific, it takes for granted certain ideas about cognition as an instrument and as a medium, and assumes that there is a difference between ourselves and this cognition. Above all, it presupposes that the Absolute stands on one side and cognition on the other, independent and separated from it, and yet is something real; or in other words, it presupposes that cognition which, since it is excluded from the Absolute, is surely outside of the truth as well, is nevertheless true, an assumption whereby what calls itself fear of error reveals itself rather as fear of the truth.[16]

In place of the words "Science" and "cognition" in Hegel's text, Brandom would put "conversation." If one makes this substitution, one

[16] G. W. F. Hegel, *Phenomenology of Spirit*, trans. A. V. Miller (Oxford: Clarendon Press 1977), paragraph 74.

will construe Hegel as saying that we should not think that there is a difference between ourselves and the discursive practices in which we are
engaged, and that we should not think that those practices are a means
to some end, nor that they are a medium of representation used to get
something right. A fortiori, we should not think that there is a goal of
inquiry which is what it is apart from those practices, and fore-knowledge
of which can help us decide which practices to have.

We should rather, as Hegel says elsewhere, be content to think of philosophy as its time (that is to say, our present discursive practices) held
in thought (that is to say, contrasted with alternative past or proposed
practices). We should stop trying to put our discursive practices within
a larger context, one which forms the background of all possible social
practices and which contains a list of "neutral" canonical designators
that delimit the range of the existent once and for all. If there were such
a context, it would of course be the proper object of study of an expert
culture charged with determining the future direction of the Conversation of Humankind. But there is no such context. "Ontology" is not the
name of an expert culture, and we should stop imagining that such an
expert culture would be desirable. Only when we do so will we put what
Heidegger called "onto-theology" behind us.

PRIVATE AND PUBLIC RELIGION

I have been arguing in this chapter that we should substitute the question
about the cultural desirability of God-talk for the ontological question
about the existence of God. But I have said little about what discussion
of the former question looks like.

As I see it, the question of whether to keep on talking about God,
whether to keep that logical space open, needs to be divided into two
sub-questions. The first is a question about an individual's right to be
religious, even though unable to justify her religious beliefs to others.
It might be formulated in the first person as "have I the right to my
religious devotions even though there is no social practice that legitimizes
inferences from or to the sentences that I employ in this devotional
practice – a lack which makes it impossible for many, and perhaps all, of
my fellow-humans to make sense of this practice?"

Aside from a few science-worshipping philosophers who retain
Clifford's antagonism to religious belief, most intellectuals of the present
day would answer this question affirmatively, just as James did. The increasing privatization of religion during the last two-hundred years has

created a climate of opinion in which people have the same right to idiosyncratic forms of religious devotion as they do to write poems or paint
pictures that nobody else can make any sense out of. It is a feature of a
democratic and pluralist society that our religion is our own business –
something we need not even discuss with others, much less try to justify
to them, unless we feel like doing so. Such a society tries to leave as
much free space as possible for individuals to develop their own sense
of who they are and what their lives are for, asking only that they obey
Mill's precept and extend to others the tolerance they themselves enjoy.
Individuals are free to make up their own semi-private language games
(as Henry James Sr. and William Blake did, for example), as long as they
do not insist that everybody else plays them as well.

But such societies have, of course, been troubled by other questions:
"what about organized religion?" "what about the churches?" Even if
one follows James's advice and ignores Clifford-like strictures against the
"irrationality" of religious belief, one might still think that both Lucretius
and Marx had a point. So it is possible to agree that society should
grant private individuals the right to formulate private systems of belief
while remaining militantly anti-clerical. James and Mill agree that there
is nothing wrong with churches unless their activities do social harm.
But when it comes to deciding whether actually existing churches in
fact do such harm, things get complicated. The socio-political history
of the West in the last two-hundred years is spotted with controversies
such as those over Jefferson's Virginia Statute of Religious Freedom, the
laicization of education in France, the Kulturkampf in Germany, and
the current controversy in Turkey about female students wearing veils
within university.

Issues like these require different resolutions in different countries and
different centuries. It would be absurd to suggest that there are universally
valid norms that might be invoked to settle them. But I would urge that
debate over such concrete political questions is more useful for human
happiness than debate over the existence of God. They are the questions
which remain once we realize that appeals to religious experience are
of no use for settling what traditions should be maintained and which
replaced, and after we have come to think natural theology pointless.

We shall not appeal to religious experiences in order to decide what
social practices to abandon or adopt if we follow Wittgenstein, Sellars,
and Brandom in thinking that there is no intermediary called "what the
experience was really *of*" in between the altered state of the nervous system associated with the onset of the claimed experience and the resulting

discursive commitments undertaken by a member of a language-using community. We shall dismiss natural theology if we see the undiscussability of God's existence not as a testimony to his superior status but as a consequence of the attempt to give him that status – a side-effect of making him so incomparably special as to be a being whose existence cannot be discussed by reference to any antecedent list of canonical designators. If we grant the Sellarsian doctrine that all awareness is a linguistic affair and the Brandomian doctrine that "existent object" is not a genuine sortal, we shall cut ourselves off from many of the traditional varieties of God-talk.

Inferentialist philosophy of language and mind helps us understand why neither appeals to "experience" nor appeals to "reason" have been of much help to us when we are choosing between alternative social practices. To move into the intellectual world to which Brandom's inferentialism facilitates access would be to treat questions of which language games to play as questions of how members of democratic societies may best adjust the balance between their responsibilities to themselves and their responsibilities to their fellow-citizens.[17]

---

[17] I am grateful to Jeffrey Stout for detailed and very helpful comments on an earlier draft of this chapter.

4

Religious belief and naturalism

Wayne L. Proudfoot

In a characteristically fresh reading of William James's article "The Will to Believe," Richard Rorty proposes a redescription of religious belief or faith so as to distinguish it from ordinary beliefs.[1] Rorty wants to disengage religious faith from the inferential links by which beliefs are justified by other beliefs. He also remains committed to the holism shared by both classical pragmatists and contemporary pragmatists like Donald Davidson, according to which we attribute content to beliefs by virtue of their inferential relations to other beliefs. Rorty's proposed solution is that we identify religious beliefs not by their place in the justification of beliefs by other beliefs, but by the role they play in the explanation of human action by attributing certain beliefs and desires to the actor.

Rorty acknowledges that his proposal differs from James's in significant ways, but he thinks it captures the spirit of what James was trying to do in "The Will to Believe." In this chapter I want to examine James's understanding of what is at stake in religious belief, show that Rorty's proposal differs more fully from James's than he suggests, and then return to assess the merits of the proposal. I agree with Rorty's conclusions about the best prospects for a philosophy of religion. I doubt, however, that the best way to achieve that goal is to draw the sharp distinctions he suggests between public and private and between the web of justifying inferences and that of the ascription of beliefs and desires to explain actions.

"The Will to Believe" is the title essay of a volume James published in 1897, just as he was negotiating to give the Gifford Lectures, which

---

[1] Richard Rorty, "Religious Faith, Intellectual Responsibility, and Romance," in R. A. Putnam (ed.), *The Cambridge Companion to William James* (Cambridge University Press, 1997), 84–102.

became *The Varieties of Religious Experience.*[2] The essays in the volume were written over a period of almost twenty years. Two-thirds of the book, including the earliest essay, "The Sentiment of Rationality," and the latest, "The Will to Believe," are addressed to how one ought to characterize religious belief in the most general terms, and what kind of inquiry is appropriate to settle it. Throughout his writings on religion, James views it as a belief that there is an order in the cosmos that is congruous with, or shaped to, the moral lives of women and men, and that they will benefit by bringing their lives into harmony with it. James's way of conceiving of this order changes over the course of his writing, and with it his idea of whether or not the harmony is guaranteed or is only a possibility, but the basic conception remains.

James writes in "The Sentiment of Rationality" that the radical question of life is whether this is at bottom a moral or unmoral universe. James is asking whether the universe is shaped to human thought and action. The sense of "moral" here is the sense in which the moral sciences (comprising what we now call the humanities and the social sciences) were contrasted in the nineteenth century with the natural sciences. The religious question, for James, is whether or not the universe is shaped to the inner lives of persons. A conception of the universe as shaped in that way is an "intimate" one.[3] The alternative, as he saw it, was the deterministic universe of materialism. "A nameless *Unheimlichkeit* comes over us," he writes, "at the thought of there being nothing eternal in our final purposes, in the objects of those loves and aspirations which are our deepest energies...We demand in [the universe] a *character* for which our emotions and active propensities shall be a match."[4]

This passage, and a later one in which James says that the "need of an eternal moral order is one of the deepest needs of our breast," echo Matthew Arnold's description a few years earlier of the idea of God in the Bible as "an eternal power, not ourselves, that makes for righteousness."[5] The word "eternal" here, in James's phrase as in Arnold's, is less a temporal designation than an indication that the ideal order is not an

[2] William James, *The Will to Believe and Other Essays in Popular Philosophy* (Cambridge, MA: Harvard University Press, 1979) and *The Varieties of Religious Experience* (Cambridge, MA: Harvard University Press, 1985).
[3] James, *The Will to Believe*, 75.   [4] *Ibid.*, 71.
[5] William James, *Pragmatism* (Cambridge, MA: Harvard University Press, 1985), 264; Matthew Arnold, *Literature and Dogma* (New York: Macmillan, 1902), 52.

artifact. It is "not ourselves," in the sense that it is not a product of human thought and action.

"The Sentiment of Rationality" was written in response to Charles Sanders Peirce's "The Fixation of Belief," which had appeared a few months earlier. While Peirce claimed that inquiry should be settled by reference to "something on which our thinking has no effect," James argued that this is impossible.[6] No inquiry is disinterested, and practical interests always come into play in choosing which of several beliefs is more rational. A rational belief, he says, is one that helps predict future experience, and that awakens our active impulses by defining the future "congruously with our spontaneous powers."[7] Later in the volume James says that some reality defined like God is the only ultimate object that is both rational and possible for human thought.[8] The most productive periods of history, he says, have been those in which people have believed that reality is "congenial" to their powers.

"The Dilemma of Determinism" in *The Will to Believe* shows what James takes to be at stake in the religious question. He regards materialism as the alternative to theism. In this essay he argues that we order the world according to our needs. Inquiry and knowledge proceed from the "desire to cast the world into a more rational shape in our minds than the shape into which it is thrown by the crude order of experience."[9] Mathematics and science are products of this ordering. James says that if a certain view of the world violates his moral demand, he will feel as free to reject it, or at least to doubt it, as if it violated his demand for uniformity of sequence. Neither demand is more subjective than the other. He goes on to argue that the moral revulsion we feel toward certain events or facts ought not to be given up in the face of arguments for determinism. This includes arguments from either science or theology. James rejects scientific determinism, but he is repulsed by theological ideas of providence in which everything is said to be for the best, and the related view that he calls gnostic romanticism and finds in some contemporary French novelists, in which even those events that seem evil to us all have their necessary place in a higher progress toward the good.[10] James's defense of pluralism, recurrent throughout his work, is motivated at least as much by this moral judgment as it is by epistemological concerns.

When he comes to write "The Will to Believe," the latest essay in the volume, James addresses a question that he takes to be about the nature

---

[6] Charles Sanders Peirce, "The Fixation of Belief," in C. J. W. Kloesel (ed.), *Writings of Charles Sanders Peirce* (Bloomington, IN: Indiana University Press, 1986), 3.253.
[7] *Ibid.*, 70.   [8] James, *The Will to Believe*, 93.   [9] *Ibid.*, 115.   [10] *Ibid.*, 132–33.

of the universe. He is not merely defending his and others' right to believe that there is a God, though the article is sometimes read that way. He is continuing the inquiry begun in "The Sentiment of Rationality": is the universe shaped to human powers and ideals, and how is that to be decided? The fact that it cannot be decided by appeal to logic, including the inductive logic characteristic of science, does not mean that we must withhold assent. A person's acceptance of any of her beliefs is affected by her "willing nature," when that is described as broadly as James describes it here, to include: "fear and hope, prejudice and passion, imitation and partisanship, the circumpressure of our caste and set."[11] This is just the point he has previously made that all of our inquiries are elicited by demands to order experience in ways that will be of use to us. Even when an issue can be decided on what James calls "intellectual grounds," the way that issue has been articulated is a product of our willing nature.

James describes the religious hypothesis in a way that sounds quite vague. Science says things are, he says; morality says some things are better than others. Religion says that "the best things are the more eternal things, the overlapping things . . . 'Perfection is eternal.'"[12] This is the question he earlier said was the most radical question of life: is the universe moral or unmoral? The formulation is vague, but a lot is at stake.

In the preface to *The Will to Believe*, which James was writing when he received the invitation to give the Gifford Lectures, he introduces the phrase "radical empiricism" as a name for his philosophical attitude.[13] Later he uses this term to refer to his metaphysics of experience, but here it is a method of inquiry, one very close to what he later calls pragmatism. Empiricism, he says, is the view that all beliefs are fallible, and radical empiricism means that that includes one's most basic assumptions and entrenched beliefs, such as the monism adopted by both positivists and idealists.

How is one to adjudicate between the claims of theism and naturalism? In *On Liberty*, John Stuart Mill had said that the choice between different ways of living in the world could not and should not be made a priori. No abstract analysis could predict that a particular way of life or of structuring society would be more beneficial than another. Mill wrote that "there should be different experiments of living; that free scope should be given to varieties of character, short of injury to others; and that the worth of different modes of life should be proved practically, when

[11] *Ibid.*, 18.　　[12] *Ibid.*, 29–30.　　[13] *Ibid.*, 5.

anyone thinks fit to try them."[14] James suggests that the same method be used to assess the consequences of living a religious life. People should be encouraged to live and act by their faiths, religious or not, and these faiths should be assessed by public criteria, including their ability to survive advances in knowledge as well as their psychological and social consequences. This is, in fact, James says, what has happened historically. "The truest scientific hypothesis is that which, as we say, works best; and it can be no otherwise with religious hypotheses. Religious history proves one hypothesis after another has worked ill, has crumbled with a widening knowledge of the world, and has lapsed from the minds of men."[15] Religious belief and practice should be assessed in this way, and not by abstract philosophical argument.

Varieties has been read as a contribution to the literature on religious experience, conceived chiefly as an epistemological issue. That literature emerged after James. He thought that the religious question could not be decided by abstract epistemological or metaphysical analysis, in the manner of his idealist colleague Josiah Royce. *Varieties* was meant as a study of the religious lives of people vigorously living out their faiths, and of the extent to which those faiths contribute to or detract from human flourishing. He begins by sketching two types of religious experience that represent two different ways of regarding oneself in relation to an unseen order, or to whatever a person considers divine. The first of these is one in which the person takes herself and her world to be continuous with that order. Whatever is is good. Religious practice is a matter of getting in touch with and appropriating that order. The second is one in which the person views herself as alienated or estranged from the good. Religious belief and practice require acknowledgment of that estrangement, along with work and hope for a transformation that will reorient her and bring her into harmony with the ideal order.

James's two types represent the two forms of religious life most salient in nineteenth-century New England. The first was articulated intellectually by the transcendentalists, and informed popular piety through various forms of spiritualism. The second was traditional theism, and underlay evangelical revivals from Jonathan Edwards down to the time in which James was writing. James argues that the second is psychologically much more complete and more adequate than the first. The first conception requires that the evil in the world be ignored or explained

[14] John Stuart Mill, *On Liberty* (Indianapolis, IN: Hackett, 1978), 54.
[15] James, *The Will to Believe*, 8.

away, while the second acknowledges the negative as well as the positive in experience. When viewed in historical context, *Varieties* is an endorsement of revivalism and its call for conversion over the superficial optimism of many in the spiritualist tradition, despite his view that religion consists in belief in an unseen order and attempts to get in touch with it.

The heart of the book consists of a description of conversion and the transformed life that results from it, along with an assessment of the deficits and benefits associated with different varieties of that life. It should be clear in light of his comments in the preface to *The Will to Believe* that all of this is in the service of discovering whether or not the religious hypothesis works better than the alternatives. In his conclusion James summarizes that hypothesis in his well-known description of what he takes to be the common core of religious experience. An individual becomes conscious that the higher part of himself is "coterminous and continuous with a *more* of the same quality which is operative in the universe outside of him, and which he can keep in working touch with."[16]

Rorty reads "The Will to Believe" in a way that lends support to his proposal to disarm any opposition between religion and science by viewing science as a public project in which everyone's agreement is necessary, in contrast to private projects, of which religious belief and practice are examples. He says that James follows Mill in defending a utilitarian ethics of belief. A person is accountable for her beliefs only to herself and to other persons. We are not responsible to some truth or reality that is independent of our fellow human beings. Beliefs need justification only when they interfere with the fulfillment of the needs of others. The underlying strategy of James's philosophy of religion, according to Rorty, is to privatize religion. This allows him to construe the proposed tension between science and religion as an illusory opposition between cooperative endeavors and private projects.

An individual is free to believe whatever she wants, Rorty says, as long as it is on her own time, or as long as it does not interfere with public, cooperative projects. He suggests that in order to accommodate this freedom we loosen up our criteria for ascribing beliefs and desires to others. We could then acknowledge that a person holds certain beliefs that do not seem to bear plausible inferential relations to other beliefs we attribute to her. We can recognize Kierkegaard's belief in the Incarnation or a parent's belief in the essential goodness of her seemingly pathological

[16] James, *The Varieties of Religious Experience*, 400.

child, even though neither of these accords with our other beliefs and the evidence we see. Charity consists not only in ascribing to others chiefly beliefs we hold to be true, but also accepting what appear to us to be anomalous beliefs in matters of personal preference, like religion and a person's private loves.

Rorty acknowledges that this is what he thinks James ought to have said, rather than what he did say. He rejects the association of religion with a belief in a power not ourselves. But I do not think he fully appreciates the difference between his position and James's. Rorty thinks it fine for someone to believe what he or she wants, so long as it does not harm others or interfere with the pursuit of their projects. He views belief in the Incarnation or love of Krishna as private matters in the sense that they are untethered to beliefs in areas in which widespread agreement is required for communication and for cooperative endeavors. Rorty thinks James agrees with him on this because James defends a kind of polytheism, in which it is acknowledged that different conceptions of the divine are appropriate for different persons and cultures.

James has a different view altogether. Although "The Will to Believe" is often read this way, he is not arguing for his right to believe in what he calls the religious hypothesis, no matter what anyone else might think. James is engaged in inquiry. In preparatory notes for "The Sentiment of Rationality," he writes, "suppose human beings so constituted that a belief in God be necessary to keep the moral world going, and yet that God does not exist. Could the success of the moral world make the existence of God in any sense true? No."[17] He wants to know whether or not the universe is a moral one, in his sense. Despite warnings to the contrary by Peirce, W. C. Clifford, Thomas Huxley, Leslie Stephen, and others, James argues that it is legitimate, under certain conditions, to adopt a belief in the absence of sufficient evidence if it satisfies one's interests better than the alternatives. His argument is as much descriptive as prescriptive. Change of belief is always motivated by interests, and one ought not pretend that they can or should be excluded from the process. When a choice between options is forced, and when it cannot be settled by appeal to logic or evidence, it will be decided by the extent to which one of the options satisfies better than the other the interests that motivated the inquiry. Even when a choice can be decided by appeal to logic or evidence, those criteria themselves are the result of prior actions of what he called "our willing nature."

---

[17] William James, *Essays in Philosophy* (Cambridge, MA: Harvard University Press, 1978), 350.

The belief James takes to be paradigmatically religious is different from the examples Rorty considers. His most general characterization of religion is belief in an unseen order, that the universe is intimate, or congruous with human thought and action. The *more* that is continuous with the higher part of the self, but operative in the universe outside it, is not a human product. This belief, which for James is the core religious belief, is for Rorty not a private matter on which individuals are free to hold any belief they desire. It is a public matter, a matter for cooperative inquiry. The inquiries into language and culture that have occupied humanities and the social sciences for most of the twentieth century, along with progress in the natural sciences, have led to beliefs that conflict with what James took to be the religious hypothesis. Any moral order, any *more* that is continuous with the higher parts of the self, any forces that might help to bring our ideals about, can be understood only as the emergent social products of the beliefs, desires, and actions of men and women. At the end of the nineteenth century, a number of thinkers subscribed to a kind of panpsychism, which they took to be compatible with the science of their day. At the end of the twentieth century, that belief is no longer plausible.

James is right that there is an unseen moral order with which we can get in touch, and which can aid us in our projects, but it is not prior to and independent of human thought and action. That order consists of the social and cultural world that is a product of history. Two years after James's death, Durkheim and Freud each published naturalistic accounts of religious belief and practice in which they sought to explain James's unseen moral order as a social product. During the century since James wrote, the humanities and the social sciences have been preoccupied with the ways in which language is constitutive of agency, experience, social practices, and everything identified as *Geist* in the *Geisteswissenschaften*.

Throughout his work, James is aware that the world is shaped by the persons living in it and is, in part, the result of their thoughts and actions. Ironically, he saw this more clearly than most of his contemporaries did. Neither Peirce nor Josiah Royce, for instance, understood as James did that language, truth, and logic are human artifacts. He was struck by the invention of non-Euclidean geometries, and regarded them as tools men and women have developed to perform certain tasks. In "The Moral Philosopher and the Moral Life," he is clear that there are no moral obligations apart from those created by the desires of others. Here he agrees with Rorty. But he is not clear that the only others with desires are our fellow human beings. In *Pragmatism*, he argues that concepts and categories, like sentences, are social and cultural products. But he thinks that does not rule out the possibility of a moral order that is not the product of human thought and action. In the final chapter of that book he writes: "I firmly disbelieve, myself, that our human experience is the highest form of experience extant in the universe . . . We may well believe, on the proofs that religious experience affords, that higher powers exist and are at work to save the world on ideal lines similar to our own."[18]

Rorty's ascription to James of his own attempt to privatize religion does not work if religion is characterized as belief in an intimate cosmos, or in an unseen order that is congruous with the inner lives of persons and that is not the product of human thought and action. The claim that anything in the universe that is shaped to our moral lives is something we have put there, and is not independent of language and culture, may be a controversial one in some circles. But Rorty can not relegate it to a realm of personal preference, analogous to a love of opera or a taste for science fiction. It is part of the cooperative project that includes Darwin's explanation of the origin of human life, and our understanding of the development of language and culture. It is integrally related to Rorty's distinction between the causes and the justification of beliefs.

Rorty asks whether we can "disengage religious beliefs from inferential links with other beliefs by making them too vague to be caught in a creed – by fuzzing them up in Tillichian ways – and still be faithful to the familiar pragmatist doctrine that beliefs have content only by virtue of inferential relations to other beliefs."[19] He is perfectly willing that this be done with beliefs he takes to be optional; for example, belief in the Incarnation or in Krishna. But he could not allow sufficient fuzzing to permit talk of a moral order that is not the product of Darwinian evolution and the development of language and culture.

Rorty offers an ingenious proposal for privatizing religious beliefs without jeopardizing the holism that is common to James, Davidson, and the pragmatist tradition. He suggests that we sever the normal inferential links by which beliefs are justified by other beliefs, and thus the holism by which we identify the content of another's belief by triangulating between our beliefs, his beliefs, and the world. Instead, we substitute the holism that arises when we attribute intentional states to another in order to explain his actions, or to coordinate our actions with his. Here

---

[18] James, *Pragmatism*, 143–44.
[19] Rorty, "Religious Faith, Intellectual Responsibility, and Romance," 95.

we have another kind of triangulation, between the attribution of beliefs, desires, and observed actions. "When we encounter paradigmatic
cases of unjustifiable beliefs – Kierkegaard's belief in the Incarnation,
the mother's belief in the essential goodness of her sociopathic child –
we can still use the attribution of such beliefs to explain what is going
on: why Kierkegaard, or the mother, is doing what he is doing. We can
give content to an utterance like 'I love him' or 'I have faith in Him'
by correlating such utterances with patterns of behavior, even when we
cannot do so by fixing the place of such utterances in a network of inferential relations."[20] Rorty intends this substitution to remove a religious
belief from the web of justification, while not isolating it completely from
the linguistic practices that give meaning to our words. The belief would
be relocated to the practice of making sense of actions by the attribution
of intentional states.

There are costs to this strategy. The words we use to attribute beliefs
and desires to others are words that have their place in inferential relations of justification, and the justifications we give for beliefs almost
always make reference to desires and actions as well as to other beliefs.
The project of radical interpretation that Davidson asks us to imagine
is one in which the field linguist attributes beliefs and desires to another
person in order to account for that person's behavior, both linguistic
and non-verbal, in an environment which they both share. This enables
her to construct a dictionary and a grammar that consist of inferential
relations between the different terms in the language she is trying to
interpret. The holism cannot be restricted to either the attribution of
beliefs or their justification. Both are involved in trying to understand
another person or culture.

Kierkegaard is a good example for Rorty, because he has his own theological reasons for wanting to disengage religious beliefs from inferential
relations with other beliefs. He uses the considerable rhetorical skills at his
disposal to decouple the terms in which Christian faith is cast from those
of any philosophical system or any non-Christian vocabulary. In *Fear and
Trembling* he says "faith" is a newly invented category that has no inferential relation to any philosophical concept, and in *Philosophical Fragments*
he considers each of the main topics in Christian doctrine, showing how
each is discontinuous with the world of Socrates and philosophy.[21] But

---

[20] *Ibid.*
[21] Søren Kierkegaard, *Fear and Trembling / Repetition*, trans. H. and E. Hong (Princeton University
Press, 1983), 60 and *Philosophical Fragments / Johannes Climacus*, trans. H. and E. Hong (Princeton
University Press, 1985).

the dramatic language Kierkegaard employs is not outside the web of inferential relations. He uses relations of negation and opposition to construct his rhetoric of transcendence, but these are well within the web. He certainly does not permit his terms to be fuzzed up.

Despite the radical disjunction he proposes between philosophy and religion, Kierkegaard's conception of faith is not independent of philosophical ideas or argument. Most of his philosophical writing is devoted to a radical deepening of the concept of freedom of the will that Kant developed in the first book of *Religion Within the Limits of Reason Alone* and that Friedrich Schelling extended in his essay on human freedom. Kierkegaard's ideas of religious belief and practice depend heavily on this radical conception of freedom. It enters into his subtle portrayals of varieties of despair and faith. Kierkegaard uses this idea of freedom to try to disengage what he calls inwardness from any inferential connections with external behavior, just as he tries to disengage the category of faith from any of our other concepts and categories. His invention of new ways to conceive of these traditional ideas is brilliant, but it extends rather than escapes the web of inferential relations.

Tillich and Kierkegaard decouple religious concepts from science and from inferential relations that they think are detrimental to them, while they also draw on the rich meanings that these concepts have in the culture. Central to those meanings is a conception of God as transcending the world that we use science to describe. Tillich supplements his concept of faith with the idealist language of participation, arguing that religious ideas participate in a reality that is otherwise beyond the reach of language. It is possible to admire Kierkegaard and Tillich as authors who found novel ways with words to generate a new kind of transcendence, while holding that the only order in the universe that is congruous with our moral lives is what they and we have put there. But they did not see it that way. They used those words to try to provoke their readers to turn away from domesticated and naturalized ideas of religious faith and its object, and to point them toward the only proper object of faith, a power not ourselves.

Rorty's proposal at the end of his article that religion be conceived as a form of romance, a product of the imagination that connects us with possibilities for self and society beyond what we can presently imagine, is excellent. Religion, along with literature, the other arts, and the sciences consists of vocabularies, social practices, and institutions that humans have invented in order to serve their needs, to criticize those needs, and to go beyond them to new desires and new possibilities. In this way we create the moral orders of the imagination with which we can get in touch and which can save us. This conception of religion should inform both the study of religion and, increasingly, the beliefs and practice of reflective religious people. This is not likely to be achieved by severing the inferential connections by which religious beliefs are justified.

The question of the origins of the moral orders in which we live is crucial, and James was right to see it as central to religious belief. Religious doctrine in most traditions has provided its own explanations for such orders. It is important that any attempt to remove religious beliefs from the web of justification not immunize them from increasing attempts to come to understand the origins of our beliefs and dispositions as well as our ideals. The web of relations by which beliefs are justified by reference to one another, the ways in which we ascribe beliefs and practices to explain human action, and the historical and social explanations we give of why certain beliefs and practices are available for ascription are all connected.

The language James uses to articulate his conception of religion is dated, but the issues it raises are not. Many religious thinkers and scholars of religion who reject supernaturalism nevertheless continue to shy away from the naturalistic alternative, that whatever there is in the universe that is shaped to our moral lives, or continuous with the higher parts of ourselves, is what we, collectively, have put there. They would not subscribe to the language of an unseen order. But they choose to brand as reductive any account of religious belief that acknowledges the object of that belief to be a product of the activity and imagination of men and women. I want to return briefly to James to look at the ways in which his view of this unseen order changed over time, at his attempts to reconcile it with his other beliefs, and to sketch some parallels in recent religious thought.

While James always takes the question of religion to be one of whether or not the world is shaped to the moral life in a way that is independent of what humans have themselves shaped, he changes his position over time on what this would entail. In the eighties and nineties this question is equivalent to the question of whether the universe has purposes commensurate with his own and powerful enough to prevail under any conditions. Writing to Thomas Davidson in 1882, he says: "All I mean is that there must be *some* subjective unity in the Universe, which has purposes commensurable with my own and which is at the same time large enough to be, among all the powers that may be there, the strongest.

I simply refuse to accept the notion of there being *no* purpose in the objective world."[22] And in *Principles*, published in 1890, religion is identified with the view that the cosmos is a realm of final purposes.[23]

In the 1898 lecture at Berkeley in which he introduced the term "pragmatism," James uses Peirce's pragmatic criterion of meaning to clarify the meaning of the word "God." The idea of God, he writes, "guarantees an ideal order that shall be permanently preserved. A world with a God in it to say the last word, may indeed burn up or freeze, but we think of him as mindful of the old ideals and sure to bring them elsewhere to fruition; so that, where he is, tragedy is only provisional and partial, and shipwreck and dissolution are not the absolutely final things. This need of an eternal moral order is one of the deepest needs of our breast."[24] By the time of *Varieties* in 1902 James has begun to doubt that religion requires a guarantee. He says that that is what most religious people believe. But when giving his own view in the Postscript he says that security may be imperfect, consolation incomplete, and some portions of the universe irretrievably lost. For practical life, he says, "the *chance* of salvation is enough."[25] Five years later, in *Pragmatism*, he drops the idea of a guarantee altogether. Royce, he says, and the absolute idealists hold to a guarantee. But they are not engaged in analysis; they build systems that stand as alternatives to the world we live in, not clarifications of it. The pragmatist needs no guarantee. Pragmatism inclines to meliorism, between optimism and pessimism, where salvation is not assured. Religious experience affords evidence that "higher powers exist and are at work to save the world on ideal lines similar to our own."[26]

By the time of *A Pluralistic Universe*, James does not even speak of higher powers. "Purpose" has yielded to "experience." He proposes that the term "intimacy," introduced at the outset of his career to characterize conceptions of the universe as congruous with the moral lives of persons, now replace "rationality" as a criterion for adjudicating between metaphysical views.[27] A metaphysics is acceptable if it portrays the cosmos as intimate rather than foreign. Idealism, as set out by Hegel and his late nineteenth-century British and American followers, is more

[22] William James to Thomas Davidson (January 8, 1882) in I. Skrupskelis and E. Berkeley (eds.), *The Correspondence of William James* (Charlottesville, VA: University Press of Virginia, 1992), 5.195 (original emphasis).

[23] William James, *The Principles of Psychology* (Cambridge, MA: Harvard University Press, 1983), 21.

[24] James, *Pragmatism*, 264.   [25] James, *The Varieties of Religious Experience*, 414.

[26] James, *Pragmatism*, 143.

[27] William James, *A Pluralistic Universe* (Cambridge, MA: Harvard University Press, 1977), 144-45.

intimate than materialism, but still foreign. Only a pluralistic pan-psychism, in which experience is ubiquitous and all cosmic relations are conceived as social relations, fulfills the criterion of being sufficiently intimate.

In this last book, James draws chiefly on the thought of Gustav Fechner and Henri Bergson to provide support for his view that the universe is experiential and social in nature. Fechner was a distinguished experimental psychologist who went on to argue that the earth has its own collective consciousness, as does the solar system, and that the universe is spiritual throughout. Bergson argued that theoretical knowledge distorts the nature of reality, which is better given by a phenomenological account of the flux of experience and of practical consciousness. A scientist and a philosopher, they provided James with contemporary examples of a metaphysics of experiential relations. Both portrayed the natural order as intimate, experiential, social, and therefore continuous with human thoughts and desires.

Like Fechner, some theologians and popular thinkers have continued to borrow images and metaphors from science to suggest that the universe is analogous to experience and mind. Alfred North Whitehead and process metaphysics offered a panpsychism that was often presented as being in special accord with contemporary science. American religious naturalists claimed to identify empirically a source of human good prior to and more fundamental than the thoughts and actions of individual persons. From the use of organic metaphors at the turn of the century to images from relativity or quantum theory to New Age speculations, religious and popular thinkers have continued this tradition. James often identified naturalism with materialism, but he knew that the issue is not one of determinism, or of the coarseness of matter, but of whether the cosmos is instinct with purpose or mind.

James says that the need for an eternal moral order is one of the deepest needs of our breast. While James was writing the articles that make up *The Will to Believe*, Friedrich Nietzsche wrote several books in which he acknowledged that need, but subjected it to critical examination. He wrote of a "supposed 'moral world order' through which the concept 'cause' and 'effect' is once and for all stood on its head."[28] James views the idea of a moral order as liberating. It provides an alternative to

[28] Friedrich Nietzsche, "The Anti-Christ," in *Twilight of the Idols / The Antichrist*, trans. R. J. Hollingdale (New York: Penguin, 1968), 136.

adapting one's desires and hopes to the values of the quotidian world. For Nietzsche, liberation comes from the gradual realization that the moral order is one we have imposed on the world, and that we are better off if we can loosen its grip on us and acknowledge the natural and historical causes of what happens to us and of our ideals.

It ought to be possible to do justice to both. We can recognize with James that imaginative ideals embodied in religious belief and experience provide leverage that can free us from some of the desires and demands that press in on us. But the unseen order that provides that leverage need not be, and is not, something "not ourselves." The moral order consists of what men and women have put there, of *Geist*, and the proper way to study it is through the humanities and social sciences, especially history. Rorty's idea of romance captures both the usefulness of religious belief and practice and their origin in imagination and action.

Nietzsche shows that the origins of our beliefs, practices, and ideals are seldom straightforward. The moral order that is the historical product of human imagination and action is often not pretty, and it provides for evil as well as for good. James often writes as if causes are irrelevant. In the opening pages of *Varieties* he says that judgments about the causes of religious experiences and judgments about their value "proceed from diverse intellectual preoccupations."[29] They need to be made separately, and can then be added together. In fact, inquiry into the causes of one's affections, dispositions, and practices is an important part of evaluating them and of the kind of self-knowledge, both individual and social, that is necessary for informed action. James is of some help with this, especially in his recognition that our concepts and categories are tools that humans have developed to serve particular purposes. But this general point needs to be heavily supplemented by Nietzsche's historical genealogy. We need to be suspicious of the too facile correlation of tools and purposes. The justification of religious beliefs, and the explanation of actions by reference to those beliefs, must be continually informed by natural and historical explanations of the moral orders within which we find ourselves.

[29] James, *The Varieties of Religious Experience*, 13.

PART II

Culture and cognition

Introduction

Several controversial features of radical interpretation in relation to religious beliefs provide the subject of the chapters in Part II by Catherine Bell, Thomas Lawson, and Maurice Bloch. Is the category of "belief" so associated with a Western and Christian bias that it has lost any value as an interpretive category? How much empirical or ethnographic evidence is there for the "coherence" that holism ascribes to the web of beliefs? Should explanation supplant "interpretation" in the study of religion? Can cognitive science models explain the inferential reasoning that leads to religious beliefs and their transmission? Should one label this inferential reasoning "counter-intuitive," as many social scientists tend to do? The answers suggested in the chapters by Bell, Lawson, and Bloch represent new research directions for these three authors, all regarded as experts on ritual. Here their overlapping interests converge on questions about cultural variations and the findings of cognitive science.

Catherine Bell's work was cited by Terry Godlove in his chapter in Part I as an example of the current tilt in favor of materiality over mentality, perhaps to counter the longstanding tilt in reverse. One of the foremost scholars of ritualization and ritual practice, Bell has contributed to the study of religion both a comprehensive historical overview of ritual theory in *Ritual: Perspectives and Dimensions* (1997) and a critical appraisal of that theory in *Ritual Theory, Ritual Practice* (1992). Analyzing what is above all a bodily activity, she has emphasized the intimate connection between mind and body, thought and action, that occurs in religious ritualization, resisting any bifurcation of these categories. Characteristic of Bell's nuanced methodological approach is an adroit avoidance of either–or dichotomies and a critical holding together of both sides of presumed antitheses. Most radically, she has resisted the idea, popular among many recent theorists, that ritual is a way of reconciling fundamental social conflicts. Such an idea, she suggests, may serve more as a legitimation of the growing field of ritual studies itself than as an accurate interpretation of the work of ritual.

In the following chapter, Bell takes up belief and believing in the study of religion, and explains why she thinks the simple report, "The Chinese Believe in Spirits," fails to capture what is most important. Questioning whether the study of religion in terms of beliefs bears any resemblance to the religion people live by, Bell draws attention to three complex problems the comparative study of religions encounters in invoking the language of belief. In particular, any theoretical orientation that flirts with "universalism" risks papering over cultural and historical variations among people and places, imposing a false appearance of "coherence." Bell credits Donald Davidson's theory of radical interpretation with holding together similiarity and difference, or "the universal and the particular," rather than dichotomizing these relations in ways that empty into either relativism or essentialism. Even so, she has reservations about focusing on sentential meaning as the level of analysis. How does this help with any "conclusions about religion in general"? And how will it be possible for the study of religion to do justice to the particularities of cultural differences without lapsing into relativism or to assess the universality of any religious structures without perpetuating essentialism?

Approaching believing as a social practice, Bell comes to conclusions that partly reinforce Stout's and Rorty's essays. At the same time, she notes "very little systematic coherence" in what constitutes spirit belief in China, Taiwan, or Hong Kong and not much more in the "bundle of behaviors" designated by "Chinese religion." The dilemma, she says succinctly, is that: "We cannot appeal to 'belief' to describe how people exist within their cultures; yet without 'belief,' it is not clear what we mean by 'religion.'"

Bell's chapter presents an implicit challenge to holism's principle of charity. The challenge may be posed by the very topic of religious belief. On the one hand, the principle of charity shows that most of anyone's beliefs are bound to be true, but this is a strange presumption to bring to religious beliefs. On the other hand, if it were less strange, it could only be because there would no longer be much of anything religious involved in religious beliefs.

In his chapter "On Interpeting the World Religiously," E. Thomas Lawson reports on the experiments he designed to test three predictions about the efficacy of rituals. Over several decades Lawson has brought to the study of religion a strong interest in interpretation and explanation, as well as an expertise in religions of Africa. His current research demonstrates how interpreting believers benefits from the revolution going on in cognitive science. Scholars not content with interpretations that begin and end in a hermeneutical circle, may seek explanations in theories that are empirically tractable and cognitively constrained. Lawson thinks such explanation is available at the intersection of cognitive science and the study of religion. His interest in accounting for religious ideas in terms of conformation to cognitive constraints places him broadly in the rational-intellectualist tradition of theorists of religion discussed by Hans Penner in Part III. Indeed, in *Rethinking Religion: Connecting Cognition and Culture* (with Robert N. McCauley) (1990), Lawson himself provided a detailed overview of the strengths and weaknesses of the rationalist or intellectualist approach in relation to the two other leading explanations of religion, the symbolist and the structuralist. *Rethinking Religion* also developed a theory of religious ritual competence analogous to Chomsky's theory of linguistic competence. Since then, Lawson has increasingly turned to the study of cognition rather than of epistemology to identify how people actually think, and with what constraints.

In his chapter here, he draws on current theories of how human beings from infancy employ cognitive resources to construct religious representations in general and religious ritual representations in particular. Cognitive science, he argues, can provide us with the methodological and theoretical tools to explain the structure of religious representations, the dynamics of their development, and the processes of their cultural transmission. "On Interpreting the World Religiously" focuses on how religious beliefs and concepts are transmitted. Why are anthropomorphic concepts of gods and goddesses standard fare across religious systems, as Stewart Guthrie's work shows in compelling detail?[1] Why does religion persist, especially if its stock in trade consists of counter-intuitive beliefs? The best theory indicated by empirical studies in cognitive psychology suggests that it is precisely the counter-intuitive ideas that are more easily remembered and culturally transmitted. That is to say, the epidemiology of ideas hinges on memory dynamics. Tweaked too far, religious ideas appear merely bizarre. Tweaked not enough, they are simply mundane. Given a conceptual optimum of intuitive and counter-intuitive properties, religious ideas are more likely to spread culturally.

Among the cognitive psychologists whose work Lawson finds helpful to the study of religion, Pascal Boyer stands out. Boyer's study of the rich inferential processes of human cognition, carried by all human minds,

---

[1] See Stewart Guthrie, *Faces in the Clouds: A New Theory of Religion* (Oxford University Press, 1993).

would seem to complement Robert Brandom's no less intricately mapped "semantic inferentialism" with respect to human language-users. In the business of inference-production, Boyer says, "many are called but few are chosen." The likelihood of acquiring and transmitting religious concepts that have staying power, according to Boyer, hinges on beliefs that both violate certain expectations from ontological categories and preserve other expectations. "Counter-intuitive" is thus a technical term Boyer uses to mean "including information contradicting some information provided by ontological categories," where the ontological categories are five: persons, tools, plants, natural objects, animals.[2]

In the next chapter, "Are Religious Beliefs Counter-intuitive?," social anthropologist Maurice Bloch takes issue with Pascal Boyer, as well as with fellow anthropologist Dan Sperber, for associating religion and religious belief with the "counter-intuitive." Like Catherine Bell, Bloch disputes the primary role given to the category of "belief" by Europeans, and, like Tom Lawson, he relates the findings of cognitive psychology with anthropology of religion. But, based on his fieldwork in Madagascar, Bloch is critical of the effort of philosophers like Davidson who devise theories of "radical interpretation," as well as of anthropologists like Pascal Boyer and Dan Sperber who employ the category of "counter-intuitive beliefs" in studying religion.

Bloch's contributions to an understanding of religion can only be called radical. His early article on "Symbols, Song, Dance and Features of Articulation: Or Is Religion an Extreme Form of Traditional Authority?" remains a classic. His account of the history and ideology of the circumcision ritual of the Merina of Madagascar in *From Blessing to Violence* (1986) theorized the indissoluble element of violence in religious ritual as having an indirect relation to political violence. In *Prey into Hunter: the Politics of Religious Experience* (1992), he gave a detailed description of the symbolism of cross-cultural rituals that construct "rebounding violence." Unlike such scholars as Girard, in *La violence et le sacré* (1972), or Burkert, in *Creation of the Sacred: Tracks of Biology in Early Religions* (1996), Bloch does not assume innate aggressiveness in humans, expressed or purged by ritual. Rather, he develops the argument that symbolic violence is itself the attempt to create "the transcendental" in religion and politics. In each case, the nature of the phenomenon is revealed by its historical behavior.

[2] See Pascal Boyer, *Religion Explained: The Evolutionary Origins of Religious Thought* (New York: Basic Books, 2001), 65. Boyer suggests that the neologism "counterontological" might be a better choice than "counter-intuitive."

In raising the question here as to whether religious beliefs are counter-intuitive, Bloch reflects on a problem that arises out of his extensive field work in Madagascar. Like Catherine Bell in connection with Chinese culture, Bloch questions whether an emphasis on belief does justice to the materials he tries to understand in Malagasy culture. Have ethnographers and philosophers alike placed altogether too much cognitive focus on "belief"? Canvassing the work of Sperber, in *On Anthropological Knowledge* (1983) and *Explaining Culture: A Naturalistic Approach* (1996) and Boyer, in *The Naturalness of Religious Ideas* (1994), in particular, Bloch suggests the answer is yes. The tendency to misrepresent a people's culture by slapping labels such as "religion" on apparently irrational "beliefs" misses what is really important to them, such as ancestor worship in the case of the Malagasy, Bloch observes. European missionaries wrongly assumed that stories about "sampy," translated as "idols," captured the most salient feature of Malagasy religion. Anthropologists are just as mistaken to place counter-intuitive beliefs automatically in the contrary-to-fact arsenal of beliefs associated with "religion," according to Bloch.

We might read Bloch's chapter as posing a challenge to theses about the holism of the mental, the principle of charity, and the overall rationality of humans. Much ethnography, after all, is written against the grain of the philosophical thesis that belief-attribution is in its nature largely truth-ascribing. But what Bloch presents as an example of bad translation and uses to suggest the dubiety of stressing the category of belief is actually, in his hands, an example of "radical interpretation." He succeeds in understanding "sampy" in relation to "medicines," even if the early Welsh Calvinist Christians arriving in Madagascar did not. At the end of the day, it seems Bloch would be willing to drop the designation "counter-intuitive" versus "intuitive" in favor of the view that religious cases of belief, though extreme, are not off the rational chart. This would bring him closer than he may suppose to the holistic thesis that theories of religion, however much they may appeal to non-rational causes and examine counter-intuitive beliefs, must be set within an overall context of encompassing rationality. Even so, Bloch's overall critique will draw sympathetic nods from many quarters. The problems of interpreting believers for him are only genuinely approached when they occur "in real situations where actors are not alone or outside historically constructed contexts."

5

"The Chinese believe in spirits": belief and believing in the study of religion

Catherine M. Bell

A recent round of books, both popular and scholarly, reveal that as a society we are, once again, fascinated with the issue of belief. While the more popular books tend to adopt a fairly straightforward and uncomplicated notion of believing and then find major problems of rationality, the more scholarly books readily accept a type of rationality to beliefs while problematizing the act of believing in other, more involuted ways.[1] Both types of argument remind the scholar of religion that the academic discipline of religious studies has not contributed much to this discussion for quite a while.[2] As described in Rodney Needham's 1972 work, *Belief, Language and Experience*, which was both a fulsome anthropological treatment of the problems and a cautionary tale for further studies, the concept of belief poses particular problems for comparative analysis

[1] Popular titles include Wendy Kaminer's *Sleeping with Extra-Terrestrials: The Rise of Irrationalism and the Perils of Piety* (New York: Pantheon, 1999); Michael Shermer's *Why People Believe Weird Things: Pseudoscience, Superstition and Other Confusions of Our Time* (New York: W. H. Freeman and Company, 1997) and *How We Believe: The Search For God in an Age of Science* (New York: W. H. Freeman and Company, 2000). Scholarly studies include Barbara Herrnstein Smith, *Belief and Resistance: Dynamics of Contemporary Intellectual Controversy* (Cambridge, MA: Harvard University Press, 1997); and Umberto Eco, *Belief or Non-Belief: A Confrontation* (New York: Arcade Publishing, 2000). Indeed, an unproblematic invocation of belief is one of the informal markers between popular and professional studies of religion and culture. For an example of a study on the edge of this divide, see Huston Smith's popular textbook, *The World's Religions* (formerly, *Religions of the World* [San Francisco: HarperCollins, 1991 (1958)]), which describes the main beliefs of each tradition.

[2] The major discussions of these issues are Robert Bellah's *Beyond Belief: Essays on Religion in a Post-Traditional World* (New York: Harper and Row, 1970); Rodney Needham, *Belief, Language and Experience* (University of Chicago Press, 1972); and Wilfred Cantwell Smith, *Belief and History* (Charlottesville: University Press of Virginia, 1977). For an interesting exchange, see Donald Wiebe, "On the Transformation of 'Belief' and the Domestication of 'Faith' in the Academic Study of Religion," *Method and Theory in the Study of Religion* 4:1–2 (1992): 47–67, reprised in "The Role of 'Belief' in the Study of Religion," *Numen* 26:2 (1979): 234–49, with a response by Wilfred Cantwell Smith, "Belief: A Reply to A Response," *Numen* 27:2 (1980): 247–55. For a useful compendium that addresses belief, see Nancy K. Frankenberry and Hans H. Penner (eds.), *Language, Truth, and Religious Belief: Studies in Twentieth-Century Theory and Method in Religion* (Atlanta: Scholars Press, 1999).

since belief does not appear to be identifiable or similarly important in religions we want to compare and from which we want to abstract more general descriptions. Moreover, it is a commonplace that many of our assumptions about the centrality of belief in religion have emerged in a decidedly Christian context, making comparison a distortion of other religious views.[3] Anthropological studies since Needham have tended to collapse belief into "culture," which has worked well enough most of the time, but it not only avoids the explicit problem of why and how "beliefs" and "believing" become prominent in the way in which many people participate in a culture, it also retreats from the problem of various ways in which any one person may appropriate parts of the culture. Recourse to the concept of culture not only leaves many of these questions to popular writers, it also tends to push anthropology into an extreme cultural relativism that is painfully dependent upon the fragile and often unarticulated nature of this idea of culture. Scholars of religion, on the other hand, generally want to use the language of belief to say that members of such-and-such a religion generally hold such-and-such conceptions that motivate their activities. While people have pointed to the overriding need for such an abstract language despite ongoing revelations of its weaknesses, we also know that a term like belief keeps tying any metalanguage to assumptions that are more culturally constrained than we really care to defend.[4]

Another reason for the field's hesitation about belief may also lie in philosophical uses of the term. Philosophical usage tends to emphasize a more individualistic version of anthropology's "culture," and in so doing deals, at least in passing, with the possibility of idiosyncrasy, madness, or the intent to delude.[5] Philosophers seeking a language with which to analyze how human beings go about interpreting their world, particularly the linguistic communications within it, often make use of the concept of

---

[3] This point is made by Donald S. Lopez, Jr. in "Belief," in Mark C. Taylor (ed.), *Critical Terms for Religious Studies* (2000), 21–35.

[4] See Jonathan Z. Smith, "Religion, Religions, Religious," in Taylor (ed.), *Critical Terms*, 169–84.

[5] For two explicit examples, see Ludwig Wittgenstein's comments in his "Lectures on Religious Belief" collected in *L. Wittgenstein: Lectures and Conversations on Aesthetics, Psychology and Religious Belief*, trans. and ed. Cyril Barrett (Berkeley: University of California Press, 1967), 54–72; his comments are also available in Ludwig Wittgenstein, "Religious Belief," in Frankenberry and Penner (eds.), *Language, Truth, and Religious Belief*, 311–28. See also the following quotes: "What is the criterion of reliability, dependability? Suppose you give a general description as to when you say a proposition has a reasonable weight of probability. When you call it reasonable, is this *only* to say that for it you have such and such evidence, and for others you haven't?" *ibid.*, 315; and "For instance, we don't trust the account given of an event by a drunk man," *ibid.*, 315. Also see Donald Davidson, *Inquiries into Truth and Interpretation* (Oxford: Clarendon Press, 1984), 153, for his remarks on the aberrant and idiosyncratic.

belief to link it to, or play it off, a notion of truth. Needham discussed the links and distinctions drawn between belief and truth in the philosophical tradition stretching from Hume to Wittgenstein, Hampshire, and Harnack. More recently, Donald Davidson has made liberal use of belief in his theory of "radical interpretation."[6] He argues that we cannot make sense of a person's utterances without understanding something of their intentions and beliefs, but "we cannot infer the belief without knowing the meaning, and have no chance of inferring the meaning without the belief."[7] His theory of radical interpretation, therefore, assumes the interconnectedness of belief and meaning as well as their formal role in interpretation. For the sake of his larger argument, essentially a theory about a theory, Davidson focuses on the belief (or "preference"), integral to interpretation, that the statements made by another are or can be true. In fact, he points out, we must grant other speakers, however aberrant or idiosyncratic, a great deal of reason and truth, or else we would have no way to conclude they are being unreasonable or untrue. Davidson goes on to propose a theory of how we infer belief and meaning, arguing that the inference that statements can be held to be true cannot be separate from this basic theory of interpretation.[8] However, philosophical discussions like Davidson's, which relate belief and meaning to truth, however truth is understood, not only seem to threaten religious studies' post-theological emphasis on the validity of different world-views, they also appear to threaten to push analysis to the level of the sentence, from where it appears hard to come to any conclusions about religion in general.

Despite these fears, the question of how to use the concept of belief, and how to identify the types of phenomenon potentially illuminated by such a concept, remains an inescapable aspect of studying religion within the language traditions that the field of religious studies inherits. This chapter, which is for me both an initial and perhaps belated foray into the topic, will explore some unarticulated tendencies in our use of the notion of belief, and tie our use of this concept to a particular way of thinking about religion. In the end, I will sketch a possible way to approach these issues from a rather different direction.

---

[6] Davidson, "Radical Interpretation" (1973), and "Belief and the Basis of Meaning" (1974) in *Inquiries*, 125–40 and 141–54.

[7] *Ibid.*, 144.

[8] In a section relevant to analyzing some forms of religious beliefs, Davidson suggests that an indeterminacy of meaning or translation should not be seen as a failure to capture important distinctions, but rather that these distinctions themselves are not that significant. In other words, indeterminacy can be important. See *ibid.*, 154.

UNIVERSAL AND PARTICULAR

A particularly provocative dimension of Davidson's analysis of interpretation is the attempt to hold on to two positions that are usually polarized in such a way as to force a choice of one over the other. On the one hand, he invokes truth (or reality) as clearly dependent on language (or culture), a stance that supports many current understandings of cultural pluralism and relativism, which are compelling and popular positions these days. On the other hand, Davidson also points to a type of shared rationalism that enables us to recognize and interpret the meaning of statements made by others even when the linguistic or cultural overlap is very thin. By holding on to both positions, Davidson attempts to find something of a middle way or, rather, as he puts it, to place theories of interpretation on a new footing. I have read Davidson primarily for this struggle to hold on to both positions in ways that make sense of what we are looking at in the study of religion: sometimes it feels like we are encountering very different realities that lead us to question our own; at other times, we experience, and point to, a great deal of similarity, although we can get nervous about that too. In both cases, we wonder what is inevitably particular and what, if anything, is, has been, or is becoming universal.

When reduced to this formulation, however, Davidson's project is one that is widely shared at the moment. Philosophical ethics, in particular, may be doing the most explicit work on how to think about cultural relativism without endorsing complete relativism, but there are and have been other engagements.[9] Among anthropologists, few have tried to imagine a more explicit convergence of relativism and universalism than Richard Shweder. In several studies in the 1980s, he groped to identify all the presuppositions of these polarized positions by delineating and classifying a wide variety of formulations of each.[10] By making transparent what he saw as the main tensions in the field, Shweder hoped to elucidate the basic stance and components of a post-positivist, postmodern anthropology. I do not think his conclusion – that anthropological

---

[9] The main studies in philosophical ethics are Gilbert Harman and Judith Jarvis Thomson, *Moral Relativism and Moral Objectivity* (Cambridge, MA: Blackwell, 1996); Richard Rorty, *Objectivity, Relativism, And Truth: Philosophical Papers* (Cambridge University Press, 1991); and David B. Wong, *Moral Relativity* (Berkeley: University of California Press, 1984).

[10] Richard A. Shweder, "Anthropology's Romantic Rebellion Against the Enlightenment, or There's More to Thinking than Reason and Evidence," in Richard A. Shweder and Robert A. LeVine (eds.), *Culture Theory: Essays on Mind, Self, and Emotion* (Cambridge University Press, 1984), 27–66; and Richard A. Shweder, "Post-Nietzschian Anthropology: The Idea of Multiple Objective Worlds," in Michael Krauz (ed.), *Relativism: Interpretation and Confrontation* (Notre Dame University Press, 1989), 99–139.

theorists should adopt a "transcendence without superiority" from which they should "take 'literally' (as a matter of belief) those reality-posits so alien in order to discover other realities within the self" – is either satisfying or successful.[11] Yet the effort was fascinating, instructive, and bold.

Religious studies, especially the history of religions, has also addressed the issue of universalism and particularism and, like most academic fields, it has probably been formed by the tension between them.[12] The differentiation of the study of religion from theology more than fifty years ago was one early engagement of the issue, by which an emerging "history of religions" approach felt its way to what was arguably a type of universalized theology and a fresh, if incomplete, particularization of Christianity and its siblings. When the field began to focus more on methods of comparison, it took another angle on these polarized options, asking several related questions: are all religions comparable manifestations of some type of universal, such as *homo religiosus* or the sacred? should we be comparing to illuminate the universal or the particular or, somehow, both? and what can be adequately compared to what for what end? With the more recent emergence of linguistic and cognitive theories, as well as studies effectively deconstructing universal narratives, one wonders if there is any other issue so responsible for what we do and how we do it today. In no small way, scholarship understands itself as both a vehicle for identifying particularism (we sometimes regarded ourselves as "liberating" it) and forging formulations of an underlying or abstract universalism. The emphasis may shift back and forth, but each, as Davidson might suggest, is impossible to infer without the other.

BELIEF

According to recent critiques, "religion" is an over-reaching folk category that misreads and even does violence to other cultures.[13] This is, of course, a corrective, and undoubtedly a slightly exaggerated one, which has the merit of addressing the many liberties we have taken with the term for so long. Yet these critiques leave two concerns unanswered.

[11] Shweder, "Post-Nietzschian Anthropology," 133.
[12] Michael J. Buckley, SJ, "The Study of Religion and the Rhetoric of Atheism: A Paradox," unpublished manuscript (1999); also see Tomoko Masuzawa, "From Theology to World Religions," in Tim Jensen and Mikael Rothstein (eds.), *Secular Theories on Religion: Current Perspectives* (University of Copenhagen Press, 2000), 149–66.
[13] Among those who have addressed this topic, let me simply note Talal Asad, *Genealogies of Religion: Discipline and Reasons of Power in Christianity and Islam* (Baltimore: Johns Hopkins University Press, 1993); and Smith, "Religion, Religions, Religious."

First, several centuries of talking about "religion in general" has created a sense of religion in many places that might, arguably, have categorized things differently without such influence. It is not so easy to recontain the term "religion" at this point in history. It may be just another form of hegemonic imperialism to claim, for example, that the Chinese today are wrong or deluded in using the word "religion" to describe either past or current practices in their culture. If we are to be clear about the historicity of such terminology, we must follow through and track how the concept is being used today beyond our own theorizing. We know there are no Platonic theoretical categories, but we keep thinking we can freeze them for this study or that critique.

Second, I work in the materials of a culture that has long constituted a good example of classifications that do not fit the Euro-American understanding of religion, namely China.[14] Yet, if one looks beyond the careful slices of Chinese culture that are usually chosen as representative, one can find much that is not completely alien to any definition of "religion," medieval, enlightenment, or postmodern. It can be refreshing, of course, to drop the notion of religion out of the picture as completely as possible, and either explore the variety of Chinese categories that have been used or fish for other ways of identifying what is either comparable or distinguishable among practices.

These concerns notwithstanding, the attempt to demote "religion" from a universal (the "consensus of nations"), a biological facility, or a cognitive structure to a theory of the specific classificatory organization of a particular culture helps to illuminate some of the problems attending our language of belief and meaning. In the same way, I want to suggest, our language about belief and meaning is part of an understanding of religion that keeps reasserting itself because a tense relationship between universalism and particularism – whether or not it is the type of solution sought by Davidson and Shweder, among others – may be integral to theoretical projects as we have culturally cast them. Even if we pay full attention to the historicity of the social system examined, as well as the historicity of the project of examining it, it is not clear that we secure a

---

[14] One has only to recall the popularity and fecundity of Jorge Luis Borges's fanciful description of a Chinese encyclopedia, which was identified as Chinese to locate such wonderfully exotic and still totally alien difference. I will only note here Michel Foucault's use of the image in *The Order of Things: An Archeology of the Human Sciences* (New York: Vintage, 1973), xv. One of the stronger arguments against the Western terminology of religion for understanding Chinese religion is given in Jordan Paper's *The Spirits are Drunk: Comparative Approaches to Chinese Religion* (Albany: State University of New York Press, 1995), especially 2–12, even though Paper argues that the comparative study of religion is still viable.

footing for scholarship that drops the allure of transcendence as another version of the particularism–universalism polarity.[15]

While we have tended to use "religion" to denote a dimension of open-ended commonality, something found in most if not all human cultures, we have used the term "belief" in the highly tailored, supporting role of denoting the culturally particular foci of a religion – specifically those things that we hold to not exist in fact. If a group "believes" in less particular or empirically problematic things like love or the tragic dimensions of life, we tend to refer to these not as beliefs, but as cultural values, attitudes, or dispositions. If a group holds convictions about astrological destiny, we are very willing to describe such attitudes as beliefs, not as culture. Belief is our characterization of the specific illusions of others. But the distinction between belief and culture is not dramatically demarcated: belief is also our shorthand for the epitome of what we see as being encultured, culture-bound, or culturally determined.

We explain a culturally particular belief, and that is a very redundant phrase, by its place in a structured system of ideas that we assemble. In this way, we see what the belief "means." Since the objects of the beliefs do not actually exist in our view, there is no other route for meaning; so the meaningfulness of beliefs is dependent upon rendering them coherent within a system of ideas. Coherent systems of belief create a meaningful structure, namely "religion," which makes sense to us of the particular and the illusionary. This can be a very circular way to work.

In connection with this tendency to identify belief with extremes of cultural particularism and determinism, we also talk about belief as a type of deeply held mental orientation or conviction. That is, belief is described as one type of thing, an all-or-nothing, on-or-off state. There is little evidence to warrant such a view outside of certain specific confessional practices. Both formulations of belief, as the illusion rendered meaningful when made part of a larger coherent system understood as religion and as a state of deeply held convictions, emerge in Shweder's argument that the interpretation of beliefs is the central anthropological question – and its fault-line. He evokes the "witch" question that lies at the root of anthropology, namely, if your informant tells you, perhaps at some risk of negative consequences, that she or he is actually a witch, what can you make of this statement when your own reality makes clear

---

[15] In his 1980 study, *Ilongot Headhunting 1883–1944: A Study in Society and History* (Stanford University Press, 1980), Renato Rosaldo's recognition of the problems with anthropological analysis led him to abandon many anthropological concepts and adopt an extremely biographical, even autobiographical approach.

there are no witches?[16] Generally, we must reconstruct the system of ideas that rationalize and render such statements coherent if we are to "interpret" them. This is a true advance, of course, on the earlier view that such statements are proof of some sort of "primitive mentality."[17] Yet it is hard to be convinced that an interpretation in which a belief, taken as a designated illusion that is nonetheless a "type" of truth, that is, as having its own particular reality, is all that different from interpretations based on a primitive mentality. Neither do I think anything is solved by concluding, as Shweder does, that unquestionably the informant is a witch.[18]

A third problematic assumption, which I have addressed at length elsewhere, is the ease with which we grant belief a prior existence in order to cast it as the a priori shaper and instigator of action.[19] While belief may well work this way some of the time, we have no evidence that this happens most of the time. Such an assumption, however, does allow us to "explain" action by connecting it to its motivating beliefs, and from there to a larger reconstructed system, understood to be "the" relevant system by its coherence and ability to explain the particulars with which the interpreter started.

COHERENCE

It is a relatively recent thing for scholars to emphasize meaningful and systemic coherence in relation to what religion is all about. Only in the second half of the twentieth century, for the most part, has the provision of coherence been seen as the defining role of religion, that is, what we theorists think it should do when religion clearly can no longer explain the nature of the universe or act as the authoritative source of morality.[20] And this is not just the stance of theorists. When I quiz my

---

[16] Shweder, "Post-Nietzschian Anthropology," 109–10. It is interesting to note the difference between the interpretive tasks represented by Shweder's witch claim, on the one hand, and Davidson's examples (*pace* Tarski?), on the other, in which he ponders the interpretive process involved in understanding Kurt's statement, *es regnet*, and Karl's statement, *es schneit* (Davidson, *Inquiries into Truth*, 129 and 141).

[17] For a thorough history of this ethnographic view and its relationship to cross-cultural interpretation of irrational statements, see Jonathan Z. Smith, "I am a Parrot (Red)" in *Map Is Not Territory: Studies in the History of Religions* (Leiden: E. J. Brill, 1978; reprint 1997), 265–88.

[18] Shweder, "Post-Nietzschian Anthropology," 109–10. For Shweder, "cultural anthropology will probably come to an end when it comes up with an incontestable answer to the witch question" (109).

[19] Catherine Bell, *Ritual Theory, Ritual Practice* (New York: Oxford University Press, 1992), esp. 13–66.

[20] Influences on the interpretive importance of coherence have been Peter L. Berger's arguments about the construction of a nomos as a meaningful order (*The Sacred Canopy: Elements of*

students, completely unread in the relevant anthropological literature, meaningful coherence is what they also have absorbed as the expected role and real contribution of religion. They lament that they have not found it or a sufficiently steady experience of it.[21] They are particularly aware of, and appalled by, what they see as the rampant incoherence – the fragmentation, hypocrisy, or compromises – in the lives of adults around them. For these students, as for most scholars of religion, religion should have a holistic coherence that delivers meaningful experiences. Yet even those who have devoted their lives to religion – the clergy of many different persuasions – rarely find those qualities in their religious experience if you ask them.[22] Coherence can be found only in some explicit self-presentations by persons, texts, or institutions. We can argue for the existence of a "deeper" coherence, of course, either in the organization of the brain, the personal psyche, the social structure, or the dynamics of culture – all universalizations that support the major theories and disciplines of the twentieth century. Awkward to use today, but still regularly invoked, these approaches contrast with attempts to see beliefs and believing as a matter of specific sets of actions or situations, that is, approaching believing as a type of social practice rather than a (true or false) linguistic statement or mental conviction.[23]

To indulge an autobiographical example, I originally thought to study religion because I was interested in how most people – that is, folks not schooled in the language and history of philosophy – made sense of their lives and worlds. I have not been heavily invested in any particular formulation of this focus, just in the general human project implied, which has to include how readily people get by without giving much attention to making any larger sense of things. It was clear to me growing up among the natives of Long Island in the 1950s and 60s – indeed, it was a striking

A Sociology of Religion [New York: Doubleday, 1967], 19); and Clifford Geertz's arguments about religions as a system ("Religion as a Cultural System," in Michael Banton (ed.), *Anthropological Approaches to the Study of Religion* [London: Tavistock, 1966], reprinted in *The Interpretation of Cultures: Selected Essays* [New York: Basic Books, 1973], 87–125); and, a bit more distant, Claude Levi-Strauss's structuralism (e.g., *The Savage Mind* [University of Chicago Press, 1966]).

21 It is interesting that theorists talk about coherence as something projected, while believers and would-be believers almost always talk of it as something found. For another discussion of coherence, also see Nancy K. Frankenberry and Hans H. Penner, "Clifford Geertz's Long-Lasting Moods, Motivations, and Metaphysical Conceptions," *Journal of Religion* (1999): 617–40, especially 626.

22 My evidence here is simply personal conversation with clergy, primarily, though not exclusively, in the Christian, Jewish, and Buddhist traditions.

23 Needham suggests this direction, belief as social action, although he does not develop it; anthropology has done a better job at grasping this stance than religious studies, although at the cost of the relativism for which anthropology is so often accused.

feature of the religious attitudes there – just how little coherence religion actually seemed to provide or was even expected to provide. Later, in the 1970s, coherence became a more explicitly stated expectation, but, as before, religiosity within the spectrum of conventional lifestyles seemed to hinge on internalizing a complex array of compartmentalizations and disassociations.

On Long Island, and in other places I have come to know well, what is thought of as religion by the natives is more a matter of loosely packaged sets of behaviors – what we can also call "bundles of behaviors" or "habits of action."[24] For Long Islanders, these packaged sets of distinct behaviors were used to deal with such events as death, serious illness, perverse misfortune, and occasionally life-crises like birth, marriage, or divorce, as well as, naturally, the ritual life of defined communities gathered at the church, synagogue, house meeting, prayer circle, or meditation group. In actual fact, family, jobs, and personal projects of service to others were more obvious overarching systems of meaning; religion appeared to be invoked simply to support them. Long Islanders' delineation and expectations of religion are not the same as those of other places that could be described. Yet neither are these other places so different that we cannot articulate similarities and differences. The commonality that allows for such articulations is the "principle of charity" defined by Davidson, a particularly felicitous if provocative basis for any new take on interpretation.[25]

THE CHINESE "BELIEVE"

In even the most sophisticated literature on Chinese religion and culture, it is readily stated that the Chinese believe in spirits. Some Chinese will say something like that, too, as I learned at a shamanic exorcism down the block from where I lived in Taipei. After the bloodied shaman was through with his spectral combat, and everyone was relaxing, the apartment owner complained that she had heard there were no ghosts in America, which seemed so unfair since large numbers of them kept bothering people in Taiwan. Analogously, there is the eloquent essay by the early twentieth-century sociologist, Fei Xiaotong, entitled "The World Without Ghosts," where he recounts growing up surrounded by ghosts

---

[24] These two phrases are used by Maurice Bloch and Richard Rorty, respectively. See Maurice Bloch, "Language, Anthropology and Cognitive Science," *Man* 26:2 (1991): 183–98; and Richard Rorty, *Philosophy and Social Hope* (New York: Penguin, 1999), xxix.

[25] Davidson expands W. V. Quine's use of this idea, see *Inquiries into Truth*, 136, n. 16.

who were as real to him as his many relatives.[26] Fei used the ghost theme
to set up a thoughtful contrast between Chinese and American cultures.
As beliefs go, believing in spirits is not a particularly strange example, and
we are very accustomed to the holistic construction known as Chinese
religion, which can make such beliefs coherent among themselves and
understandable as a type of meaningful truth.

Yet if the Chinese "believe" in spirits in anything like the way my
Long Island community believed in papal authority, or even the way
Christian colleagues believe in a central doctrine like the divinity of
Jesus Christ, then the statement that the Chinese believe in ancestral
spirits is, at best, a very vague generalization that ignores everything
interesting.[27] It ignores the great differences from one person to another,
awareness of the possibility of other positions, the individualized inner
juggling and tensions, as well as pragmatic non-judgments and refusals
to engage. Most language about belief, and about Chinese religion in
general, leaves little room for these features and certainly does not begin
to account for them.[28]

There are, as you would imagine, *many* Chinese positions on spirits.
Just a sampling of the most famous and familiar ones can demonstrate
the complexity of believing, at least in regard to this one topic in Chinese
history. In the fifth century BCE, for example, the sage Mo Tzu argued
that the degeneration of civilization since the sage-kings was due to only
one thing, doubt about the existence of ghosts and spirits. Those who
say "of course there are no spirits," he argued, bewilder the people and
bring disorder to the empire. In fact, he continued, people can know
that spirits exist in exactly the same way that they know anything exists –
through reliable testimony, the consensus of textual sources that have
proven their authority in other matters, and personal experience by the
senses.[29] Several centuries later, the Han dynasty writer, Wang Ch'ung,
made the opposite argument in order to refute Taoist teachings. With

---

[26] Fei Xiaotong, "The World Without Ghosts," in R. David Arkush and Leo O. Lee (eds.), *Land Without Ghosts* (Berkeley: University of California Press, 1989), 175–81.

[27] The purpose of such sweeping generalizations, so rarely noticed as such, may be to establish a contrast that creates "Chinese-ness," even for Fei Xiaotong. See "Acting Ritually: Evidence from the Social Life of Chinese Rites" in Richard Fenn (ed.), *Blackwell Companion to the Sociology of Religion* (London: Blackwell, 2001), 371–87.

[28] For a provocative engagement of related issues, see Maurice E. F. Bloch, *How We Think They Think: Anthropological Approaches to Cognition, Memory, and Literacy* (Boulder, CO: Westview, 1998).

[29] Mo Tzu, "On Ghosts," in Victor Mair (ed.), *The Columbia Anthology of Traditional Chinese Literature* (New York: Columbia University Press, 1994), 31–39. These are, of course, exactly the reasons that I "believe" in nuclear physics, space travel, many medical treatments, or the usefulness of "talking things out" in a marriage – to name just a few common examples.

what has been characterized by later readers as admirable rationalism, Wang argued that "man is a creature. His rank may be ever so high . . . but his nature does not differ from other creatures. There is no creature who does not die" and soon become dust.[30] Hence, for Wang Ch'ung, there can be no ghosts, spirits, or gods. In the medieval period, Han Yü (768–824 CE) admonished the emperor for his public attentions to the "bone of the Buddha" in an essay that became well known among the literati.[31] More widespread were the ubiquitous tales of the supernatural, such as those collected by Hung Mai in the twelfth century, which all turned on the moment when someone who did not believe in spirits personally experienced their intervention and came to realize the truth of their existence.[32]

Any village or urban neighborhood in China, Taiwan, or Hong Kong also yields a wide spectrum of positions on spirits. What is important about the variety, I think, is the evidence that individuals are very aware of the number of possible opinions and thus have located their own position – if it is clear enough to be called that – as a matter of some choice and deliberation. These people know that others hold different ideas, that many reject the whole thing, that people may act contradictorily, or some feign belief for self-serving reasons. There is little to suggest that a belief in spirits comes with the culture or is any one sort of belief. There is, in other words, very little systematic coherence.

As interpreters of texts and cultures, scholars of religion know that a Chinese text preaching filiality to one's ancestral spirits cannot be taken as descriptive of the actual state of cultural affairs in China, any more than a Long Island sermon about loving the poor can be taken as descriptive of Catholic life as it is really lived there. It is much more accurate, and certainly more interesting, to read admonishments and affirmations as argumentative practices, perhaps involving some complex sharing of ideals, but not as representations of a static or coherent situation.

If we argue that a person's options are still culturally limited in the forms and degrees of belief possible, clearly the limit is much further

---

[30] Wang Ch'ung, "Taoist Untruths," in Mair, *The Columbia Anthology*, 62–77, esp. 65–66.

[31] Han Yü, "Memorial on the Bone of the Buddha," in various anthologies, including William Theodore de Bary, Wing-Tsit Chan, and Burton Watson, *Sources of Chinese Tradition*, vol. 1 (New York: Columbia University Press, 1960), 372–74.

[32] See Robert Hymes, "Truth, Falsity, and Pretense in Sung China," unpublished paper, which engages a debate in circles that study Chinese philosophy and religion (notably, Chad Hanson, *A Taoist Theory of Chinese Thought* [New York: Oxford University Press, 1992] and A. C. Graham, *Disputers of the Tao* [Chicago: Open Court, 1989]) about whether "Chinese religion" is actually concerned with "truth" or not.

out or more blurred than we usually acknowledge. Of course, Chinese culture is extremely diverse, and even by the medieval period it had seen a great deal of cultural trafficking. Perhaps this plurality influenced the boundaries of what could be thought in the culture, let alone what constituted belief and its systemic coherence. A possible counter-example dealing with a relatively more isolated society is suggested by Renato Rosaldo's account of headhunting among the Ilongot.[33] He implies little or no debate, doubt, or discussion among the Ilongot about the efficacy, and meaningfulness, of headhunting; but he does note discussions of its necessity and periods when young men did not take heads prior to marriage. If there is no evidence of various shades of conviction and degrees of involvement in headhunting practices, then that would seem to be an unusual situation warranting study as such.

RELIGION

All native statements about belief can be seen as concerned with the nature (classifying and boundaries) of religion in the sense that people on Long Island and in Beijing are constantly asking themselves what to believe, how much to believe it, and with what specific investments or commitments. This is true not just for so-called religious ideas, of course, but also for personal affairs or economic and political matters. People regularly ask questions that deal with what we might call the cultural boundaries and definition of religion. There are some familiar examples, such as the famous Rites Controversy provoked by the Jesuits in seventeenth-century China, which revolved around the question whether ancestor worship was religion as such and had to be abandoned by converts, or

---

[33] Rosaldo tried to explore the practice without the usual judgments of the time by attempting to see the rationality of headhunting and by looking to find aspects of his own experience illuminated by his encounter with Ilongot culture. See his *Culture and Truth: The Remaking of Social Analysis* (Boston: Beacon Press, 1989; 1993). In *Ilongot Headhunting 1883–1974*, particularly 55, Rosaldo describes the Ilongot concept of history and Ilongot unwillingness to accept the veracity of stories of the past, as well as the lack of any uniformity to their accounts. "In general," Rosaldo writes, "Ilongots are unlikely to accept as true any narrative about events they neither saw for themselves nor heard about from an eyewitness" (55). Of course, in this passage Rosaldo is assessing attitudes toward stories and explanations, not toward activities that are considered (by whom?) central to the culture, like headhunting. In terms of comparative ethics, one approach to all the other problems of cultural comparison and objectivity, Rosaldo has addressed the "ethics" of Ilongot headhunting. In "Of Headhunters and Soldiers: Separating Cultural and Ethical Relativism," *Santa Clara Magazine* 42:2 (Fall 2000): 18–21, Rosaldo argues that the acceptance of cultural differences, even extreme ones, does not lead to an acceptance of the chaos of ethical relativism.

whether it was an aspect of customary etiquette and no more threatening to converts than the bow given in greeting.[34] Of course, this was a more critical question for the foreign missionaries than for most, though not all, Chinese. A careful ethnography by Margery Wolf details the extended deliberations in a small village in Taiwan over the question of whether a particular woman was a shaman-to-be called by the spirits or a batty and unsympathetic outsider to be shunned.[35] Drawing on more recent examples, members of the recently outlawed group, the Falundafa (Falungong), to some extent like other *qigong* societies in China since the 1960s, have had to decide to what extent their practices are religious or simply therapeutic physical exercises that do not threaten other religious affiliations or fall under government control of religion. For various political reasons and agendas, their deliberations and articulated positions are carefully calibrated to keep the line between religion and therapeutic exercise more unclear than clear.[36]

[handwritten margin note: Falun gong]

When a coherently organized systemization of beliefs is proposed by a Chinese source, then a very specific argument is being made about the way things really are. The creation of a broadly designed system of coherence is a particular rhetorical project, one undertaken indigenously as well as by outside scholars. And the difference between the practices of these two groups is, perhaps, one of the many distinctions that should lose its importance in our analyses.[37] For example, coherence is an important part of the argument made by a subset of Chinese texts known as morality books (*shanshu*), which emerged in twelfth-century China among the opportunities of easy wood-block printing, inexpensive paper, and manageable distribution; they are still produced and circulated today. These texts are explicitly engaged in an enormous polemical effort to provide a totally comprehensive and coherent understanding of the workings of the world, both visible and invisible, in terms of universal and inexorable laws of cosmic retribution – despite evidence available to all that appears to contradict such a system. In this project, these morality books reinterpret a wide variety of local and regional practices in terms

---

34 On the rites controversy, see David E. Mungello, ed., *The Chinese Rites Controversy: Its History and Meaning* (Nettetal: Steyler Verlag, 1994); Jonathan D. Spence, *The Memory Palace of Matteo Ricci* (New York: Viking, 1984) and *The Search for Modern China* (New York: W. W. Norton, 1990); and Lionel M. Jensen, *Manufacturing Confucianism* (Durham: Duke University Press, 1997).

35 See Margery Wolf, "The Woman Who Didn't Become a Shaman," in *A Thrice Told Tale* (Stanford University Press, 1992), 93–126.

36 Catherine Bell, "Exercise, Ritual, and Political Dissent: The Falun Gong," untitled volume, ed. Christoph Wulf, Surkamp, forthcoming, 2003.

37 For an example of what this might look like as analysis, see Susan Friend Harding's *The Book of Jerry Falwell: Fundamentalist Language and Politics* (Princeton University Press, 2000).

of a system said to underlie the otherwise incoherent or incomplete cosmologies attributed to Buddhism, Taoism, Confucianism, and folk religion.[38] As such, this project often echoes scholarly studies that present a coherent overview, at least more coherent than the last scholarly attempt, of a definable cultural tradition, although such overviews can be found particularly unhelpful come a real encounter with some aspect of the said tradition.

As a type of test of the hypothesis I am proposing, one can look again at a well-known example of an underlying and apparently determinative cultural structure, namely, Arthur Wolf's ethnographic account of the different grades of spirit currency burned to ghosts, ancestors, and gods – coarse yellow paper, paper with a silver appliqué, and finer paper with a gold appliqué, respectively. Although focusing on one part of Taiwanese rural society, Wolf argued that this system of paper types demonstrates a more basic and wider cultural understanding of the organization of the cosmos, one "that mirrors the social landscape of its adherents."[39] His ethnography is often cited as evidence of a latent structure in Chinese folk practice, in reference to which a particular belief, such as the existence of ancestral spirits, makes sense to people and accounts for a variety of related actions. However, it is equally persuasive, and correct, to argue that Wolf represented this practice as more coherent and routine than it really was or is. Extended ethnographic observation adds so many qualifications and regional differences that the original assertion can be regarded, at best, as heavily generalized, that is, as much suggestive as descriptive.[40]

Several sociological studies have attempted to assess the degree of coherence among the beliefs to which people are willing to attest, and their results reinforce each other: there is surprisingly little coherence among people's formulated beliefs and it decreases as one moves from more educated and articulate people, comfortable with narrative or

---

[38] What is most striking about these texts is not their cosmic message, but their juxtaposition of esoteric talismanic properties with mass distribution. See Catherine Bell, "Printing and Religion in China: Some Evidence from the *Taishang ganying pian*," *Journal of Chinese Religions* 20 (Fall 1992): 173–86 and "'A Precious Raft to Save the World': The Interaction of Scriptural Traditions and Printing in a Chinese Morality Book," *Late Imperial China* 17:1 (June 1996): 58–200.

[39] Arthur P. Wolf, "Gods, Ghosts, and Ancestors," in *Religion and Ritual in Chinese Society* (Stanford University Press, 1974), 131–92, particularly 131.

[40] I develop this argument, citing the conflicting ethnographic studies, with regard to the "universal" Chinese practice of domestic ancestor worship in Bell, "Performance," in Mark Taylor (ed.), *Critical Terms in the Study of Religion* (University of Chicago Press, 1998), 205–24.

abstract categories, to the less-educated, who are not as apt to use them.[41] Two of these studies also inquired into the "meaning" of various ritual practices and found little consensus among the explanations given, even when people were asked about ritual features that had well-known, even memorized, doctrinal explanations associated with them. Instead of these formalized and accessible explanations of belief, which informants could volunteer when pressed, people routinely preferred to use their own, fairly personal "takes," which used very loosely related ideas and claimed to be rooted in experience.

My own research into ritual activity tends to make me think of beliefs not as something prior to or separate from action, that is, not as something mental, cognitive, or linguistic in opposition to the physical or active. If there are habits of the body, there can be habits of thought and expression as well as speech and self-presentation. They are all social activities. While I use terms like "religion" – albeit with all the historical qualifications and hesitations shared by others – when talking about Chinese materials, the language of belief seems *more* distorting, in particular, by specifically imposing a false sense of coherence, conviction, systemization, and meaning. We cannot appeal to "belief" to describe how people exist within their cultures; yet without "belief," it is not clear what we mean by "religion." If it seems easier to talk about Chinese religion, rather than Chinese beliefs, it may be simply because one is more comfortable today attributing a working coherence among cultural phenomena rather than implying the illusion and falsity of specific ideas.

This problem brings up an interesting association, namely, the strange fortunes of what would seem to be a particularly Chinese "bundle of behaviors," the prognostications of feng shui (wind and water), which are ubiquitous in California and becoming familiar elsewhere in the United States. Going beyond the dabbling of "new-agers" or the concerns of transplanted Chinese, feng shui is also being used by all sorts of serious people as a type of back-up system of cosmic control and insurance. It is possible that one day we may compare its global spread to such other cultural practices as food spicing and tea drinking. A similar phenomenon

[41] See David K. Jordan, "The jiaw of Shigaang (Taiwan): An Essay in Folk Interpretation," *Asian Folklore Studies* 35:2 (1976): 81–107; Peter Converse, "The Nature of Belief Systems in Mass Publics," in David Apter (ed.), *Ideology and Discontent* (New York: Free Press, 1964), 206–61; and Peter Stromberg, "Consensus and Variation in the Interpretation of Religious Symbolism: A Swedish Example," *American Ethnologist* 8 (1981): 544–59.

can be seen in the enduring popularity of the Asian martial arts, especially
taiqi, begun in the late 1970s and early 80s, or Japanese Zen meditation,
begun in the 1930s. Feng shui, *taiqi,* and *zazen* are closely tied to ritual
postures considered very basic to Chinese and Japanese culture, yet they
have been readily translated to the more pluralist sections of American
society. The viable translatability and subsequent longevity of these sets of
practices indicate the existence of something not readily caught in either
universals or particulars, something both more durable and mutable and
much less hindered by incoherence with other sets of practice.

In short, such packaged sets of behaviors blur "religion" as such. As
a feature of a global society and culture, the translatability of feng shui,
taiqi, and *zazen* is evidence of cultural properties going in many directions – perhaps too many for our notions of religion and culture to track.
In the end, religion may vanish as any sort of empirical entity in one
place, only to emerge in another, as attested by the growing numbers of
Christian evangelicals in Beijing as well as the government officials trying to control them with a stretched classification schema. To appreciate
these issues is to be more fully historical in our understanding and use
of theoretical categories.

Feng shui is not particularly illuminated by being regarded as a belief or
part of a more comprehensive religion, terms that return to the defining
polarities of universalism and particularism. Nor do the activities of
members of the Falundafa fit traditional theories of religion, although
they do evoke many older models in Chinese history. Theorists do not
need to stop using the terms belief and religion, but their historical freight
must be made part of them. And theorists do not need to stop theorizing,
of course – after all, it is a distinct cultural practice to seek universal
explanations and doing so must be as legitimate as offering incense to
one's ancestors – as long as no one gets hurt. But the coherence or
incoherence of practices can be explored on a more realistic footing if
scholarship can let go of the transcendent status still clutched by Shweder
and the quest for a logically prior theory of interpretation still sought by
Davidson. Without the panorama provided by these perspectives, we will
have to spend a lot more time figuring out how to situate ourselves, but
the alternatives do not seem to take us very far either.

6

On interpreting the world religiously

E. Thomas Lawson

Humans come into the world with a problem: how to interpret what is going on out there and in here. Of course, unless they have a disorder (for example, autism), they seem to handle the situation quite well. They learn very quickly about the ordinary kinds of things that there are in the world. They also learn about the properties of things.[1] And they seem to acquire linguistic skills effortlessly. They even read minds: the curl of the lip, the raised eyebrow, the look of scorn, the eyes sparkling with joy. They also see faces in the clouds, meaning in the drop of a glove, and God in the eye of the storm. Cognitive science has spent the last five decades theorizing about the processes that lead to the acquisition of such knowledge. With the aid of cognitive scientists' clever experiments we now seem to know at least a little bit more about intuitive physics, intuitive biology, intuitive psychology, and intuitive quantification. My interest lies in the areas of the structure and acquisition of religious knowledge as this relates to such intuitive systems. I am particularly concerned about peoples' intuitive knowledge of agents and their actions and how this form of cognition undergirds religious concepts about culturally postulated superhuman agents.[2]

My point would be that the process that leads to the development of religious ideas is the same process that leads to the development of ordinary ideas with minimal "tweaking" that makes it possible for us to distinguish the former from the latter. Bluntly put, religious ideas are parasitic on ordinary ideas.

[1] Psychologists such as Frank Keil (1989) investigating concepts, categorization, and cognitive development have shown that human beings possess intuitions about the kinds of properties different things have based upon ontological category membership. For example, when presented with an animal they have never seen before, young children make a number of assumptions about the unobserved characteristics of the animal in question. These assumptions involved the physicality, the animality, and the goals of the animal. The children assume that the animal cannot pass through solid objects, it needs to eat, it moves purposely to fulfill its desires.

[2] Melford Spiro, "Religion: Some Problems of Definition and Explanation," in Michael Banton (ed.) *Anthropological Approaches to the Study of Religion* (London: Tavistock 1966).

Among these religious notions, ideas about agents with special qualities play a particularly important role in religious systems. Religious systems typically possess concepts about agents with special qualities and the actions they are thought to perform (gods create worlds and destroy them, spirits rattle dishes and possess bodies, ancestors punish the people for failing to fulfill their obligations and reward them for their good deeds).

Philosophers have spent a great deal of intellectual energy arguing about whether there are such agents and what it would take to confirm their existence. In fact the philosophy of religion has had such issues as its focus for a very long time. While not particularly interested in the concept of *religious* agency, some philosophers of science have even gone so far as to argue that the concept of agent itself has no scientific application. And more than one historian of science has pointed to the fact that the development of science has relegated agency to less and less of a role in accounting for what happens in the world. The more we learn the more impersonal the world appears.

Cognitive scientists, particularly those interested in cognitive development, however, are much more interested in the processes that lead to the postulation of such agents, even if such notions have no scientific application. They are much more concerned about what goes on in the head, even if there is nothing out there to correspond to the products of the internal workings of the human mind.

Psychologists of religion operating within the framework of William James have approached the problem of religious agency by focusing upon religious experience as the mechanism that might account for the emergence of such concepts. Some cognitive neuroscientists (who have recently decided that religious concepts and religious experiences are interesting after all) have even argued for a G(od)-spot in the brain. I and a number of other investigators (both cognitive psychologists and cognitive anthropologists), have followed a different route.[3] We have argued that our ordinary cognitive resources are largely sufficient to account

3 See E. T. Lawson, "Religious Ideas and Practices," in Frank Keil and Robert Wilson (eds.), *The MIT Encyclopedia of the Cognitive Sciences* (Cambridge, MA: MIT Press, 1999); E. T. Lawson, "Towards a Cognitive Science of Religion," *Numen* 47 (2000): 338–49; P. Boyer, *The Naturalness of Religious Ideas* (Berkeley: University of California Press, 1994); E. T. Lawson and R. N. McCauley, *Rethinking Religion: Connecting Cognition and Culture* (Cambridge University Press, 1990); H. Whitehouse, *Inside the Cult* (Oxford: Clarendon Press, 1995) and *Arguments and Icons* (Oxford University Press, 2000); J. L. Barrett, "Exploring the Cognitive Foundations of Religion," *Trends in Cognitive Sciences* 4:1 (2000): 29–34; J. L. Barrett and F. Keil, "Anthropomorphism and God Concepts: Conceptualizing a Non-natural Entity," *Cognitive Psychology* 3 (1996): 210–47; and R. N. McCauley and E. T. Lawson, *Bringing Ritual to Mind: Psychological Foundations of Cultural Forms* (Cambridge University Press, 2002).

for the processing and structure of religious ideas. Religious concepts conform to cognitive constraints. Our assumption is that such ideas are not only relatively easy to acquire with the cognitive machinery at our disposal, but also have practical consequences for how people come to terms with their natural and socio-cultural environments. These cognitive resources that we seem to possess do not require either special mechanisms or extraordinary experiences to ensure the acquisition of such religious ideas and the practices they inform. When we focus upon the aggregate of concepts that people employ in their religious representations, both theoretical work and empirical research seem to show that religious concepts of agents and their actions are the kinds of idea that are intuitively compelling, particularly memorable, and, therefore, culturally transmittable even if they have no scientific application.

In their empirical research, cognitive psychologists such as Justin Barrett and Frank Keil have dealt with some of the properties of such agent representations that are intuitively compelling.[4] Barrett and Keil have shown, for example, that, even though a theological system may contain rather abstract concepts of a non-temporal god, nevertheless when religious participants, committed to such a theological system, and quite knowledgeable about many of its details, are required to make judgments about such gods during real-time problem solving or causal reasoning, such participants will employ temporal notions in their representations of the agents in question. It seems that religious ideas about such agents come more "naturally" than the far more complex and abstract ideas characteristic of theologies precisely because they conform to human expectations about what agents are like.

What the Barrett and Keil studies appear to show is that people systematically *misremember* the properties of gods. For example, in one of their studies (conducted in both India and the United States of America) Barrett and Keil found that when their subjects were asked to reflect on their theological ideas about the gods, they described them as having neither spatial nor temporal properties. The gods were quite capable of being in more than one place at the same time and attending to many things at once. However, when presented with stories about the gods responding to human situations, the gods were cognitively represented as possessing the limitations of any ordinary intentional agent. They attribute to the gods the properties that any ordinary person would possess. When required to remember certain features of the stories that they had

---

[4] Barrett and Keil, "Anthropomorphism and God Concepts."

been told, the subjects misremembered the properties of the gods in an anthropomorphic direction. Such anthropomorphic representations are standard fare across religious systems.

While religious systems differ in significant ways in both their concepts and their practices, they do (as Pascal Boyer has argued[5]), possess recurring features and such recurrence requires explanation. Boyer argues that if, in fact, people do have a natural receptivity to religious concepts, then this susceptibility makes it highly probable that such concepts will become widespread and that they will be widely shared in various cultural contexts. Boyer places his argument in the framework of the epidemiology of ideas advanced by Sperber.[6] Boyer's project on intuitive ontologies attempts to account for why it is that some ideas are more easily transmissible than others.

Religious ideas about agents with special qualities seem to be particularly capable of cultural transmissibility. Boyer argues that the issue involves memory dynamics. In one of his studies, Boyer has focused upon the kinds of idea that are more likely to be recalled.[7] He argues that ideas that are minimally counter-intuitive are more likely to be recalled, and therefore transmitted. Concepts with such counter-intuitive features are more easily remembered than either mundane or bizarre ones. Minimally counter-intuitive concepts attain a conceptual optimum. This means that they are intuitive enough to be understood and represented without placing an undue strain on our cognitive machinery and yet are interesting enough to capture human attention. Any idea (or practice for that matter) that grabs human attention by having a combination of intuitive and counter-intuitive properties is more likely to spread culturally. Of particular interest are people's capacity to recall and transmit ideas about agents with minimally counter-intuitive features. Boyer and his colleague Ramble have devised recall studies to test these claims.[8]

Stewart Guthrie has argued that both ethnographic and psychological research shows that people have a tendency to attribute agency to various features of their environment even when there are perfectly natural ways to account for the situations in question.[9] He thinks that we possess cognitive mechanisms that bias us toward explaining events as being

[5] *The Naturalness of Religious Ideas.*
[6] Dan Sperber, *Explaining Culture: A Naturalistic Approach* (Blackwell, 1996).
[7] P. Boyer and C. Ramble, "Cognitive Templates for Religious Concepts: Cross-cultural Evidence for Recall of Counter-intuitive Representations," *Cognitive Science* (2001).
[8] *Ibid.*
[9] S. Guthrie, *Faces in the Clouds: A New Theory of Religion* (Oxford University Press, 1993).

the consequence of the intentional action of agents with special qualities even when the evidence is hardly capable of supporting such over-attributions. And work in social psychology seems to support Guthrie's claims. According to Ross, people seem to be particularly susceptible to attributing agent causality in interpreting events even when the facts show otherwise.[10] One way of talking about this is to argue that, for evolutionary reasons, people have a hyperactive agent detective device. Such a device would seem to confer a selective advantage. It is better to be safe than sorry.

Both in present[11] and in previous[12] work, McCauley and I have argued that, even though they involve our ordinary representations of action, the representation of religious rituals are distinguished from acts of other kinds by their presumption of the causality of agents with special (i.e., superhuman) qualities. We argue that a structural description of religious rituals enables us to see that the elements of the ritual can be represented as agents acting upon patients with the goal of bringing about a consequence by means of instruments. In such a description, either the agents, the instruments, or the patients may be regarded as possessing superhuman qualities. Which of these elements in the representation of the elements in the structural description of the ritual possesses the special qualities will make a difference to the religious representations of the participants and, therefore, to the judgments that these religious participants will make with regard to the type of ritual it is. For example, on the basis of information provided to them, religious participants will judge not only whether a ritual is well formed, but also whether it is repeatable, reversible, permits substitutions, and so on.

Because the claims that McCauley and I made in *Rethinking Religion* were theoretically motivated but only anecdotally plausible, Barrett and I decided to conduct a study[13] that was designed to test three empirical predictions that could be derived from our analysis in *Rethinking Religion*. These predictions were that:

1 individuals unfamiliar with a particular ritual, religious system, or any religious rituals at all, still would have converging intuitions about whether or not a particular ritual is well formed;

---

[10] L. D. Ross, "The Intuitive Psychologist and His Shortcomings: Distortions in the Attribution Process," in L. Berkowitz (ed.), *Advances in Experimental Social Psychology* 10 (1977): 173–220.

[11] McCauley and Lawson, *Bringing Ritual to Mind*.

[12] Lawson and McCauley, *Rethinking Religion*.

[13] J. L. Barrett and E. T. Lawson, "Ritual Intuitions: Cognitive Contributions to Judgements of Ritual Efficacy," *Journal of Cognition and Culture* 1:2 (2001): 183–201.

2 ritually naive individuals still will appreciate the central importance
    of superhuman agency being represented somewhere in the ritual
    structure; and
3 subjects will judge having an appropriate agent for a given ritual most
    important to the success or failure of a ritual action.

These studies were designed to tap participants' intuitions regarding
ritual structures by presenting fictitious rituals to the subjects that were
described as successful. The rituals were then altered in some specific
way. Then we asked the subjects to make relative judgments about what
changes in the ritual would most likely undermine their effectiveness.

In the first experiment, the subjects were students recruited from intro-
ductory psychology courses at a Protestant college in the United States.
Each item consisted of a fictitious ritual prototype that was claimed to
be successful in bringing about a specific state of affairs; for example,
"a person blew sacred dust on a field and the field yielded good crops."
A second, different version of the ritual then was described; for example,
"a bird kicked dust on a rock and the field did not yield good crops."
(Notice that we changed "person" to "bird" and "blew" to "kicked.") All
eight rituals in the first section of the study had a change that related to
superhuman agency (hereafter referred to as an S-marker), such as sacred dust no longer being sacred, a priest being replaced by laypersons,
or an agent change, such as a person being replaced by a bird as the
initiator of the action. In addition, all but one of the rituals also had a
change in the action, for example, "blew" replacing "kick."

The second section of the first experiment contained four fictitious
rituals. Here, after having been presented with a successful prototype
ritual, the subjects were asked to rate the likelihood of success of the
many variations, including changes in S-markers, changes in agents,
changes in actions, and changes in instruments.

The results of the first experiment were encouraging but raised some
questions. The fewer S-markers, the more likely the subjects would
judge that the ritual was more likely to fail. In addition, items in which
there were S-marker changes were regarded as being more likely to fail.
The results of section 1 had subjects rating S-marker changes as the most
likely explanation for ritual failure. The results of section 2 showed that
the more S-markers the better. These results support the first prediction, namely that a ritual is likely to succeed, that is, is well formed, if
superhuman agency is represented in the ritual structure.

The second prediction tested was that removing S-markers would
have more deleterious effect on judgments of ritual efficacy than other

changes, for example, action or instrument changes. This, too, was born out by the results.

Third, we predicted that changes in the agent slot of the ritual structure should affect the judgments of ritual efficacy more than the specific action involved. The results here were less satisfactory, partially due to the design of the experiment. For example, the S-marker used for non-human agents was "magical," which may have introduced unwanted bias. Another part of the problem was that, unlike action, agent, or single-S-marker changes, when both S-markers were removed, the resulting sentence with which the subjects were presented differed from the prototype in the number of words used. This means that the data could have been generated by a simple heuristic giving lower scores to items that best matched the prototype and higher scores to items that deviated from the prototype.

Although the first experiment showed promise, it was problematic enough to call for a redesign. The second study was devised to correct these problems. Because it was possible that words such as "sacred," "magical," and "priest" could very well have introduced unwanted bias, and, furthermore, since these words have a range of popular meanings that may not indicate any special properties associated with superhuman agents, these words were omitted and replaced with "special." Even the word "ritual" used in the first experiment was replaced with "action" in order to eliminate potential culturally induced bias. And, finally, to eliminate the problem of different lengths of sentences, the twelve ritual sets in the second experiment had an equal number of prototype rituals with one S-marker in the agent slot, one S-marker in the instrument slot, S-markers in both slots, and no S-markers.

The results of the experiment confirmed the first prediction by showing that two S-markers were better than one, and that one was better than none. They also confirmed the second prediction by showing that not having S-markers would more likely damage the efficacy of an action than either action or instrument changes. And the results confirmed the third prediction that changes in the agent slot were more damaging than changes in any other aspect of the ritual structure.

In summary, these two experiments were designed to test three general predictions in Lawson and McCauley's *Rethinking Religion*: (1) that people have converging intuitions about the efficacy, i.e., well-formedness, of rituals; (2) that, when judging the efficacy of a ritual, superhuman agency will be more important than any other aspect of ritual; and (3) that people will regard having an appropriate agent as relatively more important than the particular action involved. The strategy we employed to test these predictions involved tapping people's intuitions by presenting them with fictitious rituals identified as effective, altering their form in specific ways, and then asking the subjects to make relative judgments about what kind of changes in the presented rituals would most likely undermine their effectiveness. The results of the experiments supported all three predictions.

Rather than guessing at random, which would have produced mean ratings around the mid-point of the scales, the subjects who were unfamiliar with the fictitious rituals seemed to possess converging intuitions about what in the ritual structure was most important for each ritual's success.

The subjects also seem to understand that, for an action to produce special consequences, superhuman agency must be involved in some way, and that a connection with superhuman agents is the best predictor of success. Rather than simply rating the rituals that best matched the prototype as most likely to be effective and ignoring the importance of S-markers, the subjects recognized the importance of superhuman agency. They favored ritual forms with "special" agents or "special" instruments when "specialness" was defined as having been endowed with unusual properties of the gods. And, finally, participants' intuitions converged on the point that having an appropriate agent for a ritual is relatively more important than the specific action involved. Having an agent that does more than merely perform the action but also intends the consequences of the action is more important than the actions themselves in determining the efficacy of the action involved.

A theory about religious ritual intuitions, then, is empirically tractable and capable of being tested to highlight the role that ritual intuitions with non-cultural foundations play in making religious ritual judgments. Religious ritual judgments are cognitively constrained. This means that a cognitive psychology of religion may begin to demonstrate that, in order to connect the cognitive and the cultural, it is worth focusing upon the non-cultural foundations of religious ideas and the practices they inform.

Such experimental work finds further support in some cognitively inspired ethnographic research. In recent work, McCauley and I have focused upon such ethnographic work and evaluated the contribution that our previously developed theory of religious ritual competence has made to the results of such investigations.[14] In order to clarify matters we have adopted a new terminology. We have distinguished among special

[14] McCauley and Lawson, *Bringing Ritual to Mind.*

agent, special patient, and special instrument rituals. Special agent rituals stand out as those rituals in which the gods are either represented as directly performing the actions themselves or as grounding the agents (such as ritual agents) who perform the actions on their behalf. Special patient rituals are those in which ordinary agents act upon the gods. Here the gods are the recipients of the ritual actions. Special instrument rituals presuppose that the instruments involved possess divine sanction and attain their efficacy by virtue of the action, either directly or indirectly, of the gods.

With such distinctions in place we have investigated the role that the ritual form hypothesis plays in accounting for certain aspects of the dynamics of cultural transmission. Before I discuss the ritual form hypothesis, however, I need to discuss a hypothesis about the role that frequency plays in cultural transmission as this has been developed by a cognitive anthropologist, Harvey Whitehouse. In both his *Inside the Cult*[15] and his *Arguments and Icons*,[16] Whitehouse has proposed the frequency hypothesis to account for the transmission of certain forms of cultural information, especially religious notions. He argues that in order for a religious notion to become an element in a religious system of concepts it either must be frequently activated (for example, by repeated doctrinal instruction) or else its mnemonic effects must be instilled by all the techniques involved in what McCauley and I have called sensory pageantry. Sensory pageantry is a powerful mnemonic aid and is typically to be found in such rituals as initiation rites. Whitehouse appeals to the flashbulb memory research by J. Kulik and R. Brown,[17] to support his claims about the role that flashbulb memories play in cultural transmission. Flashbulb memories involve events that are unique and emotionally arousing. For example, an older group of Americans can remember where they were and what they were doing when they heard of the assassination of John F. Kennedy.

Now it is a truism to say that religious ideas are either remembered or they disappear. Before the advent of literacy the major way for ideas to be transmitted was orally. On the basis of archeological evidence, it seems to be the case that religions were around long before the advent of literacy, and the majority of religious participants to this day rely primarily on oral tradition. Oral traditions rely overwhelmingly on human memory for the transmission of cultural knowledge. McCauley and I are particularly interested in the memory for actions rather than the memory

---

[15] Whitehouse, *Inside the Cult*.   [16] Whitehouse, *Arguments and Icons*.
[17] J. Kulik and R. Brown, "Flashbulb Memory," in U. Neisser (ed.), *Memory Observed: Remembering in Natural Contexts* (San Francisco: W. H. Freeman, 1982).

for verbal materials. While religious rituals often include words (people do things with words) very often these words are brief and even cryptic and sometimes even nonsensical. Some rituals, of course, contain no words at all.

What we have argued is that religions evolve so as to exploit the variables that contribute to the recall of religious ritual actions. As Whitehouse has shown, one of the variables is surely frequency. People who are subjected to frequent types of event tend to remember such types even when they might forget some of the details. Whitehouse argues that such events are encoded in our *semantic* memory, that is, the knowledge we have of the world that does not depend upon the memory of specific episodes. So, for example, we will remember that at times of elections good citizens are supposed to vote, but we might not remember whom we voted for in the governor's race in the state of Michigan twenty-five years ago. But psychologists of memory also talk about *episodic* memory, that is the recall for specific events. And Whitehouse argues that, for those religious practices that are only infrequently performed, the religious ritual system faces a particularly important challenge to ensure its transmission. This is where sensory pageantry plays a very significant role.

The best way to increase the probability that a practice or set of practices be remembered if it is an infrequent event is to stimulate the emotions, because they play a crucial role in laying down memories. And one of the best ways to stimulate the emotions as a memory aid is by stimulating the sensory modalities of the human body by dancing, feasting, deprivation, punishment, scarification, circumcision, and so on. Infrequent rituals such as initiation rites are emotionally provocative because they typically are accompanied by smells, sounds, and sights that are extraordinary in their power to appeal to, or have an effect on, the human senses. Such emotional provocation has a significant mnemonic effect. In simple terms, these episodes prove memorable for the religious ritual participants because they have been enhanced by sensory pageantry. Such memorability increases the probability of their transmission. Ten years down the road the initiates will remember what to do to the next generation whether or not any particular initiate will perform the actual initiation.

But now there is an issue: which rituals will involve sensory pageantry and which will not? Is it just willy nilly? Or are there are other variables that need to be taken into account? In *Rethinking Religion*, McCauley and I developed a theory of religious ritual competence analogous to Chomsky's theory of linguistic competence. The motivation for the analogy was twofold: (1) we thought that the success of generative linguistics was significant enough with regard to one set of cultural materials that showed considerable variability, namely human languages, to warrant investigations into other cultural systems, and (2) we thought that having available some of the formal tools employed by linguists would make it possible for us to far more precisely describe relationships among the elements of religious ritual representations as well as the relationships between various ritual representations. Our goal, of course, was to argue that religious ritual participants possessed deep intuitions about ritual form even if they had never been subject to explicit instruction. We were after the non-cultural foundations of religious ritual intuitions. This endeavor led us to postulate certain principles that inform ritual form (such as the principle of superhuman agency and the principle of superhuman immediacy) and to show the role that such principles played in the specification of certain ritual types such as special agent and special patient rituals. Since then we have focused much more rigorously than we could in this earlier work on the theoretical work and empirical research in cognitive science, as well as on the results of ethnographic research which we thought bore directly on our claims about religious ritual competence. Because Whitehouse's ethnographic work was significantly informed by cognitive research, specifically memory dynamics, we saw the opportunity to test our claims about religious ritual form on the specific cultural materials that his work so ably provides. We could also confer with Whitehouse to check whether we had accurately represented the materials which he had discussed in his writings. We were particularly interested in the role that the tacit knowledge of religious ritual form (as well as emotion and memory) plays in the transmission of cultural materials of a religious nature.

In *Bringing Ritual to Mind*, McCauley and I discuss where we agree and disagree with Whitehouse's account of the cultural transmission of religious ritual representations. We quite agree with Whitehouse that the most obvious variable in the transmission process is frequency. Where we find ourselves in disagreement is *which* rituals contain the sensory pageantry that I have alluded to above. We argue that it is religious ritual participants' knowledge of the differences in *ritual form* that determines which rituals will have higher levels of sensory pageantry. In other words, people will have intuitions about what is more or less important, what is more or less central in the ritual system. These intuitions will play an important role in the cultural transmission of specific religious ideas and practices.

Obviously, much research needs to be done in both psychology (especially in memory dynamics) and anthropology (especially on the mechanisms of cultural transmission) before claims such as these can be thoroughly evaluated. What is clear is that, in order to understand how people interpret the world religiously, we need to do a great deal more theoretical and empirical research (including experimental work) especially about the recurrent features across cultural systems. While the variability is real, the underlying story that accounts for the variation promises to be far more interesting than idealizing differences. Searching for generalizations about any form of human behavior is still a major concern of the sciences in general and of cognitive science in particular. A cognitive science of religion is in the making.

7

Are religious beliefs counter-intuitive?

Maurice Bloch

Anthropologists are great suppliers to the general public, and to certain philosopher clients, of strange beliefs said to be held by remote people. These seem to furnish raw material for thought experiments concerned with the question: how is it possible to hold such beliefs? Or, in the fashion of Davidson: how can one interpret statements by people who apparently believe such bizarre things about the world? On the other hand, most anthropologists, who have studied remote people and who have been engaged in the practice of understanding those foreign others who say this type of thing in real situations, are keen to stress, often to the very same philosophers, that the strangest thing about strange people is how easy interpretation turns out to be.

One way of dealing with this anomaly, one to which I partly subscribe, has been developed by Sperber[1] and then greatly elaborated and somewhat modified by Boyer.[2] It consists in questioning the apparent strangeness of these beliefs. This position involves stressing that, before one considers the content of bizarre belief statements, one should consider the pragmatic cues which mark how they are intended to be understood in the real world. More particularly, both writers stress that the many strange belief statements reported by anthropologists, which have employed the time of a number of philosophers, are merely intended as tentative propositions about the world and that some intention of the sort is always pragmatically indicated, if only by the obvious counter-intuitive aspect of the assertions of belief. These statements, it is argued, are really understood, and are intended to be so understood, as if in inverted commas, i.e., as: "I don't know this on my own authority, but I hold it as an intriguing possibility since I have been told this by people whom I have every reason to trust, but, on the other hand, I am not

---

[1] D. Sperber, "Apparently Irrational Beliefs," in M. Hollis and S. Lukes (eds.), *Rationality and Relativism* (Oxford: Blackwell, 1982).

[2] P. Boyer, *The Naturalness of Religious Ideas* (Berkeley: University of California Press, 1994).

going to drop my mental inverted commas as the proposition remains strange and counter-intuitive to me and I don't want to muddle myself by merging it with what I take as obvious." Sperber and Boyer then point out that these counter-intuitive propositions are only counter-intuitive in very limited ways and so easily remain overwhelmingly within types of knowledge bounded and formed by human-wide, genetically inscribed predispositions which make us all see the world in a particular way. These authors could support a Davidsonian view of radical interpretation on ethnographical grounds, since all humans, by their common nature, already share so much, and what they do not share is so severely constrained that the problem of radical interpretation would only occur when people meet Martians.

The Sperber–Boyer position further attempts to show that it is precisely the intriguing, indicated, counter-intuitive character which makes religious-like beliefs catchy, so that such beliefs become easily established as part of a shared culture within a given population.

Boyer says that this catchiness explains the weird fact that "religion" exists, since these counter-intuitive beliefs are, for him, what it consists of. He apparently denies what most anthropologists would now maintain, that there is no such *thing* as religion, other than the somewhat, but only somewhat, similar phenomena one finds in different places, and which remind the observer, in a theoretically insignificant way, therefore, of what we have been brought up to understand by the term (see Bell: this volume). He implies that the various counter-intuitive beliefs weave together to create a whole of linked representations and practices.

Boyer and Sperber's ideas about counter-intuitive statements are very important. I entirely support their key point, which is that, before we can consider the rationality, or otherwise, of representations, we need to grasp how they are meant to be understood in real situations. Furthermore they are right, when they stress that a number of belief-type statements have often wrongly been taken, by ethnographers and others, as straightforward affirmations about how the world is, while it is clear that their implicatures are of a totally different order. It is probable that such famous cases as the Nuer assertion that "twins are birds"[3] or "we are red Macaws"[4] are of this type.[5] Sperber illustrates his position with

---

[3] E. Evans-Pritchard, *Nuer Religion* (Oxford University Press, 1956), 77.

[4] C. Crocker, "My Brother the Parrot," in G. Urton (ed.), *Animal Myth and Metaphors in South America* (Salt Lake City: University of Utah Press, 1985), 34.

[5] Turner gives ethnographic evidence that the statement about macaws is indeed to be taken in a way which could not be guessed out of context.

a story about dragons. He shows how he was, at first, mistaken in taking a request to kill a dragon as the same sort of speech act as a mundane request to carry a basket, for example, while in fact he should have realized the implicit presence of pragmatic inverted commas which marked the statement to be understood as "far from ordinary." More recently, Sperber has emphasized his position again by arguing that, come what may and given human innate dispositions to see the world in a particular way, such beliefs can never become intuitive-like.[6]

I have no problems with his argument for this example, but I am uncomfortable about how ethnographers can know, in general, when to assume the presence of implicit inverted commas and therefore when to set in motion the "further scrutiny" deemed necessary for interpretation according to Sperber. He seems to think this scrutiny is triggered simply by the evident counter-intuitive character of the belief, like the switch of register required for understanding a live metaphor brought about by the obviously outrageous character of the statement.[7]

The story of the dragon is straightforward, because there is clearly a bizarre element in someone declaring a belief in the existence of dragons for us and, it also turns out, for the people concerned. But what if a statement seems to us apparently odd, but not so to the people concerned? And what if nobody is very clear? Thus, I have often been told by sophisticated Malagasy, something like the following story: "Europeans go around the country secretly stealing blood, or other vital constituents, from poor people in Madagascar by means of techniques which are those of flying witches; they do this while moving around mysteriously and unseen by everybody. These Europeans then use the stolen bodily elements to diminish the life force of the Malagasy and to increase their own, or that of third parties, usually other rich Europeans, to whom the Malagasy hearts, blood or bones are sold." Some will also add that they have heard warnings, through a European-sponsored media campaign, intended for the Malagasy, that, however poor they are, they should have nothing to do with such trade in organs, especially kidneys. Indeed, a Swiss doctor, broadcasting in Madagascar, has been heard on the radio, by me and some of my informants, saying precisely this.

Such statements constitute much more awkward examples than Sperber's story about dragons. How much of this story would be treated by an ethnographer, working according to the criteria implicitly

---

[6] D. Sperber, "Intuitive and Reflexive Beliefs," *Mind and Language* 12:1 (1997): 67–83.
[7] See R. Thourangeau and R. Sternberg, "Aptness in Metaphor," *Cognitive Psychology* 13 (1981): 27–55.

suggested by Sperber and Boyer, as counter-intuitive? First of all, the part about the trade in organs is very unlikely to be considered by such an ethnographer as an example of the statements she suspects are taken as counter-intuitive and therefore worthy of special treatment. On the other hand, the part about witchcraft-like thefts is likely to arouse this type of suspicion, but both elements are clearly an inseparable whole, at least as far as the informants are concerned. In fact, I, and, I believe on the basis of my empathetic ethnographic observation, they, as hearers of such statements, as well as other recipients, will not be sure how the story is intended by the speaker or intended to be heard by the hearers. Is the speaker claiming that it is something she has heard from others, but that she treats with the greatest of caution because it appears counter-intuitive? After all, removing blood from a person without being seen to do it, or having direct contact with them, or leaving any trace on their body, is extraordinary. Or, on the other hand, is this story treated as a statement of an apparently intuitive fact about the world, passed on through reliable sources, which therefore needs no particular precautions or scrutiny, like my being told by a doctor that I have caught a virus? After all, when people steal things from you, they try to hide what they are doing so you will not be aware of what is happening; if reliable people tell you that such thefts are taking place, there is nothing counter-intuitive in this information. Finally, it is possible that the first time one hears such a story about heart thieves one treats it as odd, but then, subsequently, one hears this story so often that, every time it comes up, it requires less and less critical attention; in the end, it becomes exactly *like* an unexamined intuitive belief, in that its hearsay aspect has been eroded. When information has become as familiar as this, it is no different from being told that if you eat too many unripe fruit you will get diarrhoea – something you may well not have experienced yourself, and for which you have no intuitive connection between cause and effect, but which seems so sensible, given the frequency of the statement and the reliability of the informers, that it is experienced "as good as." In the case of the blood and heart thieves story, the confirmation comes from the evident fact that Europeans are richer and healthier than Malagasy peasants for no very obvious other reason.

These indeterminacies of translation seem to me characteristic of much that we find in the field, indeed, they are more typical than Sperber's story about the dragon. How any story will be heard, whether about dragons, blood thieves, or stomach aches is an empirical question, which Sperber and Boyer do not address, perhaps because they assume an a priori way of knowing what kind of propositions are counter-intuitive in terms of their content. But, if the content is context-dependent and the real contexts are as fluid, as changing, and as uncertain as I have suggested, merely declaring a proposition to be counter-intuitive, on the basis of what they acknowledge is a highly speculative psychology, is not sufficient. This does not mean, however, that we should not use, as Sperber and Boyer certainly do, our interpretative intuition and examine such claims critically to analyze what might be happening. But interpretation is only possible in terms of an existing state of affairs where the communication takes place.

THE OLD ANTHROPOLOGICAL PROBLEM WITH "BELIEF"

There may be another, even more fundamental problem, which lies at the back of all this. This is whether the focus on "belief," counter-intuitive or not, as the core concern in dealing with religion, is not misleading for the type of phenomena under examination. Both Boyer and Sperber have a strong background in anthropology and in the kind of field work from which the "twins are birds" stories have originated, but I wonder if, as a result of trying to address a mainly philosophical audience, they have not forgotten something which we anthropologists teach to our first-year students: that is, that the very stress on "belief" may be misleading for the kind of religions studied by anthropologists, such as myself.

The anthropological challenge to the usefulness of "belief" for the study of religion has a long history. It was first formulated by Robertson Smith, and subsequently echoed by Durkheim, and explored in depth by such writers as Needham,[8] Pouillon,[9] Lenclud,[10] and others. The problem seems to involve two elements. First, philosophers are interested in the types of mental states roughly indicated by the phrase (in English) "to believe that," while anthropologists are often concerned with phenomena indicated by the phrase "to believe in." Secondly, the phrase "to believe in" is only appropriate for a particular type of counter-intuitive claim, typical of certain religions, of which Christianity is the most obvious example, where "to believe in" *should* be, but *is* not, the same as "to believe that." Or to put the matter as would a number of philosophers

---

[8] R. Needham, *Belief, Language and Experience* (Oxford: Blackwell, 1972).

[9] J. Pouillon, "Remarques sur le verb 'croire,'" in M. Izard and P. Smith (eds.), *La Fonction Symbolique* (Paris: Galimard, 1979).

[10] G. Lenclud, "Vues de l'Esprit, Art de l'Autre," *Terrain* 14 (1990).

such as Davidson and Dennett, both discussed by Lenclud,[11] we are not dealing with simple beliefs but with reflexive beliefs on reflexive beliefs to the nth degree.

However, these distinctions, often made by the writers cited above, seem to get forgotten when philosophers and anthropologists enter into a dialogue. That is usually when talk of belief and/or representations and/or interpretation comes to the fore, while the flesh of the context from which this data is issued fades out of sight, becoming forgotten in ethereal thought experiments.

A MALAGASY EXAMPLE

One way to begin to illustrate the problem and discover what might be its origin, is by recounting a little of the history of Madagascar in the early nineteenth century.[12] This was the time when European Christian missionaries arrived on the island. They saw their primary task as demonstrating the errors of "savage" religion, which they understood as most probably the work of the devil, and replacing such paganism with true Christian beliefs. However, the missionaries soon found themselves faced with an unexpected problem, created by this very programme. They simply could not work out what were the erroneous *beliefs* the Malagasy held, which they were to counter. They found little that fitted the bill of their understanding of "primitive," or "demonic," or "pagan" religion. The issue was, to a certain extent, resolved when a kind of dialogue was established between the Malagasy and the missionaries, which gradually led them to agree together about what they thought they disagreed about.

The missionaries were led to direct their attention to the *belief* in "idols" which, they claimed, was held by the Malagasy. As Welsh Calvinist Christians, or as Lutheran Norwegians, whose history had been so centrally concerned with denouncing the idolatry of the "whore of Rome," and the even more insidious idolatry of the Anglican quislings, this was a very comfortable stance. They had found their golden calf which they could destroy according to a venerable tradition. Once the missionaries had decided that what they were to eradicate were the "idols," the Malagasy, for their part, at last understood what the Europeans were objecting to with such vehemence – they were against what the Malagasy

---

[11]   G. Lenclud, "Beliefs, Culture and Reflexivity," unpublished manuscript (n.d.).
[12]   M. Bloch, *From Blessing to Violence* (Cambridge University Press, 1986), ch. 2.

called *sampy*, the word the missionaries had been led to translate as "idol." This word designated objects and cults which were often of foreign origin, and which are referred to in the Africanist literature as "medicines." One characteristic of such cults, which are typically imports from outside, is that they are always "in question."[13] New "medicines" were and are continually introduced, others are dismissed as ineffective or harmful. This means that the issue whether one "believed," or "chose," or simply tried out a particular medicine was always relevant and no doubt furnished the occasion for statements of the kind: "I believe you should try this particular medicine and not this one." The missionaries' attack on *sampy*/idols appeared sensible to the Malagasy also, since it could be understood in this way.

The fact that the missionary–Malagasy dialogue led to the focus on the eradication of *sampy* was to have great historical significance. When the Merina (the dominant group in Madagascar when the missionaries first came) converted to Christianity in the mid nineteenth century, they duly burned the Idols/*sampy* in great *autos da fe*. It made perfectly good sense since, by then, it was agreed all round, this was what was to be changed and replaced by Christianity. But, at the same time, far more important rituals and practices, such as those concerning ancestors, were hardly called into question at all, either by the missionaries or by the Merina Christians. This was because, for the missionaries, these "beliefs" had an ontological status which looked quite unlike what they expected from "religion," and, for the Malagasy, the ontology of ancestors was not a suitable subject of reflection. Thus the ancestors were largely ignored; these still continue to be barely challenged by the strong Christian commitments of most present-day ordinary Merina Christians. This fact explains much of characteristic contemporary religious activity in Christian Madagascar, which is accompanied by what looks very much like ancestor worship. It is as though, since the missionaries had not been sure what to say about ancestors, these "beliefs" were unaffected by conversion.[14]

The nature of the dialogue between the Malagasy and the missionaries and its legacy is thus explicable by two factors, one from either side. The first concerns the nature of Christianity itself. The second is the nature of "beliefs" concerning entities such as ancestors.

---

[13] For a history of the *sampy*, see Dominichini, *Les Dieux au Service des Rois. Histoire Orale des Sampin' Andriana* (Paris: Editions du centre national de recherche scientifiques, 1985).

[14] This corresponds exactly to the problem faced by the Christian missionaries in China discussed by Bell in this volume.

Christianity is a "believe-in religion." At least that is how it would be represented by adherents, i.e., believers, who are asked about it. They would say "As Christians we believe in . . . " Thus, the most typical aspect of Christianity, something which it shares to a relative extent with the other Semitic religions, is its stress on the importance of *emphatic* statements of "belief" of which the creed is perhaps the most obvious example.

It is as though Christians feel so unsure of what they declare that they have to repeat, emphatically and endlessly, what they believe *in*, to convince themselves and others that they believe *that* the world is so, rather like a child coming back home in the dark might repeat to herself "I am not afraid of the dark." Christianity seems to say there are things which are so, and are indeed normally *taken* to be so, but that this is not good enough for religion; some extra reflexive and counter-intuitive beliefs have to be added on top and these have to be *taken* as so, in an exaggerated kind of "belief" act, sometimes called "faith."[15]

The other side of the Missionary–Malagasy dialogue concerned the nature of people's involvement with ancestors. What that involvement was and still is cannot be known, either from thought experiments or sketchy historical accounts, precisely because of its largely implicit character. Therefore, I have to draw on what I have known through long-term field work as an anthropologist in Madagascar on and off between the 1960s and the 1990s. This is obviously a risky procedure but, given what I know of Madagascar, far less risky than just guessing without any specific ethnographic experience. In ordinary contexts, the Malagasy are simply not interested in whether they, or anybody else, "believes" in ancestors in the Semitic religions' sense, any more than they are interested in whether they, or anybody, believes in "fathers." Indeed, this comparison is particularly relevant since ancestors are treated in ways which are very reminiscent of the way living ascendants are treated. Writing about Africa, Kopitoff [16] stresses, in a way that would be equally appropriate for Madagascar, that behavior toward dead ancestors is apparently fundamentally no different than it is toward living fathers or elders. The motivations, emotions, and understanding of elders and ancestors are assumed to be the same. Ancestors are simply more difficult to communicate with. Thus, when rural Malagasy, in perfectly ordinary context, want to be overheard by the dead, they speak more loudly, something

[15] See Pouillon, "Remarques sur le verb 'croire.'"
[16] I. Kopitoff, "Ancestors as Elders," *Africa* 41:11 (1971): 129–42.

they often also do when they want elders to take notice, since these are also often deaf. I would not go as far as Kopitoff in saying that there is *no* difference in how ancestors and elders are evoked, especially in rituals, as I shall discuss below, but he is right insofar as, in many ordinary situations, the difference never becomes salient. The ancestors are not as close as living parents or grandparents, but they are not all that distant, and differential closeness is, after all, typical of all kinship systems.

In a similar vein, the famous Chinese anthropologist Fei Xiaotong, also referred to by Bell in this volume, writing in the 1940s, describes an encounter with his grandmother's ghost in this way:

> One day not long after her death, I was sitting in the front room looking toward her bedroom. It was almost noon. Normally at that time grandmother would go to the kitchen to see how the lunch preparations were coming along . . . This had been a familiar sight for me, and after her death the everyday pattern was not changed. Not a table or chair or bed or mat was moved. Every day close to noon I would feel hungry . . . The scene was not complete without grandmother's regular routine, and so that day I seemed to see her image come out of her bedroom once more and go into the kitchen.[17]

In ordinary contexts when one does not really want to involve the ancestors very actively, for example, when offering a libation to them before a shared bottle of rum or when asking for their blessing before a minor journey – people's behavior does not seem to be marked as different, or as concerned with counter-intuitive beings. To implicitly assume the ancestors' existence does not seem to require a special type of effort, as would be necessitated by the understanding of a counter-intuitive proposition. Knowing ancestors, therefore, is not an act of value, or duty, or daring, as Christians would claim is the case for Christian belief. Thus, to the Malagasy even today, after total familiarization with a Semitic religion, the idea of "converting" somebody to a belief in ancestors is ridiculous, like converting them to a belief in the existence of fathers. People are not normally interested in what ancestors are like and, unless pushed very hard by an ethnographer, they have nothing much to say about such things as the way the ancestors spend their time, where they might be located, their way of existence, or how to account for their powers. What does concern the Malagasy are such things as how they can get ancestors to help them and whether ancestors are the agents behind diseases or other unpleasant occurrences happening to them, at

---

[17] Fei Xiaotong, "The World Without Ghosts," in R. David Arkush and Leo O. Lee (eds.), *Land Without Ghosts* (Berkeley: University of California Press, 1989).

a particular time. The ancestors' usual ontological and rhetorical status is no different from that of rain. Normal people, normally, do not take the fact that rain can get one wet as a subject of thought or discourse. Indeed, I suspect, they would be at a loss for words to explain how this happens; rather they are concerned whether they will get wet if they go out, now, without an umbrella. Christianity and Islam, on the other hand, seem concerned, above all, with what humans *do to* God, i.e., believe in him. Malagasy concern with the ancestors is the other way round. What matters is what ancestors *do to* you.

This fundamental difference between the way ancestors are conceived and the way God is conceived in Christianity meant that the missionaries, with their belief-focused religion, could simply not get a grip on ancestors since these were not the kind of phenomena they expected, given the type of religion they knew. They could not convert the targets of their missionizing away from a belief in ancestors, since the Malagasy could not understand what the missionaries were talking about or what they wanted. This explains the fact that many present-day Malagasy, who are clearly devout Christians and who therefore believe that they believe *in* God and in the divinity of Christ and do not believe *in* ancestors, because they know Christians do not, surprise themselves and others by being suddenly involved with ancestors in ways requiring rituals of which they thought they disapproved. The Christian business of belief and disbelief has not given them the tools to address their relation with their dead forebears which is, therefore, "untouched" by what they consider "religion."

On the other hand, something closer to the Christian emphasis on belief was involved with the *sampy*, since the attitude toward them, as it is revealed in social practice and talk about them, was, and still is,[18] one which emphasizes their counter-intuitive nature. I suspect that the missionaries felt not only comfortable, but also relieved, when they hit upon the *sampy* as likely targets for translation, because when they tried to eradicate *sampy* the Malagasy could react to them as sensible people who made sense. After all, this type of attack was familiar and had been going on a long time. People who attacked particular *sampy* were as comprehensible to the Malagasy as someone who tells us that a particular brand of headache medicine we have been using is ineffective and that they have a better one we should try. By contrast, people who attacked

---

[18] Some new *sampy* have reappeared at times, like now, when Christianity seems to be failing many people.

the belief in ancestors would be as weird as Martians turning up, trying to convince us that eyes were not true.

DIFFERENT SUPERNATURAL BELIEFS AND DIFFERENT COGNITIVE ATTITUDES

My argument is that Sperber and Boyer are misled in thinking that all religious manifestations are cognitively and saliently counter-intuitive, in the same way the missionaries were misled in only looking for that type of belief. On my reading, when Sperber and Boyer identify the religious with the counter-intuitive, they are unwittingly thinking in the terms of Christian, or Semitic, religions, perhaps because they are addressing interlocutors who know nothing else. I suspect that, if they were considering the Malagasy case, they would rightly have found their type of counter-intuitive in the *sampy* and their cults and also, wrongly, in the ancestors – two types of phenomena which accordingly they would lump together. The reason why they would not be able to differentiate is because they would not have based themselves, as here, on an approach informed primarily by the nature of the actual evocation of these two very different types of agents in natural situations; something which ethnographic field work enables us to do particularly well.

However, there seem to be a number of related counter-objections to my criticisms of the Sperber–Boyer stance. First, these two authors might well defend themselves by arguing that the taken-for-granted character or familiarity of a belief concerning entities such as ancestors is irrelevant to the attitude people have toward the object of that belief. They might also argue that, if Malagasy people fear diseases sent by the ancestors, which they certainly do, and do things which are *out of the ordinary* to contact them, i.e., perform rituals, then the oddity of this means of communication demonstrates the counter-intuitive nature of ancestors.

Even though ancestors are said to speak, and it is an unchallengeable fact, for the Malagasy as for anybody else, that dead bodies do not speak, the problem with taking entities such as ancestors as counter-intuitive is that this ignores the usual *attitude* that people display toward the supernatural entities in question. Most speakers of statements about ancestors do not, most of the time, indicate that they are referring to counter-intuitive beings, and, therefore, to interpret their statements as indicating this type of mental state seems unwarranted. To classify ancestors as counter-intuitive beings implies something which is ethnographically wrong: that, *to the ordinary Malagasy*, they are experienced as the same sort of beings, with similar types of attributes, as those evoked in the creed, or, for that matter, belief in particular *sampy*. By ignoring the difference, we would be merging phenomena which, while perhaps superficially potentially cognate in one way (because they seem odd to the ethnographer), could not, as we saw, be more contrastive from the social, cultural, communicative, or cognitive point of view. This categorical difference is revealed by the acid test of their differential reaction to history.

The basis of the problem is that a stance which identifies the counter-intuitive with a priori characteristics, that can be inferred from the nature of the entities proposed, ignores the role of communicative practice in real situations. This was precisely what Sperber and Boyer were criticizing others for omitting. Furthermore, such an approach ignores the ever-changing evolution of attitudes of people toward these entities through time and in different circumstances. Thus a representation, which a particular person might understand as counter-intuitive when they first come across it, out of the blue, so to speak, clearly does not have the same cognitive significance as it does when it has become totally familiar, and has been held as valid by oneself and everybody else around for as long as anyone can remember.

As an additional problem, the case of an accepted proposition, such as the existence of ancestors for the Malagasy – something never even discussed as an issue or rhetorically marked in any way as peculiar – is totally different from the content of those assertions of belief that are continually marked as being in doubt or out of the ordinary by being prefaced on Sundays with the phrase "I believe." In a society such as pre-Christian Madagascar, it is the former state of affairs which is typical of most aspects of the religious, though not all. In fact, the matter may be even more complex, since it may be that some people, all the time, consider the ancestors as counter-intuitive, while other people, all the time, never have an attitude toward the ancestors with a whiff of anything counter-intuitive, and that still other people, some of the time, suddenly feel the statements made about the ancestors to be counter-intuitive while, most of the time, they do not. In fact, for the Malagasy, on the basis of the most anecdotal of evidence, the third case seems to me to be the most common, but this does not mean that the two attitudes are not sharply contrasting.

These fundamental differences in attitude should not be ignored by the Sperber–Boyer type theories of religion since it is precisely the arresting cognitive presence of the counter-intuitive in certain representations which the two authors see as the explanation of their historical and evolutionary destiny. Thus Sperber and Boyer argue that, if certain representations are counter-intuitive in the way they appear to *the people who hold such representations* (N.B. not in themselves) then such representations will be somehow stimulating and interesting to entertain, and will then spread and stabilize through the population, becoming part of the culture. But I am arguing that, if the representations they are talking about are, for the people concerned, of totally different cognitive types and seem to display very great differences in degree of counter-intuitiveness, then, their catchiness, or otherwise, will also be totally different. Furthermore, if some of these representations are so familiar as to be just like intuitive beliefs, then the special catchiness attributed to the stimulation of the counter-intuitive will be nullified.

The second objection to my criticism of the Sperber–Boyer theory of religion is somewhat similar and can be phrased as follows. One could argue that, although the Malagasy are not normally much concerned with the ontological status of beings like ancestors on a day-to-day basis, when they want to contact these supernatural entities, for example when they want to ask them to remove a disease which the ancestors have sent, then, by the very act of attempting communication, they expose the counter-intuitive nature of their belief, since such contact cannot be established in the straightforward way one would with regular creatures.

According to this objection, the way such entities as ancestors can be communicated with, in moments when it is really important to do so, contrasts drastically with the way one would communicate with a person, such as a neighbor, with whom one might, for example, engage in a two-way conversation. With dead ancestors, such straightforward reciprocal intercourse is not possible and, instead, exchange must take place through ritual. This fact, it can be argued, must bring to the fore the counter-intuitive nature of ancestors in that what we call rituals are characterised, precisely, by the *oddness* of the means of communication employed. For example, in rituals the typical means/ends rationality of everyday life is abandoned for one that is obscure for all concerned, including the ritual practitioners, were they to be obliged to explain it (which, in normal circumstances, not faced by an ethnographer, they do not have to do).[19]

However, on the interpretation I am advancing, ritual, far from enabling the participant to become aware of the intuitive or counter-intuitive nature of the entities addressed, does precisely the opposite.

[19] E. R. Leach, *Political Systems of Highland Burma* (Cambridge MA: Harvard University Press, 1954), 11.

If anything, it is the use of ritual as a means of communication which itself becomes the focus of the awareness of the counter-intuitive element, while the beings evoked in the process almost completely fade from view.

This is because ritual removes the possibility of intellectual discursive evaluation of the forces involved or of the reasonableness of the exact nature of communication. Certain rituals are indeed "addressed" to the ancestors and so they imply the strange fact that people who are dead get up to things and do these things in unseen and unheard ways, yet the very nature of rituals, as many anthropologists, including myself, have pointed out, involves such actions as singing rather than speaking, such unexplained symbols as lambs and fishes, rather than straightforward signs, and this places them in the category not of semantics but of pragmatics. One cannot be sure whether any proposition in a ritual context asserts anything in particular about the world which, even implicitly, could be taken as either "intuitive" or "counter-intuitive." What makes it reasonable in English to label the acts I am talking about as rituals, therefore, is the out-of-the-ordinary character of the communicative mode they employ, but not the-out-of-the-ordinary character of their semantic content. Rituals involve communicative practices which are *alternatives* to normal understandings and meanings, and which hinder and interfere with the tools we normally think we need to make ourselves understood (and through which we can interpret what we and others believe). One enters a ritual mode of communication by radical modifications of ordinary behavior. Speech becomes singing, even wordless singing. Customary adaptation of means to end is obscure. The Gricean requirements are nowhere on the horizon. One cures by killing. One often synchronizes one's bodily and linguistic movements with those of others. This is so to the extent that one is not sure whether it is oneself or another inside oneself who is acting and using one's voice and one's body. Thus, in rituals concerned with the ancestors, one floats off in a highly emotive but semantically obscure world; rituals are attempts to achieve this state. One needs to go through the looking glass, but, once there, one loses all reference points. In other words, in the practice of ritual, the cognitive effect of the fact that the ancestors might be counter-intuitive is irrelevant.

There is a further aspect. Rituals cannot, by definition, be spontaneous. They are conventional actions where the intention to mold what one is saying or doing for the sake of transmitting representations is impossible, since the molding has already been done, long before, by person, or persons, unknown. The Davidsonian preliminary requirement for interpretation, *viz.* that what the speaker utters is intended by herself to be true, or rather to be understood by the hearer as intended to be understood as true by the hearer, is absent in ritual action, since one cannot identify the originator of the message who might have made such a commitment and whose intentionality could be read. Furthermore, most rituals are done in a group, and so participants find themselves doing, singing, or saying things that are willed in part by others, too, and only afterwards can one try to work out what all this "means." In other words, linguistic statements of belief concerning the ancestors evoked in rituals, which could be interpreted as counter-intuitive (e.g., those that anthropologists might succeed in extracting from their informants) are merely *post hoc* reflections or rationalizations of what cannot, by its very nature, be put in ordinary language because it is not an ordinary language matter. Whether these rationalizations are to be interpreted as counter-intuitive or not is irrelevant to the experience itself.

Thus, the phenomenon of the ancestors evoked in rituals is a thousand miles removed from being told intriguing stories about dragons, the choosing of *sampy*, and the implicit or explicit testing of one *sampy* against another. It is a thousand miles removed from saying, in the cold light of morning, perhaps to an anthropologist, "we are all red macaws," or "twins are birds." This is not to say that this type of reflective activity is unimportant in places like Madagascar or that it never occurs in myth, where the arresting quality of the counter-intuitive representations might well account for its spread. But this is not the case in ancestor worship.

To sum up, the English term "religion" normally indicates phenomena which imply a consideration of strange "beliefs" with an explicit and clearly emphasized counter-intuitive element (for example a stress on life after death as a subject of reflection). This is what is salient in general discussions of "religion" in Euro-America. This is because the particular history of the Semitic religions, especially Christianity, influenced as it was by Platonism, made faith in the not-fully-knowable the touchstone of what religion is.[20] People like the pre-Christian Malagasy do, and did, also have practices focused on stressed counter-intuitive beliefs. But the most important aspects of the kind of thing they did, which we would readily label religion, are simply not there and this fact has enabled it to survive attacks in the name of the alternative "religion" which Christianity presented itself as. And, therefore, just as it was for the missionaries, discussions of the content of "the beliefs of the Malagasy,"

[20] Pouillon, "Remarques sur le verb 'croire,'" 51.

in the European sense of the words, such as might be found in the work of Sperber, Boyer, and the philosophers who have interested themselves in anthropological records, would either pass by most of what are normally labelled as "religious" practices, or place on the same level quite different phenomena.

THE COUNTER-INTUITIVE IS EVERYWHERE

Finally, in this chapter, I turn to another side of the problems raised by the Sperber and Boyer theory. If we were, for the sake of argument, to accept their characterization of the counter-intuitive and, like them, to identify religious-like phenomena with the counter-intuitive, this would seem to imply that the counter-intuitive, in their sense, is only, or mainly, to be found in certain specified areas of the socio-cultural process that are rather exceptional, such as in religious phenomena.

Yet, if we turn again to the discussion concerning ancestors, and if we, once again, if only to a certain extent, follow the lead of Kopitoff when he argues for the identity of elders and ancestors, we realize that, if we were to label ancestors as counter-intuitive, we would justifiably have to do the same for elders or any other traditional office holders. This is because behavior toward elders, and indeed toward anybody for that matter, is far from straightforward. An elder is not treated as only the person in front of you, understood simply through the cognitive means which we all share as humans and which enable us to understand such phenomena as human intentionality, but as an *elder*, that is, an entity which appears to be merely an old man, or sometimes an old woman, but is, in fact, endowed with a mysterious, non-empirical aura which means that they deserve respect. Furthermore, manifesting respect is, in many places in Africa, not merely politeness, since not to offer this respect will, through a mysterious unexplained causality, not of the conscious volition of the elder, cause disease, in exactly the same way as offended ancestors cause disease. Elders, therefore, must also be considered to be as much counter-intuitive as dead ancestors. Moreover, a moment's reflection will reveal that, although this is a particularly clear case, there is nothing special in this since the whole of social life involves behaving toward other human animals in terms of social roles and statuses. That is, in ways which are therefore informed by non-empirical, inferred characteristics which cannot possibly be directly derived from a hard-wired intuitive tool kit which we might possess for general understandings of the world and people. Thus, an element of the counter-intuitive, in the non-discursively marked sense of the term, is everywhere.

Of course, an objection to the argument developed in the previous paragraph could be that, while ancestors are *only* counter-intuitive beings, elders are counter-intuitive beings and *also* intuitive beings. But this would be an awkward defense for a writer such as Boyer, since he insists that ancestors, too, are beings that can be understood intuitively apart from their little counter-intuitive extras. But the general point I am making in this chapter sweeps such questions aside for much more fundamental reasons. I argue that neither ancestors nor elders are normally perceived as counter-intuitive, since in ordinary circumstances their counter-intuitive potential is not cognitively salient because they are so familiar, while *sampy* and Christian "beliefs" are protected from growing familiarity by a variety of devices such as the repetition of the phrase "I believe." This, of course, does not rule out the possibility that, in certain circumstances, *both* ancestors and elders may be temporarily realized as counter-intuitive in moments of metaphysical or political reflection, perhaps occasioned by the presence of an ethnographer.

I also accept, as noted earlier, that certain other phenomena can be and, most of the time, are given a counter-intuitive discursive prominence. This is the case with the *sampy*. A sign of this is that *sampy* are put in question and made a subject of talk, while the nature of ancestors usually is not. In other words, while the nature of ancestors and elders normally "goes without saying,"[21] that of *sampy* and dragons does not. But this difference cuts across all kinds of phenomena, including religious-like phenomena, and therefore cannot be one of its distinctive features.

For example, recent studies on the understandings of kinship by Astuti[22] and myself[23] have led the authors to argue that what is discursively salient concerning the transmission of characteristics between parents and children cannot be taken as expressing the principles of understanding of folk genetics among the people studied, since these normally "go without saying." The basic principles of folk genetics are taken for granted, like the nature of ancestors, while the focused subjects of discourse are quite different, often counter-intuitive, in the sense that

[21] M. Bloch, "What Goes Without Saying: The Conceptualisation of Zafimaniry Society," in A. Kuper (ed.), *Conceptualising Society* (London: Routledge, 1992).
[22] R. Astuti, "Are We All Natural Dualists? A Developmental Cognitive Approach," *Journal of the Royal Anthropological Institute*, n.s., 7 (2001): 429–47.
[23] M. Bloch, M., G. Solomon, and S. Carey, "Zafimaniry Understanding of What is Passed on from Parents to Children: A Cross-Cultural Approach," *Journal of Cognition and Culture* 1:1 (2001): 43–68.

they add a further intriguing and challenging reflection to the unspoken general principles.

Thus, in a domain such as folk genetics we find the same mixture of occasionally evoked counter-intuitive elements and normally un-expressed intuitive assumptions as we find in what is, loosely and con-ventionally, called religion. The contrast between simpler beliefs and more reflexive beliefs which might be counter-intuitive is thus marked, not by the intrinsic character of the subject matter, whether genetics, ancestors, dragons or *sampy*, but by how it is treated and presented in certain discourses.[24]

[24] I would like to thank the following for important and constructive comments on earlier drafts of this chapter: R. Astuti, P. Boyer, N. Frankenberry, G. Lenclud, E. Keller, R. Rorty, and D. Sperber.

PART III

Semantics

Introduction

The chapters in Part III have in common a concern with the semantics of religious belief. Hans Penner explores the flight from the literal meaning of myths and rituals, Nancy K. Frankenberry critiques the very idea of the metaphorical or symbolic meaning of religious propositions, and Jonathan Z. Smith presents "manna" and "mana" as two "false friends" whose case histories illustrate the perils of interpreting believers among Hebrews and Durkheimians alike.

As a Hindologist and historian of religions, Penner's longstanding interest in methodological impasses and theoretical resolutions is well known.[1] As a radical voice in the academic study of religion, he has dissented from theologically motivated interpretations of myth and ritual, and mounted critiques of the widespread use of phenomenology and functionalism in religious studies. His leading premise is that a religion is structured like a language, so that a full explanation of any religious system requires setting out both its syntax and its semantics. Appropriating Lévi-Strauss's structural anthropology and Donald Davidson's semantics, Penner has specified the distribution of labor he thinks is most fruitful. Structuralism provides the tools for explicating the syntax of religion, but the structure of a myth is not synonymous with its meaning, despite Lévi-Strauss's assumption that it is. Davidson's truth-conditional theory of meaning supplies the theory of semantics needed by the study of religion, according to Penner. His appreciation of holism, therefore, derives as much from Davidsonian semantics as from structuralism and linguistics.[2]

---

[1] See in particular Hans H. Penner, *Impasse and Resolution: A Critique of the Study of Religion* (New York: Peter Lang, 1989).

[2] For his account of the contemporary meaning of structuralism for the study of religion, see the "Introduction" to *Teaching Lévi-Strauss*, ed. Hans H. Penner (Atlanta, GA: Scholars Press, 1998). For one of the first apprehensions of the significance of Donald Davidson's work to the semantics of religious belief, see Hans H. Penner, "Why Does Semantics Matter to the Study of Religion?" in *Method and Theory in the Study of Religion* 7: 3 (1995): 221–49.

The approach to myth, ritual, and religion that Penner has recommen-
ded in recent years embraces at least three additional premises. First,
rather than studying isolated or separated elements, the explanation of
myth and religion should state how the various mythical figures or religious elements are related to each other. Second, it is the relation among
the elements of a religion or between mythical figures that defines the "nature" of both. Third, myth and religion cannot be studied apart from the
material and social conditions of society, but neither are they constituted
by or reducible to historical or social conventions and events. Penner
maintains a clear distinction between language and speech, meaning
and use, competence and performance, semantics and pragmatics, along
with an understanding that the first term in each pair cannot be derived
from the second. If the proper object of study for linguistics is competence, rather than performance, then the proper theoretical object of the
study of religion is the system or its structure, not its practice in the daily
lives of adherents, who may be unaware of what the system is.

Penner's reading of structuralism, as a development out of modern linguistics, and his interest in the explanation of myth, ritual, and religious
symbolism, converge in his chapter here. It will be obvious to readers
that he does not really believe that, in the language of his title, "You
Don't Read a Myth for Information" – he only believes the Romantic
Movement gave rise to such a view and that the enduring modern
dialectic between Romanticism and rationalism continues to be played
out in our most influential theories of myth and ritual. Penner's chapter
exposes the roots in the Romantic Movement of a set of assumptions
about myth and ritual that would interpret them as expressivist, non-
cognitive, performative, and symbolic. Tracing the rise of the modern Romantic tradition of interpretation in religion to Georg Friedrich
Creuzer's multivolume *Symbolik und Mythologie der alten Völker*, Penner's
chapter offers not so much an exegesis as an overview of Romanticism.
Even Lévi-Strauss provides some shelter to this legacy. Perhaps the most
important assumption in Penner's chapter is the one glossed only at the
end: the "given" has been as much a myth in religious studies as it has
been in philosophy (Sellars, *Empiricism and the Philosophy of Mind*, 1997).
Like other contributors to this volume, Penner sees clearly that without
a "given," there is no "organizing" of a given by religious schemes, and
without a pre-conceptual content, there is no expressivist or representationalist function to be performed by religious language.

Frankenberry's chapter takes up where Penner's leaves off. Should
religious studies adopt Penner's conclusion that the best way to interpret

believers is to take their statements literally? Doesn't this fly in the face of a long history of theological hermeneutics in which religious language is regarded as symbolic language that cannot be understood literally, due to the very nature of its subject matter? In "Religion as a 'Mobile Army of Metaphors'" Frankenberry's topic is the symbolic treatment of religious meaning, located squarely on the Romantic side of the rational–intellectualist/expressive–symbolist division Penner has sketched. Frankenberry offers a Davidsonian critique of the very idea of symbolic or metaphorical meaning in religion. Reliance on the notion of a special, second, symbolic truth for religious language over and above "first" or literal meaning has been an essential element of what she calls The Theology of Symbolic Forms. Her critique, therefore, may appear as controversial in philosophy of religion as Davidson's essay, "What Metaphors Mean," has been in the discussions of metaphor to which she is indebted. In addition to the work of Davidson, Frankenberry's chapter makes use of the work of Richard Rorty. From Davidson she takes the emphasis that there is no such thing as metaphorical meaning. From Rorty she borrows the emphasis on the use of metaphor in conceptual revolutions, extended to cases of theological or religious change and innovation.

In conclusion, Frankenberry shows how the logic of Davidson's argument in his classic paper "On the Very Idea of a Conceptual Scheme" can be adapted to apply to the category of the Wholly Other/Sacred/Deus Absconditus that much Western religious literature posits as approachable only symbolically. The "no radically untranslatable language" argument thus suggests the incoherence of religious language about a "Wholly Other" as found in Western theology. From another direction, this chapter can be read as a reinforcement of Rorty's conclusion in "Cultural Politics and the Question of the Existence of God," that "there is no such thing as a certain kind of object demanding a certain kind of language," a point that Brandom has demonstrated in meticulous detail.

In the final chapter, Jonathan Z. Smith epitomizes the preceding chapters by Penner and Frankenberry when he quotes Durkheim's linguistically illegitimate conclusion that: "Religious forces are real, no matter how imperfect the symbols with whose help they were conceived."[3] Master of the comparative method and the telling detail, Smith is concerned in "Manna, Mana, Everywhere and / ⌣ / ⌣ / ⌣" with the two primary, linear, linguistic behaviors of narrative and argument. Using the biblical narrative of the miraculous manna feeding and debates over

---

[3] Emile Durkheim, *The Elementary Forms of Religious Life*, trans. K. E. Fields (New York, 1995), 206.

the meaning of the Polynesian sacred term "mana," he addresses issues of fact and interpretation in history of religions. There is nothing here pertinent to "reality," only to thought, he says. The mysterious mana is a linguistic category, not an ontological one, according to Smith; and it possesses no intrinsic symbolic value, but rather a semantic function. Similarly, its "false friend," the biblical manna, as ambrosial divine food, is not a matter of entomology, Smith shows, but of philology in which entirely new connotations get introduced within the linguistic realm.

After Smith, no one will read Durkheim in the same way again. In the trajectory of interpretation Smith charts, mana moves from being a mysterious force or secret power for Mauss and Durkheim to having a semantic function for Lévi-Strauss. Durkheim "risked his argument on a mana that was not there," while Lévi-Strauss "proposed mana as a category for objects that had no 'where.'" Smith is not content simply to understand native terminology about "mana" or compile comparisons of "manna" narratives. His radical interpretation aims to have explanatory power as well. Subtly, he takes the reader to that end in his closing paragraphs.

The notorious gap between theoretical explanation and native phraseology is a difference Smith would have students of religion embrace rather than abjure. In a striking claim likely to be quoted for a long time, Smith once argued that "while there is a staggering amount of data, of phenomena, or human experiences and expressions that might be characterized in one culture or another by one criterion or another, as religious – there is no data for religion. Religion is solely the creation of the scholar's study."[4] In that light, much of what students of religion have come to understand in the last twenty-five years about the religions of late antiquity has been the creation of Smith himself. Few scholarly works are as original or indefatigably researched as his *Drudgery Divine* (1990), *To Take Place* (1987), *Imagining Religion* (1982), or *Map is Not Territory* (1978). Although he thinks of himself primarily as an historian, Smith is also a geographer, illuminating the significance of *place* in religion, a ludic spirit, drawing attention to the role of *play* in religion, and a cartographer, providing maps with which to explore the territory of others, reminding us of Alfred Korzybski's dictum: "Map is not territory" – "but," Smith adds, " maps are all we possess."[5]

4 Jonathan Z. Smith, *Imagining Religion: From Babylon to Jonestown* (University of Chicago Press, 1982), xi.
5 J. Z. Smith, *Map Is Not Territory: Studies in the History of Religions* (Leiden: E. J. Brill, 1978), 309.

8

You don't read a myth for information

Hans H. Penner

At first glance the study of religion appears to be a many-splintered thing. In fact, a growing number of scholars think that there is no such subject matter, that religion, or, more specifically, Hinduism, for example, is a figment of scholars' imaginations. However, one has only to survey the last two-hundred years of scholarly writings about religion in order to discover a very interesting fact: the study of religion is anything but splintered; on the contrary, I find there is massive agreement on its essential meaning. The familiar disagreements usually express only different variations, not the fundamentals, of the prevailing agreement. My purpose in this chapter is to expose some of the pitfalls that attend that agreement.

In general, two primary theories of religion have competed with each other in the modern study of religion: the rational–intellectualist theory and the expressive–symbolist theory. The first holds that religion, consisting of beliefs, myths, and rituals, is rational and false. E. B. Tylor's *Primitive Culture* (1871) and Emile Durkheim's *The Elementary Forms of Religious Life* (1912) are two classical examples. It is not a popular theory at the present time. It requires that religious beliefs be taken literally and most rituals viewed as rational, means–ends actions. In brief, this theory explains religion as entailing propositional attitudes whose significance is not unique, special, or distinct from ordinary, natural language, thought, and action. This last assumption cannot be overemphasized in the interpretation I want to advance.

One of the central problems for this theory has been the troublesome question: why do so many people persist in holding false beliefs? Although this question changes the subject from what religion is to why people hold false beliefs, most scholars have answered it by invoking another theory, known as functionalism: people persist in holding on to a religious system of beliefs and actions because of certain needs that must be satisfied.

153

However, since it has been amply demonstrated that functionalism is illogical if not false when applied to cultural systems, we way well wonder why this doctrine persists, and what needs it fulfills among scholars in the academy! Whatever one's verdict on the merits of functionalism, the persistence of false beliefs remains troublesome for all rationalist theories of religion. One popular attempt to solve this problem is the relativist argument that "what is true and what is not true is given in the sense that a language has." However, it does not take much reflection to notice that such arguments entail a contradiction that leads to incoherence. Most rationalist theories of religion usually put the question to one side and turn to interpretations of the symbolic meaning of religion.

Rationalist theories of religion frequently produce accusations of eth-nocentrism and racism. Marshall Sahlins at Chicago, Edward Wilson at Harvard, Melford Spiro at the University of California at San Diego, and Robin Horton in Nigeria learned first hand how bitter these criti-cisms can become. Although the accusation is valid in some cases, most rationalist theories of religion make it clear that to say that religious beliefs are false does not entail that persons who hold such beliefs are irrational, mentally deficient, or indicative of an early childlike stage of evolutionary development. The use, abuse, and criticism of this theory in our intellectual history still deserves a thorough analysis.

The second theory of religion – the expressive–symbolist – has been by far the most popular. This theory claims that religion is *not* rational. That is to say, religions, religious belief, myth, and ritual are best explained as neither true nor false. Lacking propositional content, or truth-value, they are at best non-rational. Nevertheless, according to most variants of this theory, religion is rich in symbolic significance. I find that this theory is the overwhelming choice of most scholars of religion today. Here, briefly, are some examples drawn from the work of well-known scholars.

The first is the classic article first published in 1966 by John Beattie. Beattie's thesis is that "when we speak of ritual we are speaking of some-thing that is basically expressive, even dramatic." He tells us that he agrees with Raymond Firth's argument that "magical and religious rites are, in consequence, very much like the arts, like poetry, painting, and sculpture, for example, than they are like science as we understand it in this century." From there Beattie concludes that whatever it is that ritual does, it "can be understood only by reference to what it says."[1] And what it says is to be taken as symbolic.

---

[1] John Beattie, "Ritual and Social Change," *Man* 1 (1966): 61, 65.

One year later Victor Turner published a volume of influential essays significantly titled *The Forest of Symbols*. I do not think it is accidental that most scholars who refer to Turner's essays overlook his definition of ritual. He defines ritual as "prescribed formal behavior for occasions not given over to technological routine, having reference to beliefs in mystical beings or powers."[2] Turner leaves no doubt about what he means by "mystical beings." In his essay on liminality he defines the *sacra* of a ritual as "absolutely sacrosanct, as ultimate mysteries. We are here in the realm of what Warner would call 'nonrational or nonlogical' symbols which [quoting Warner] do not have their source in rational processes."[3] In the large literature that Turner's work has spawned, I have found no critical reference to these essays that challenges his fundamental hypothesis about the nature of religion and ritual.

Almost a decade later, Maurice Bloch published "Symbols, Song, Dance, and Features of Articulation," an essay that stands in direct opposition to Turner's theory of symbol, Weber's work on religion and power, and Lévi-Strauss's work on the logic of myth. In this essay, Bloch uses a theory of language that stresses the identity of syntax and semantics. For scholars using this theory, Bloch says, semantics "becomes the study of the rules of combination of speech, the propositional content of speech." Bloch then makes the following inference:

If semantics and syntax are the same, the logical potency of language depends on the creativity of syntax. This does not constitute a restriction precisely because syntax is so creative... However, it also follows from such a conclusion that if we are dealing with a language use where syntax does not articulate freely, the potential of language for carrying arguments becomes reduced and the propositional force of language is transformed.[4]

Ritual and myth, according to Bloch, are such formalized languages. Formalized language strips language of its creativity, its capacity to describe specific events or actions, restricting what can be said. Normally, the statements we make are open to contradiction and replacement. In formalized language, however, these features of language are reduced to zero. "To put it simply," Bloch says, "we can say that logic depends on the flexibility of the features of articulation in language and if there is no such flexibility there can be no argument, no logic, no explanation, and

---

[2] Victor Turner, *The Forest of Symbols* (Ithaca, NY: Cornell University Press, 1967), 19.
[3] *Ibid.*, 107–08.
[4] Maurice Bloch, "Symbols, Song, Dance and Features of Articulation," *Archives Européennes de Sociologie* 15 (1974), 56.

in one sense of the word, no semantics."[5] Thus, the language of religion involves a restriction of logic and propositional force. As Bloch says, religion both "excludes explanation and hides this exclusion."[6] Religion, and ritual in particular, are "mis-statements of reality."[7]

It would be wrong, however, to conclude that religion is meaningless. Bloch stresses that there is a second, different kind of meaning he calls "illocutionary" or "performative force" that is strictly contextual. What we should focus on, according to Bloch, is the *"disconnection"* between religious statements and the real world. After all, he reminds us, "circumcision ceremonies do not, as van Gennep was at pains to point out, make adults out of little boys, curing ceremonies do not cure, etc., and any attempt to pretend that they do (as is done in the work of so many anthropologists) is wrong from the first."[8] Thus ritual language varies inversely with ordinary language on the principle that "with increasing formalisation propositional force decreases, and illocutionary force increases. In other words, the two types of meaning vary inversely."[9]

I think it is fair to say that the identity of semantics with syntax is loaded with problems. Performative force as a "second, different kind of meaning," also seems problematic insofar as it lacks semantic properties. Although these problems are relevant in any discussion of religion, myth and ritual, they are not my primary focus here. What is of more general interest, and what I find most fascinating, is that, even though there is wide disagreement among the scholars I am citing, there is also a fundamental, essential agreement about the nature of religion: religion and its two basic components, myth and ritual, are regarded as non-rational.

In a cautious and complex 1985 essay entitled "A Performative Approach to Ritual," Stanley Tambiah gave John Austin's notion of "performative utterance" and Bloch's use of "illocutionary force" primary place in his description of ritual as performative. Tambiah notes that, according to Austin, "the saying of the illocutionary speech act is 'the doing of the action'; this act, 'conforming to a convention' in 'appropriate circumstances' is subject to normative judgments of felicity or legitimacy and not to rational tests of truth and falsity."[10] Tambiah makes his position crystal clear by citing Tylor, Frazer, Evans-Pritchard, and Horton, all of whom misjudge rituals "solely against the perspective and truth canons of Western scientific rationality"; they thus miss the insight

---

[5] *Ibid.*, 66.   [6] *Ibid.*, 67.   [7] *Ibid.*, 77.   [8] *Ibid.*, 77.   [9] *Ibid.*, 67.
[10] Stanley J. Tambiah, "A Performative Approach to Ritual," in *Culture, Thought, and Social Action* (Cambridge, MA: Harvard University Press, 1985), 143–35.

that since rituals are "constitutive and persuasive acts they cannot be 'falsified,' though individual instances of them may be declared normatively infelicitous or illegitimate."[11] From Tambiah's point of view, there is no conflict between "western science" and religion precisely because religion does not entail truth-conditions. The normative judgments of "felicity or legitimacy" to which rituals may be subject are not the same as rational tests of truth and falsity.

Of course it is true that Tylor thought that Western history is primarily a history of the development of reason from the personification of nature through metaphysics to science, that Frazer called magic a "bastard science," that Evans-Pritchard described the Azande belief in witches as "not in accord with reality," that Horton holds that African religious beliefs and rituals are like Western scientific theories, and that Sahlins has argued that the Hawaiians took Captain Cook to be a god. There seems to be no doubt that both Frazer and Tylor thought that Western civilization was far superior rationally and ethically to life among "primitives" and "savages." Yet, to their great credit, they employed a theory of religion that emphasizes that religious beliefs and rituals entail truth-conditions. In brief, I am arguing that if we want to understand the meaning of the language of religion, myth, and ritual, we must take it literally.

The problem with Tambiah's opposition to Tylor and his criticism of Bloch's theory that ritual contains no propositional force is that it contradicts his own Austinian position that ritual as a performative act is neither true nor false. What, we may ask, does Tambiah think rituals communicate? We are never told. Catherine Bell is certainly right, in her comprehensive review of ritual studies, to point out that the emphasis on communication by such performative theories of ritual "has nothing to do with the efficacy that the ritual acts are thought to have by those who perform them."[12] This is indeed a very odd communication system; it seems to entail a language spoken by people who do not understand its meaning. Moreover, when we are told what the message is, it seems that the goddesses and gods have nothing to say.

Once again, what is interesting here is Tambiah's insistence that ritual performances are both performative acts in Austin's sense and also communicative, indexical, if not ontological in some symbolic sense that remains theoretically opaque. Dan Sperber is the only contemporary

---

[11] *Ibid.*, 135–36.
[12] Catherine Bell, *Ritual Theory, Ritual Practice* (Oxford University Press, 1992), 43.

scholar I know of who has argued for a theory that draws the inescapable positivist conclusion. If religious language, ritual, and myth are void of propositional content, if religious statements and symbols are neither analytic nor synthetic, then religion is meaningless.[13] I agree with him that it simply does not make much sense to talk about "hidden meaning."

My fifth example comes from the anthropologist of religion Roy Rappaport. Consider what he has to say about religion:

> It is of interest that sacred propositions and numinous experiences are the inverse of each other. Ultimate sacred postulates are discursive but their significata are not material. Numinous experiences are immediately material . . . but they are not discursive. Ultimate sacred propositions are unfalsifiable; numinous experiences are undeniable . . . That this is logically unsound should not trouble us for, although it may make problems for the logicians, it does not trouble the faithful . . . The unfalsifiable supported by the undeniable yields the unquestionable, which transforms the dubious, the arbitrary, and the conventional into the correct, the necessary, and the natural. This structure is, I would suggest, the foundation upon which the human way of life stands, and it is realized in ritual.[14]

Rappaport was not joking when he wrote that paragraph, for shortly before his death he repeated the claim. In a discussion of "levels of meaning," he described the "higher-order" level of meaning as "grounded in identity and unity." It is not so much "intellectual," he emphasized, as "experiential." That is: "It may be experienced through art, or in acts of love, but is perhaps most often felt in ritual and other religious devotions." The highest order of meaning is, according to Rappaport, "beyond the reach of language; it seems enormously or even ultimately meaningful even though, or perhaps because, its meaning is ineffable."[15] Ineffable meaning? When Rappaport wrote that striking paragraph, either he was writing nonsense, or he had reached Beattie's conclusion: "religion is expressive."

As a sixth and final case, Caroline Humphrey and James Laidlaw set out, in *The Archetypal Actions of Ritual* (1994), to challenge much of the received theory. Lamenting the fact that "anthropology is littered with theories of ritual: a welter of labyrinthine arguments and complex, multiclause definitions," they argued that most of these theories are

[13] Dan Sperber, *Rethinking Symbolism* (Cambridge University Press, 1975).
[14] Roy A. Rappaport, "The Obvious Aspects of Ritual," in *Ecology, Meaning, and Religion* (Richmond, CA: North Atlantic Books, 1979), 217.
[15] Roy A. Rappaport, *Ritual and Religion in the Making of Humanity* (Cambridge University Press, 1999), 71.

"trying to explain the wrong thing."[16] Although pleased with Lawson and McCauley's use of cognitive research, they disagree with their formalist–linguistic model and are most unhappy with the Lawson–McCauley definition of religion as belief in superhuman agents, citing against them the case of Theravada Buddhism.[17] Unfortunately, Lawson and McCauley do fall into this snare by admitting that Theravada Buddhism "may prove troublesome for our approach," and adding, "but such cases are hardly prototypical by anyone's lights!" (As if that solves the problem.) They tighten the snare by asserting that religions that do not entail postulated superhuman agents are "extremely unlikely to have much ritual at all."[18] I pause to dwell on this issue because I am in complete agreement with Lawson and McCauley's definition of religion though not with their interpretation of it with respect to this case.

The use of Theravada Buddhism as empirical evidence that falsifies a definition of religion in terms of belief in superhuman agents is at least as old as Durkheim's use of it in *The Elementary Forms of Religious Life* in connection with his criticism of Tylor. Melford Spiro was the first to point out that Durkheim was quite mistaken. Theravada Buddhism, in all of the countries in which it is thriving, clearly entails belief in superhuman agents, as the belief and rituals involving the *nats* in Burma and the *phi* in Thailand will confirm. One can reply, of course, that these beliefs were grafted into Theravada Buddhism as it moved into Burma and Thailand from India, where it originated without such beliefs. Quite so! What neither Durkheim, Spiro, Lawson, nor McCauley notice, however, is that there is no greater example of a superhuman agent than the Buddha himself. He fairly leaps from the pages of the Theravada Buddhist Pali canon, an Indian production if there ever was one, with all the marks of a superhuman being, comparable to what we find in the myths of Moses, Jesus, Krishna, and Muhammad. Why scholars have overlooked this data is in itself a fascinating problem having to do with the modern quest for the historical Buddha, a quest that dates to about the same time biblical scholars began their search for the historical Jesus.[19]

---

[16] Caroline Humphrey and James Laidlaw, *The Archetypal Actions of Ritual* (Oxford: Clarendon Press, 1994), 65.

[17] *Ibid.*, 82, n. 4.

[18] E. Thomas Lawson and Robert N. McCauley, *Rethinking Religion* (Cambridge University Press, 1990), 7–8.

[19] I am putting aside for another occasion the parallels between the quest for the historical Buddha and the quest for the historical Jesus, as well as the problem of the relation between myth and history, or myth and fiction.

Asking "what kind of theory do we need?" Humphrey and Laidlaw answer that rituals are not acts of communication, and that rituals do not inform us of anything. Rather, rituals are acts that have been ritualized, that is to say, stripped of intentionality and meaning. The authors' main objective is "to establish that there is an important sense in which [action] in general has meaning, but ritualized action does not"; they will refer to meaningful action as "intentional meaning."[20]

If ritual is lacking it, what then is "intentional meaning"? Humphrey and Laidlaw stipulate that in order

... to understand the behavior of our fellows we need to grasp the intentional content of action, and to do this we have to rely on the implicit ascription to them of beliefs, desires, and prior intentions (or purposes). These prior intentions or motives must be clearly distinguished from "intentional meaning." An intention *to* do something is not the same as an intention *in* doing it. Intentional meaning is not what someone intended to do before doing it, but what they understood themselves to be doing as they did it ... Thus it follows that if we want to understand what is going on we must grasp his or her "intentional meaning." *It is one of the central claims of this book that when an action is ritualized, this is not the case.*[21] (italics original)

To recapitulate: action which is not ritualized has intentional meaning (warning, delivering, murder), and this is understandable by means of the ascription of intentional states to its agent. Ritualized action is not identified this way, because we cannot link what the author does with what his or her intention might be. Instead of being guided and structured by the intentions of actors, ritualized action is constituted and structured by prescription, not just in the sense that people follow rules, but in the much deeper sense that a reclassification takes place so that only following the rules counts as action.[22]

The authors believe that this is a radical theory of ritual and they are careful to point out where they disagree with Beattie, Bloch, Tambiah, and Turner. What they fail to see, however, is that they remain in essential agreement with the dominant view that regards religion as non-rational in the sense that it does not contain propositional content. In other words, religion and ritual are neither true nor false.

It is this assumption that I find puzzling. Why is it the case that religious language, belief, and action are thought to be exempted from truth-conditions? Why are most religious people ignorant of the fact, if it is a fact, that their religious beliefs and actions are neither true nor false, but

---

[20] Humphrey and Laidlaw, *The Archetypal Actions of Ritual*, 91.
[21] *Ibid.*, 93 and 94.   [22] *Ibid.*, 106.

instead entail a symbolic meaning to be decoded by specialists? Simply to attribute it to a variation on the legacy of logical positivism only conceals the problem under the illusion that it has been solved. After all, most scholars are aware of the theoretical turn away from empiricism and verificationism and the reasons why that path has been shown to be a dead-end. What should be alarming in the study of religion is that a theory of religion could put the object of its study so thoroughly beyond rationality, beyond the possibility of truth or falsity, and therefore beyond criticism.

As one reflects upon the implications of such a theory, one realizes that the relativist attempt to solve some of the problems in a rationalist approach to religion also reaches a very similar conclusion. If what is true and what is false is given in the sense that a language has, and languages are incommensurable, then Peter Winch is quite right to rebuke Evans-Pritchard for asserting that the Azande belief in witchcraft is "not in accord with reality."

Few of us read the Romantics anymore. That may be a mistake. It is easy to forget that the Romantic tradition, perhaps more than any other, was explicitly concerned with religion, myth, ritual, and, in particular, with biblical criticism. Studying this literature, one finds an almost perfect fit between what the Romantics say about myth and religion and the way in which Eliade or Otto, for example, characterize "archaic religion" and "the Sacred." The strong emphasis on the non-rational from Beattie and Turner to Bloch, Tambiah, Rappaport, Humphrey, and Laidlow, however, is enough to prompt deeper reflection on just what it is that accounts for the continuous construction of theories of religion, ritual, and myth on a non-rational foundation – a basis never doubted as the origin of religion for most of the Romantics.

It was Jonathan Z. Smith whose investigations pointed the way in *To Take Place: Toward Theory in Ritual*, a book that, along with Lévi-Strauss's *The Savage Mind*, surely ranks among the rare virtuoso performances in our profession. Calling attention to the Indian sociologist who dated the rise of a distinctive Western worldview to Zwingli's insistence that the word "is" in "this is my body" was not to be taken in any real or literal sense, but "only" in a symbolic sense, Smith encapsulates the literature of sixteenth- and seventeenth-century religious controversies: "No matter what the format, the matter and the message remained the same. In Erasmus's blunt formulation, 'To place the whole of religion in external ceremonies is sublime stupidity.'" Smith then adds:

I insist on this point, in part, because the usual histories of the study of religion conceal it. They speak... as if the major task of rectification was to disabuse the notion that myths were false or that they were lies. Not so! The history of the imagination [a favorite word in this essay: HHP] of the categories myth and ritual was sharply divergent. To say myth was false was to recognize it as having content; to declare ritual to be "empty" was to deny the same.[23]

Smith does not stop here, but goes on to point out that the Protestant insistence on the "emptiness" of ritual was often linked to the "Romantic (and equally Protestant) theory of origination on ritual... its first instance... awe-filled, spontaneous [and] dramatic... that subsequently became 'depleted' by repetition."[24] Turner's phrase – "prescribed formalized behavior" – immediately comes to mind here.

The problem the Romantics faced was twofold. First, how do we justify religion, myth, and the arts as mimetic, as representation, as a mirror of nature when, in fact, the happenings do not exist in nature? The usual answer to this question, as Smith makes clear, was to argue that the fabulous world of myth and poetry is false, or "an ingenious lie." This solution to the problem of the meaning of the supernatural and the superhuman became the foundation for such classical works as E. B. Tylor's *Primitive Culture*, in which he defined religion as "the belief in supernatural beings." Such beliefs could be understood as false but still rational. Although no longer the paradigm model for the study of religion, this remains, as I noted, the basic semantic principle in the work of such scholars as Durkheim, Evans-Pritchard, Spiro, and Horton.

The second problem was more troublesome since it involved the very heart of Protestant Christianity and the doctrine of biblical revelation. We need only recall that Robert Lowth, Christian Gottlob Heyne, Johann Gottfried Herder, Johann Gottfried Eichhorn, Gabler, and F. W. J. von Schelling were all theologians in order to grasp the significance of their revolutionary work on the mythological status of the Bible, the study of Hebrew and Greek poetry, the comparison of Sanskrit myth with the mythologies of antiquity, as well as the comparison of the Laws of Manu, newly discovered in India, with the Mosaic Code. These Romantics had to face the question: is the Bible false or an "ingenious lie" from cover to cover? It is ironic that their use and development of the critical and cultural sciences brought them to such an impasse. The irony is compounded when we recall that Tambiah thinks that the use of "Western science" is a mistake when applied to religion. Trapped by the evidence

---

[23] Jonathan Z. Smith, *To Take Place: Toward Theory in Ritual* (University of Chicago Press, 1987), 99–101.
[24] *Ibid.*, 102–03.

of their own scientific research, the Romantics produced a revolution whose effects persist in our time. Rather than face the stark conclusion of their own scientific practice, they placed religion outside the domain of rationality, raising it to a "higher" level of meaning, a symbolic value "beyond" truth and falsity.

It is poetry in mythic form, the Romantics declared, not revelation in prose, that comprises the earliest language of humanity in its childhood. It is poetry – an expressive, spontaneous, iconic or symbolic "picture language" – that precedes prose and literacy. Heyne's statement that "all history as well as philosophy proceeded from the myths of ancient men" became the motto quoted by most scholars who wrote on religion from Eichhorn to Strauss. We find it still reflected today in essays on language, art, poetry, and semiotics. In *Basics of Semiotics,* John Deely, for example, puts it this way: "the whole of our experience, from its most primitive origins in sensation to its most refined achievements in understanding, is a network or web of sign relations."[25] Anyone familiar with Eliade's writings will easily detect the Romantic sources of his nostalgia and thirst for the archaic as well as his fascination with the myth of eternal return.

The Romantics severed religion from the principle of imitation, representation and allegory. Religion, myth, and ritual were no longer representations of the empirical world. The meaning of religion, poetry, art, was not to be explained by the standards and rules of scientific theory or truth since religion was an object-in-itself. The test of religion, therefore, was not "is it true to nature?" but "is it true to itself?" One of the most important recurrent words in the literature to explain this kind of truth is "creation." God as creator is the original poet. The world is God's poem. Religion and art are a second creation, a second nature, a "heterocosm." For Schelling it is very obvious that myth precedes poetry: "Poetry is the natural end," according to Schelling, "the necessary product of mythology; it cannot be the cause or source of the gods."[26] In a footnote to *Die Philosophie der Mythologie,* Schelling refers to the "well-known Coleridge," whose lecture on Prometheus employs the word "tautegorical" to distinguish myth from allegory. Myth, says Schelling, is not allegorical, but tautegorical:

Since the representations and expressions [of mythology] are not governed or created by consciousness, it is the case that mythology is born directly as such, that is to say, everything in mythology must be understood just as it expresses

---

[25] John Deely, *Basics of Semiotics* (Bloomington: Indiana University Press, 1990), 13.
[26] F. W. J. von Schelling, *Werke,* vol. 6 (Munich: Beck, 1924), 22–23.

itself, and not as if something else was being thought or said. Mythology is not allegorical, it is tautegorical. The gods, for mythology, are beings that really exist, they are not something else, nor do they signify something else, they signify only what they are.[27]

In other words, the meaning of myth, for Schelling, cannot be separated from what it conveys. Both are, as Umberto Eco puts it, "self-presentations, and instead of signifying an idea, they are that idea *in themselves*."[28]

There is nothing new here. Heyne, Eichhorn's mentor, would certainly approve of Schelling's description of myth, and so would Eichhorn and Gabler who asserted that the Bible from its first to last page is myth in this tautegorical sense. For Eichhorn, myth was the language of preliterate civilizations, the language of mankind in its childhood. For de Wette, the language of myth was the first and natural form of the religious life, the unification of the eternal with the infinite, the primal source for inspiration, resignation and devotion. As de Wette put it: "Religion ist somit Ahnung," simply a presentiment or feeling that is represented through images or symbols.

Georg Friedrich Creuzer, Schelling's friend, produced the first full systematic text on myth, symbol, and religion in 1810. *Symbolik und Mythologie der alten Völker* went through three editions. Often cited as the founder of *Symbolwissenschaft*, Creuzer's description of the symbol as a unification of concept and sensation, the awakening of consciousness, and a necessary condition of the very foundation of thought, can be traced through many contemporary essays on symbol and religion. For example, Victor Turner's analysis of symbol as consisting of both an ideological and a sensory pole provides an exact copy of Creuzer's notion that symbols are composed of two elements, ideas and sensations. In other words, symbols contain both condensed and multiple meanings, according to both Creuzer and Turner. A careful analysis of Turner's ritual concepts of "liminality" and *sacra* will show, I believe, the full extent to which the Romantic tradition's view of religion is alive and at work. "Liminality" for Turner is the center of all rites of passage, and "liminality" is opposite and opposed to logic and structure. Similarly, one may read Eliade's work as a classic expression of the Romantic notion that myth is a "heterocosm."

---

[27] *Ibid.*, 197–98.
[28] Umberto Eco, *Semiotics and the Philosophy of Language* (Bloomington: University of Indiana Press, 1984), 1.

For the Romantics, religion, poetry, and art are a self-sufficient whole that, in the words of Karl Phillip Moritz, "have no need to be useful."[29] Thus religion, myth, and art can be severed from the empirical world, and if we must speak of the truth of religion or myth it will only be in terms of their consistency and self-coherence. As Goethe said, "artistic truth and natural truth are entirely distinct." For John Stuart Mill, "the logical opposite [of poetry] is not prose, but matter of fact or science."[30]

This distinction between the two kinds of truth, one that corresponds to the empirical world of sensation, and one that is the coherent and consistent expression of the union of sensation and thought, has the apparent advantage of dissolving any conflict between religion and science. After all, why should there be conflict? If religious language is non-propositional, there is nothing to be wrong about, but then, at the same time, there is nothing to be right about either.

What seems clear is that the modern stress on the lack of propositional content in religion, myth, and ritual is as true of Eliade, Turner, and Rappaport as it is of Schelling, Schlegel, and Coleridge. Myths and rituals are considered intrinsically symbolic; they are self-generating and constitute a unified meaning. From here it is but a short step for functionalists like Malinowski to conclude that "since we cannot define the object of myth [since it has none], perhaps we can explain its function."[31]

For the Romantics, the tautegorical entailed the symbolic doubling of myths, pan-symbolism, and the disconfirmation of any unique revelation. As E. S. Shaffer wrote, in a slightly different context:

All mythological systems except that of one's own community [are] thought of as a heresy . . . to "encounter" another system within one's own is heretical, and produces a slight "shock"; and to claim that all are reducible to one "internal" system is regarded as the greatest heresy for all systems. The internal system, however, can have no independent full expression; "original revelation" is lost.[32]

The point to notice here is that "the internal system can have no independent full expression"; symbols refer to symbols, myths refer to other myths, the gods refer to other gods. As Lévi-Strauss has repeatedly emphasized, the meaning of a myth refers to other myths. "Myths think

[29] Cited in M. H. Abrams, *The Mirror and the Lamp: Romantic Theory and the Critical Tradition* (Oxford University Press, 1953), 327.
[30] *Ibid.*, 278, 321.
[31] Branislaw Malinowski, *Magic, Science and Religion* (New York: Doubleday Anchor Books, 1954), 37.
[32] E. S. Shaffer, *'Kubla Khan' and the Fall of Jerusalem* (Cambridge University Press, 1975), 184.

themselves through us." The "internal system," the "presentiment" that precedes all knowledge, is given by means of what Merkelbach called a "mythological doubling" of a particular mythological system, the observance of which requires that we adopt a standpoint outside of any particular system. In Shaffer's words: "to the Egyptians, the Greek gods were only emanations of their own. But from the universal comparative mythologer's point of view, all gods are 'emanations' of all other gods."[33] Theoretically speaking, "imagination" (*einbildung*) becomes the central term for both the origination and interpretation of myth, religion, and symbol.

The Romantic tradition's stress on *ahnung* (presentiment or feeling) and "imagination" in the context of an internal, non-referential system helps to clarify the assertion made by Lévi-Strauss that "man has from the start had at his disposition a signifier–signifier totality which he is at a loss to know how to allocate to a signified." That is because, according to Lévi-Strauss:

in the ascent of animal life, language can only have arisen all at once ... from a stage when nothing had a meaning to another stage when everything had a meaning ... [this] radical change has no counterpart in the field of knowledge, which develops slowly and progressively. In other words, at the moment when the entire universe all at once became *significant*, it was none the better known for being so, even if it is true that the emergence of language must have hastened the rhythm of the development of knowledge. So there is a fundamental opposition in the history of the human mind, between symbolism, which is characteristically discontinuous, and knowledge, characterised by continuity ... What people call scientific knowledge, could only have been and can only ever be constituted out of processes of correcting, and recutting of patterns, regrouping, defining of relationships of belonging and discovering new resources, inside a totality which is closed and complementary to itself.[34]

As far as I can see, the Romantic tradition is in total agreement with this point of view. Not even the structuralism of Lévi-Strauss escaped the effects of the Romantic revolution.

In the year that Schelling died, Feuerbach wrote:

Feeling is the dream of Nature; and there is nothing more blissful, nothing more profound than dreaming. In dreaming, the active is the passive, the passive the active ... Dreaming is a double refraction of the rays of light; hence its indescribable charm ... Feeling is a dream with the eyes open; religion the dream of waking consciousness: dreaming is the key to the mysteries of religion.[35]

33 *Ibid.*, 184.
34 Claude Lévi-Strauss, *Introduction to the Work of Marcel Mauss*, 65.
35 Ludwig Feuerbach, *The Essence of Christianity*, trans. George Eliot (London: 1854), 140.

This emphasis on *ahnung*, presentiment or feeling, and imagination in the age of Romanticism is not simply a reaction against the Enlightenment preoccupation with reason, but also a critical response to Kant's refutation of the ontological proof, in which Kant demonstrated, according to Feuerbach, that "Human reason cannot constitute itself an object of sense."[36] Many years later Cassirer will write that: "Not the world, not objective existence and happenings are the scene of myth and religion, nor do religious tales pretend to be giving information on that score . . . the active subject of mythology is to be sought in human consciousness and not somewhere outside it."[37] And Lévi-Strauss will tell us that:

We have to resign ourselves to the fact that the myths tell us nothing instructive about the order of the world, the nature of reality or the origin and destiny of mankind. We cannot expect them to flatter any metaphysical thirst, or breathe new life into exhausted ideologies. On the other hand . . . lastly and most importantly, they make it possible to discover certain operational modes of the human mind, which have remained so constant over the centuries . . . that we can assume them to be fundamental . . . and show nature is thereby illuminated.

Finally, Lévi-Strauss will conclude that: "Ritual is not a reaction to life; it is a reaction to what thought has made of life. It is not a direct response to the world, or even to experience of the world; it is a response to what man thinks of the world. What, in the last resort, ritual seeks to overcome is not the resistance of the world to man, but the resistance of man's thought to man himself."[38]

As Alexander Smith wrote: "the essential character, however, of a poetical narrative or description, and that which distinguishes it from a merely prosaic one, is this – that its direct object is not to convey information."[39] Malinowski only updated Alexander Smith when he wrote that "Studied alive, myth . . . is not an explanation in satisfaction of a scientific interest, but a narrative of a primeval reality . . . it is not an intellectual explanation or an artistic imagery, but a pragmatic charter of primitive faith and moral wisdom."[40] In brief, you do not read myths for information.

---

[36] *Ibid.*, 200.
[37] Ernst Cassirer, *The Problem of Knowledge* (New Haven, CT: Yale University Press, 1950), 304.
[38] Claude Lévi-Strauss, *The Naked Man* (New York: Harper & Row, 1981), 639, 681.
[39] Quoted in Abrams, *The Mirror and the Lamp*, 152.
[40] Malinowski, *Magic, Science and Religion*, 101.

Throughout all the modifications, complexities, and disagreements among scholars in the study of religion for the past two-hundred years, one basic, theoretical, assumption has endured for interpreting religion. Its names are legion – "religious experience," "presentiment," "numinous feeling," "pre-rational," "non-rational," "non-logical," "collective unconscious," or "non-propositional." In any of these forms, it assumes the status of "the given," as endorsed by C. I. Lewis and H. H. Price, and critiqued by Wilfrid Sellars. The "given," according to scholars who appeal to it, is one of the oldest, most universal insights we have. It is thought to be made up of two components: the immediate data of experience (sensation or feeling, for example) and the form, structure, or conceptual scheme which interprets this immediate content. The two, content and schema, are independent of each other and thus it seems evident why the immediately given must be "non-rational" or "non-propositional."

But this is fatal since it renders the content of "the given" ineffable and incomprehensible. Moreover, what is ineffable and incomprehensible cannot provide us with any clue to the meaning of religion, let alone knowledge of the foundation on which religion, according to this assumption, itself has its origin. If the content of the given is non-propositional, then translation or interpretation becomes impossible. It is not only myths, rituals, and religious beliefs, but also all interpretations of them that would be beyond the truth-conditions of ordinary language. To borrow Feyerabend's phrase, "anything goes." One could equally conclude that the history of religions is a "rationalization" of the flux of the given (Weber), or that religious beliefs and practices are best interpreted "as if" they were true models of and for "reality" (Geertz), or, most simply, that religion is meaningless (Sperber).

The best evidence for the failure of what could be called the Romantic tradition of interpretation is the complete lack of agreement on an adequate theory of symbol and symbolic meaning since the time of Creuzer's multivolume *Symbolik und Mythologie der alten Völker*. (Creuzer never defined the term and most scholars follow his practice.) Once we understand the basic assumption and the problems raised by thinking of religion as non-rational, as "the given," we can easily understand why this is the case even though the notion of "symbolic meaning" becomes crucial for anyone who accepts this theory.

I think the Tylorian tradition is on the right track. E. B. Tylor may have been mistaken in his stress on religion as a false science, but he was right in thinking that religion, myth, and ritual do indeed claim to provide us with information and do entail truth-conditions. I fully endorse the basic definition of religion that Tylor, Spiro, and Lawson, among others, have defended. My revised version reads as follows:

1 *Religion is a communal system of propositional attitudes and practices that are related to superhuman agents.* Explanation: "superhuman agents" refers to beings that can do things you and I cannot do. The term does *not* automatically refer to "God," "theism," the "supernatural," or "the sacred," still less to metaphysical or theological notions such as "the transcendent," "the ultimate," or "the unconditioned."

2 *A myth is a story with a beginning, middle, and end which was or is transmitted orally about the deeds of superhuman agents.* Explanation: no story, no superhuman being(s), no myth. The salience of "oral transmission" places certain genres, such as novels and science fiction, out of bounds as myths.

3 *Ritual is a system of communal actions consisting of both verbal and non-verbal interactions with a superhuman agent or agents.* Explanation: most habits are not rituals. Ants, bees, birds, and dolphins do not perform rituals since, as far as we know, although they can communicate, they neither interact with superhuman agents nor have a belief system. The life of an ascetic is not excluded from this definition.

The central issue in each of these definitions has to do with the semantics of "superhuman agents." There is a sense in which one can view the entire 200-year history of the study of religion as concerned with this question. The Romantic tradition along with its heirs fashioned one of the most important theories for dealing with the questions concerning belief and action related to superhuman agents. We tend to forget that the notion that religion is non-rational, neither true nor false, is a *theory* of religion. The central point of my argument has been that this very theory, born with and developed by the Romantics, was a direct outgrowth of a confrontation with the language of "superhuman agents." The confrontation originated from within the development of the cultural sciences.

Once we reject the theory of "the given" along with its demand for symbolic meaning as an adequate theory for the interpretation of the language of superhuman agents, we are forced back to a fundamental principle – sentence meaning is literal meaning. Adopting that principle from within a holistic theory, we can conclude that myth and ritual do indeed entail information and the information is false. How this information is *used* is a different issue. There may be as many different uses of religion as there are uses of language within the constraints of a particular language and community.

In conclusion, there are two important points to be stressed for the study of religion. First, we have yet to fully understand the revolution brought about by the disclosure of the error in accepting "the myth of the given." The power of this doctrine is widespread among students of religion. It is assumed in most interpretations of religion as a representation, symbol, projection, worldview, or ideology of certain feelings or experiences. It can also be found in interpretations of religion as a representation or projection of an infrastructure, or of the sacred, or of anything else the scholar believes is "the given" found in the schemas of the history of religions. There is a sense in which one can interpret what has become known as "postmodernism" as an attempt to correct the error of appealing to "the given." We need not become mired, however, in the many avenues of "incommensurability" constructed by this movement. The correction I have proposed is the construction of a semantics of religion that fully acknowledges the satisfaction of truth-conditions in the meaningful discourse and narrative that we call religion. There is a simple test, consisting of one question, that determines where an author stands on this issue: what is the meaning of superhuman agents in religious belief and discourse?

Finally, we have yet to fully grasp the theoretical importance of clearly distinguishing between sentence meaning and sentence use, between competence and performance, semantics and pragmatics, or, as Saussure put it, the difference between language and speech, the synchronic and the diachronic. When we do, we will also understand that the best explanation of the meaning of religion begins by taking its sentences literally.

9

Religion as a "mobile army of metaphors"

Nancy K. Frankenberry

> What then is truth? A mobile army of metaphors, metonyms, and anthropomorphisms – in short, a sum of human relations, which have been enhanced, transposed, and embellished poetically and rhetorically, and which after long use seem firm, canonical, and obligatory to a people.
>
> Nietzsche[1]

Since Nietzsche, the mobile army conscripted for duty under the banner of "religious truth" has been thought to be largely "symbolic." As linguistic phenomena, metaphors, metonyms, and anthropomorphisms make their appearances in sentences, whose meaning is now widely regarded as "symbolic meaning." But, whereas Nietzsche's description of truth is redolent with denunciation and nostalgia ("metaphors which are worn out and without sensuous power; coins which have lost their pictures and now matter only as metal, no longer as coins"), the vitality of notions of "symbolic truth" and "symbolic meaning" remains undisturbed among most students of religion today.

Various reasons have been given for the inescapability of symbolic language in religion, but few writers have distilled these into methodological principles for the comparative scholar of religion as unequivocally as Mircea Eliade. His recommendations boil down to the following six assertions: (1) Religious symbols reveal a "modality of the real" that is not evident on the level of immediate experience. (2) Religious symbols point to something "real," equivalent to "the sacred," and imply an ontology. (3) Religious symbols are multivalent, expressive of a number of simultaneous meanings. (4) Religious symbols disclose a certain unity of the world, and provide a "destiny" and "integrating function"

---

[1] Friedrich Nietzsche, "On Truth and Lies in an Extra-Moral Sense," in Walter Kaufmann (ed.), *The Portable Nietzsche* (New York: Viking Press, 1954), 42.

for human agents. (5) Religious symbols have the capacity for expressing paradoxical situations or structures of "ultimate reality" that are otherwise inexpressible. (6) Religious symbols not only unveil a "structure of reality" or a "dimension of existence," but they also bring "a meaning into human existence."[2]

Every one of these statements is contentious. So influential has been Eliade's approach, however, that this set of assumptions has congealed in the shape of what might be called The Theology of Symbolic Forms. Under the large umbrella of this school, a variety of symbolic formists in addition to Eliadeans find shelter. I would include, for example, Geertzians, Tillichians, Ricoeurians, as well as champions of "perennial philosophy" and various proponents of apophatic theology.[3] The Nietzschean view that truth and metaphor come to the same thing surfaces in The Theology of Symbolic Forms as the idea that "religious truth" consists in a mobile army of metaphors. No one denies, of course, that extensive use of metaphors and metonyms and their transformations occurs in all religions. If metaphors are defined as conventional symbols of similarity across domains, and metonyms are symbols of similarity within the same domain, then *A* stands for *B* by association in metaphor, and as parts stand for a whole in metonymy. Non-linguistic symbols also abound in religious traditions and pose no deep problem of interpretation; symbols of place, for instance, such as the Temple Mount or Westminster Abbey serve as symbols for Israel or England. It is important, however, to distinguish the commonplace and unproblematic claim that religious systems use objects, events, or geography representationally, from the very different and problematic claim that religious language has symbolic meaning. The argument of this chapter is that the role played by metaphors, metonyms, and anthropomorphisms in linguistic communication cannot

[2] Mircea Eliade, "Methodological Remarks on the Study of Religious Symbolism," 86–107 in Mircea Eliade and Joseph M. Kitagawa (eds.), *The History of Religions: Essays in Methodology*, with preface by Jerald C. Brauer (University of Chicago Press, 1959). I am indebted to Hans Penner for calling this source to my attention. Cf. his "Interpretation," in Willi Braun and Russell T. McCutcheon (eds.), *Guide to the Study of Religion* (London and New York: Cassell, 2000): 62–63. For a critique of Eliade along these lines, see Ivan Strenski, *Four Theories of Myth in Twentieth-Century History* (University of Iowa Press, 1987).

[3] Here I am not concerned to analyze the work of particular theologians or schools of thought, but to critique a generalized picture on the part of writers who agree with Paul Ricoeur's theory that expressions have multiple, or second, symbolic meanings in addition to a primary, literal, manifest meaning. According to Ricoeur, "symbols have their own semantics, they stimulate an intellectual activity of deciphering, of finding a hidden meaning." See Paul Ricoeur, *Freud and Philosophy: An Essay on Interpretation* (New Haven, CT: Yale University Press, 1970), 19.

properly be understood as comprising something called "symbolic meaning."

Radical interpretation, as I will develop it here, offers a challenge to the very idea of symbolic meaning in religion and to the presumption that there is another *kind* of meaning over and above, and in addition to, literal meaning. Sometimes termed "symbolic meaning," or "religious meaning," or "metaphorical sense," the target of my critique is anything presumed to offer a second, different, hidden meaning or code that needs to be interpreted or decoded.

As a rule, the chief perpetuators of Symbolic Formism have been theologians and anthropologists. Both groups have undertaken the task of probing behind or beneath the literal meaning of words or sentences in order to bring forth a symbolic or metaphorical meaning. Neither theology nor anthropology, however, has succeeded in explaining the puzzling phenomenon of "thinking mythically" or why people would think "symbolically" in the first place. Certainly mythic thinking does not always recognize itself as a symbol for something else. Native speakers commonly dissent from symbolist interpretations of their beliefs. But The School of Symbolic Forms supposes that *inquiring minds* have always known the gods to be symbols. Anthropologist John Beattie flatly declares that if the natives would only "think deeply" enough about their rituals they would see them as symbolic.[4] Historians of the study of religion are not so sure. Jonathan Z. Smith points out that it was a rare figure during the Enlightenment who recognized that the religion of both the "primitive" and the "ancient" was never allegorical or symbolic. Hans Penner notes that Beattie and other symbolists, well aware that their informants actually authorize a literal reading, wind up denying that the natives know what they are doing; they also overlook the salient detail that "the beliefs are mistaken" if taken as hypothetico-deductive or instrumental.[5]

Anthropologist Robin Horton, another critic of symbolist interpretations of religion, puts the point forcefully: "Surely all the evidence from fieldwork in religious cultures is that, when men talk about the gods, they are talking about beings that are as real to them as men and women, sticks and stones, rivers and mountains. Surely all the

---

[4] John Beattie, "Ritual and Social Change," *Man* 1 (1966): 69–70.
[5] See J. Z. Smith, *To Take Place* (University of Chicago Press, 1987), 101–02; and Hans H. Penner, *Impasse and Resolution: A Critique of the Study of Religion* (New York, Bern: Peter Lang Publishing, 1989), 70–71.

evidence is that when people say their crops have been destroyed by the anger of the gods or prospered by their approval, they are talking literally."[6] Still more emphatically, physicist Richard Dawkins has inveighed against liberal theologians who insist that nowadays religion has moved on from the man with a long white beard who resides in a physical space called heaven. Heaven is not a physical place, and God does not have a physical body where a beard might sit, Dawkins says he has been told. "Well, yes, admirable," he responds, "separate magisteria, real convergence. But the doctrine of the Assumption was defined as an Article of Faith by Pope Pius XII as recently as November 1, 1950, and is binding on all Catholics. It clearly states that the body of Mary was taken into heaven and reunited with her soul. What can that mean, if not that heaven is a physical place containing bodies?" He repeats: "This is not a quaint and obsolete tradition with just a symbolic significance. It has officially, and recently, been declared to be literally true."[7] Perhaps it was with such examples in mind that Leszek Kolakowski could open his ardent little book, *Religion*, by announcing: "The questions I am going to examine will be discussed on the shallow assumption that what people mean in religious discourse is what they ostensibly mean."[8]

Post-Enlightment liberal theological interpretations of religious systems have been dominated by the symbolic method of interpretation, as earlier ones were by allegorical interpretation. Modernity's shifting plausibility conditions, along with recognition of the constitutive role of metaphors, metonyms, and anthropomorphisms in religious language, left liberal theology with little choice but to treat the language of religion symbolically and not literally. When it came to something like kinship systems, explanation could be sought in empirical infrastructures and their social and economic relations, but when it came to explaining the gods, goddesses, spirits, angels, demons, and heavenly realms that populate religious literature, no such explanation was available. The method of interpreting religion in terms of symbolic forms assumed the presence of hidden meanings, indirectly expressed in symbolic representations. It was largely a defensive posture on the part of liberal theology in the wake of the masters of suspicion whose causal explanations aimed to uncover the "real" meaning of religion in symbolic representations of society (Durkheim), or consolation and legitimation (Marx), or infantile

---

[6] Robin Horton, *Patterns of Thought in Africa and the West* (Cambridge University Press, 1993), 114.
[7] Richard Dawkins, "Snake Oil and Holy Water," *Forbes ASAP*, October 4, 1999.
[8] Leszek Kolakowski, *Religion* (London: Collins/Fontana, 1982), 15–16.

illusion (Freud). Liberal theology proved powerless to show the superiority of its interpretations over these alternatives so long as it held that "something" is given in religious experience or texts that "has" a definite meaning content interpreters must grasp if they are to get the message. Symbols thus came to be treated as though they were vehicles that carry meaning, like cargo on a freight train, or a virus in a computer program. A laborious amount of intellectual labor went into the study of symbolic systems as though they harbored hidden meanings and encoded messages that needed to be cracked. This assumed, in some form, the existence of a language from which the code was constituted and from which it could be decoded. But what was that language? And what was the means for extracting it?

For the study of religion, the principal problem with The Theology of Symbolic Forms has been twofold. The assumption of hidden meanings or uncracked codes makes it difficult to explain (1) why people invest time and effort in an obscure form of communication rather than using more direct expressions; and (2) how it is that most believers remain ignorant of the real meaning, all the while participating in symbolic systems whose meaning is hidden from them and which they do not (on this assumption) comprehend. Several decades ago, anthropologist Dan Sperber presented a persuasive critique of traditional semiotic approaches to symbolism, highlighting this twofold explanatory difficulty.[9] Approaches to semantics concerned with arriving at appropriate interpretations by decoding the symbolic material fail for several reasons, according to Sperber. First, symbols are so multivalent that it is impossible to pair them with their interpretations. The underlying code is not essentially the same for all, and there is too much variability of symbolic material and of individual appropriation to allow it to be construed in terms of a code. Second, symbol systems fail to supply their own algorithm for assigning interpretations to symbols on any systematic basis; they never wear their meanings on their sleeves, and attempts to interpret them only produce additional layers of symbolic material rather than elucidation of the original layers, thus extending the problem but not solving it. Third, religious actors like the Dorze of Ethiopia typically do not worry about the correct exegesis of symbols but will engage in symbolic activities without any interpretative schemes for them at all. The standard semiotic approach would cast doubt on the rationality of the participants, committing what one anthropologist has

9 See Dan Sperber, *Rethinking Symbolism* (Cambridge University Press, 1994), esp. ch. 2.

called "the cardinal interpretative sin of flouting the actor's point of view."[10]

In sum, two main paths diverge in the interpretive road and one cannot travel both. Either the interpreter attempts to naturalize or rationalize the meaning of beliefs about superhuman agents in conformity with conditions in the actual world (the path of liberal theology), or the interpreter takes religious utterances at face value and accords literal meaning to language about superhuman agents. The first method saves the appearances, but flouts the actor's point of view.[11] The second method, more common in historical or anthropological studies of religion, saves the actor's point of view, but flaunts the "patent falsity" of religious language.

In Sperber's analysis, particular symbols have *no* meanings to decode, and we should not therefore be surprised that most natives employ meaningless symbol systems uncomprehendingly. Whether one finds Sperber's conclusion too pessimistic or not depends on one's estimate of the possibilities for developing a semantic theory of symbolic meaning.[12] Those who prefer Sperber's verdict (symbols do not *mean* at all) to The Theology of Symbolic Forms (symbols mean something transcendent) should find the case for holism compelling.[13]

Common to versions of holism is the claim that meaning is located, not in isolated elements that form building blocks, but in the relations among the elements. The primary bearers of meaning are sentences, and sentences have meaning only in relation to other sentences. Scholars

[10] Robin Horton, "Tradition and Modernity Revisited," in M. Hollis and S. Lukes (eds.), *Rationality and Relativism* (Oxford: Blackwell, 1982), 201–60. Of course Horton's own way of drawing an analogy between the Kalabari gods and waterspirits and "Western" theoretical entities commits the same sin. The Kalabari regard the gods and waterspirits as real objects, with undoubted existence, hardly theoretical, whereas Horton claims they are analogous to theoretical objects.

[11] I have in mind here primarily Wiemanian, Whiteheadian, and historicist naturalisms that expressly eliminate superhuman agents from their theology. See, for example, Charley Hardwick, *Events of Grace: Naturalism, Existentialism, and Theology* (Cambridge University Press, 1996), David Griffin, *Reenchantment Without Supernaturalism: A Process Philosophy of Religion* (Ithaca, NY: Cornell University Press, 2000), and Sheila Davaney, *Pragmatic Historicism: A Theology for the Twenty-First Century* (Albany: State University of New York Press, 2000).

[12] See Sperber, *Rethinking Symbolism*, ch. 1; and Sperber, *On Anthropological Knowledge* (Cambridge University Press, 1983), 72, 83–84. Penner, in *Impasse and Resolution*, criticizes Sperber's verdict on the "meaninglessness" of symbols as a mistake, based on a theory of meaning derived from logical positivism.

[13] This section summarizes material in my chapter, "On the Very Idea of Symbolic Meaning," in J. Harley Chapman and Nancy Frankenberry (eds.), *Interpreting Neville* (Albany: State University of New York Press, 1999). Robert C. Neville's theology is the most sophisticated development available of a theory of religious symbols. See R. C. Neville, *The Truth of Broken Symbols* (Albany: State University of New York Press, 1996), as well as his reply to my criticisms, in Neville, "Responding to My Critics," *Interpreting Neville*, 299–304.

across a wide variety of disciplines using holistic analysis in semantics have demonstrated that the elimination of reference does not imply that symbolic–cultural systems and religious systems in particular have no *meaning* at all.[14] While traditional (i.e., empiricist) techniques for the semantic analysis of natural language in terms of reference and truth have not proved productive in the treatment of symbolic systems, it has become clear that holistic strategies are able to purchase meaning without reference.[15] As one variation on holism, Donald Davidson's holism, truth-conditional semantics, and "anomalous monism" provide important resources for considering central issues in the study of religion, in particular for the question I am raising about "symbolic meaning."

Reinforcing Sperber's conclusion from another direction, Davidson's controversial essay, "What Metaphors Mean," argues for a metaphors-without-meaning view. As encapsulated by Eva Kittay, the argument runs as follows:

(1) Meaning in language is context-free. (2) Aspects of language which are not context-free are not questions of language meaning but of language use. (3) Metaphorical interpretation is context-bound, hence it is not a question of meaning but a question of use. (4) Therefore there is no meaning of metaphorical utterances beyond their literal meaning. (5) If there is only literal meaning of metaphorical utterances, then any cognitive content they possess must be expressible in a literal utterance. (6) Whatever is interesting about metaphor must therefore lie in a use of language and cannot be a question of an unparaphraseable cognitive content.[16]

Two major conclusions emerge here. The first has to do with what metaphor *means* and the second with what metaphor *does*. For *semantic theory*, there is nothing at all interesting about metaphors beyond the

---

[14] See, for example, E. Thomas Lawson and Robert N. McCauley, *Rethinking Religion: Connecting Cognition and Culture* (Cambridge University Press, 1990).

[15] See, for example, Donald Davidson, "The Inscrutability of Reference," in *Inquiries into Truth and Interpretation* (Oxford University Press), 227–41 and "Reality Without Reference," *ibid.*, 215–25. The holism of the mental implicates not only beliefs but also wishes, hopes, desires, emotions, and fears.

[16] See Eva Feder Kittay, *Metaphor: Its Cognitive Force and Linguistic Structure* (Oxford: Clarendon Press, 1987), 97–98. Kittay uses this argument as a foil to her own "relational theory of meaning" that challenges Davidson's truth-theoretic semantics and hence his view of metaphor. Although I cannot resolve the differences between Kittay and Davidson here, I think that the general requirement that a semantics be truth-conditional offers an option worth exploring in the study of religion. For what it is worth as a theory of truth, Davidson's account seems to me to be already deflationary, fully recognizing the folly of offering any definition, explanation, or property of truth. For doubts about the importance of truth-conditions, see Michael Williams "Meaning and Deflationary Truth," *Journal of Philosophy* 96:11 (1999): 545–64. Among the authors in the present volume, Stout, Godlove, Rorty, and Penner have all disputed Kittay's first claim that Davidson holds that meaning in language is context-free.

literal meaning of the utterance or proposition. For a theory of language *use*, on the other hand, the interesting feature of metaphor is its ability to make us see things in a new light. Depending on which of these conclusions one emphasizes, two different paths open up with respect to the interpretation of religious language. As most commentators have emphasized the second conclusion, I want to call attention to the first argument that metaphor, "the dreamwork of language," only means "what the words, in their most literal interpretation mean, and nothing more."[17] This aspect of Davidson's work is important for critiquing the idea of symbolic and metaphorical meanings as special *kinds* of meaning. The relevant argument occurs in a striking passage in "What Metaphors Mean" where Davidson says:

Where [previous theorists] think they provide a method for deciphering an encoded content, they actually tell us (or try to tell us) something about the *effects* metaphors have on us. The common error is to fasten on the contents of the thoughts a metaphor provokes and to read these contents into the metaphor itself... If what the metaphor makes us notice were finite in scope and propositional in nature, this would not in itself make trouble; we would simply project the content the metaphor brought to mind onto the metaphor. But in fact there is no limit to what a metaphor calls to our attention, and much of what we are called to notice is not propositional in character. When we try to say what a metaphor "means," we soon realize there is no end to what we want to mention. If someone draws his finger along a coastline on a map, or mentions the beauty and deftness of a line in a Picasso etching, how many things are drawn to your attention? You might list a great many, but you could not finish since the idea of finishing would have no clear application.[18]

Rejecting the idea of metaphorical meaning as "encoded content" opens up a new avenue for the critique of religious utterances regarded as having or expressing "symbolic meaning." Over and above the literal meaning, such utterances have nothing in the way of a distinct cognitive content that it is necessary to grasp. Metaphors are uses of language and not the carriers or containers of "meanings" that need to be retrieved, deduced, or decoded. Beyond the literal meaning of the sentence, there is no other second, different, higher, or hidden meaning. In metaphor, words do not lose their literal meaning, Davidson argues, or the force of the metaphor would be lost. Moreover, rationalization of the sentence's metaphoric quality is not accomplished by adverting to speaker's meaning. Instead, the interpretative activity is located in the reader of

[17] Donald Davidson, "What Metaphors Mean," in *Inquiries into Truth and Interpretation*, 245.
[18] *Ibid.*, 262–63.

the metaphor, who must calibrate a series of novel and provocative jux-
tapositions of objects and ideas. The metaphoric function consists in
prompting precisely those novel relationships, which the patently false
expression causes one to notice.

What Davidson says of metaphor may be applied to its use in religious
language: there is no fixed content or meaning to be retrieved. If there is
only the literal meaning of metaphorical utterances, then any cognitive
content that religious metaphors and symbolic statements possess must
be expressible in a literal utterance. What catches our interest or causes
our puzzlement in the case of religious language, then, cannot be a
matter of an unparaphrasable cognitive content, but rather of "what we
are caused to notice."

Extending this analysis to include theological language, we would expect to find that symbolic language, if this is the language of theology,
may at best suggest, intimate, or get people to notice things, but *it does not
carry meaning*. From this perspective, much standard Christian theology
appears to be involved in the very confusion promoted by I. A. Richards'
and Max Black's "usual view" of metaphor. "On the one hand,"
Davidson complains, "the usual view wants to hold that a metaphor
does something no plain prose can possibly do and, on the other hand, it
wants to explain what a metaphor does by appealing to a cognitive content – just the sort of thing plain prose is designed to express."[19] Treating
metaphorical meaning as a different *kind* of meaning is troubling, according to Davidson, because it suggests a second track alongside of and
yet somehow beyond literal meaning, one in which "the message may be
considered more exotic, profound, or cunningly garbed."[20] But if what
distinguishes metaphor is not meaning but *use*, it cannot be used to "say
something" more profound, not even indirectly. "For a metaphor *says*
only what shows on its face – usually a patent falsehood or an absurd
truth."[21] This criticism illuminates the semantic confusions created, for
example, by Paul Tillich's systematic theology of God as "Being-Itself"
beyond conceptualization, by Reinhold Niebuhr's rehabilitation of biblical symbols so that they could be taken "seriously but not literally," and
by Rudolf Bultmann's demythologizing program that was unable to say
what "Resurrection" meant once it was no longer thought of as the resus-
citation of a dead corpse. Symbolists and non-literalists must deny the
possibility of paraphrase, but, as Davidson points out, the only way they
or we can say what the metaphorical meaning is, is by paraphrasing it, in

[19] *Ibid.*, 261.   [20] *Ibid.*, 246.   [21] *Ibid.*, 258.

which case we would make it literal, thus denying that it is metaphorical or symbolic after all. A better reason for maintaining that metaphors are not paraphrasable, Davidson suggests, is because a metaphor does not *say* anything different from its literal meaning. Symbolic Formists, perhaps reluctant to reverse the logic by which the decline of religion's literal sense permitted the discovery of its symbolic sense, falter when asked what their exotic tropes and symbols *mean*. Most answers tend to posit the presence of a non-language-like meaning that lies beyond speech.

On the metaphor-without-meaning view, religious metaphors and symbolically expressed statements are like lies or jokes. They can be treated like the use of italics, or illustrations, or odd punctuation, rather than as a way of conveying a message. Special *use* of literal meaning may intimate a new insight that might cause something to be seen in a new light. But religious speakers who utter metaphorical sentences can *mean* only what those sentences mean literally. Metaphors and symbols may make us see one thing as another, or the same thing in a different light, and thus cause us to alter our belief about it, as when, in John Wisdom's classic paper "The Logic of God," one woman says to another who is trying on a hat: "My dear, it's the Taj Mahal." The meaning is literally false, but the novel usage prompts insight. Like Wittgenstein's duck–rabbit example, this "dawning of an aspect" induces a "seeing-as" experience. What is the character of that insight? Wittgenstein arrived at no notable or clear conclusions as to this phenomenon, but Davidson is definite: "The difficulty is more fundamental. What we notice or see is not, in general, propositional in character."[22]

For example, the metaphorical invitation in the sentence "the world is the body of God" can *mean* only what the sentence means literally, namely, that the world is a biodegradable physical system that forms the corpus of a superhuman agent. As uttered or written by ecological theologians, process theists, and Gaia enthusiasts, however, the sentence can be used to *intimate* something about the world. Like the Wordsworthian intimation of "something far more deeply interfused," the metaphor of the world as the body of God may prompt a seeing-as process of a vaguely pantheistic vision. There is no reason why that vision could not be conveyed by literal statements of the author's or speaker's pantheistic beliefs. It seems unlikely, however, that anything formal or general can be said about such visions or intimations. Neither hermeneutical theory

---

[22] *Ibid.*, 263. See John Wisdom, *Paradox and Discovery* (Oxford: Blackwell, 1965).

nor theological construction stands to gain much here, for if there can be no formal account of *use*, there can be no possibility of a theory of religious metaphors. What a metaphor "conveys" is a causal effect of its use, largely non-propositional, the product of a non-rule-governed creative skill on the part of individual theological poets. It would be odd to ask for a "theory of intimation" in religion.

Taking up this view of metaphor in religious language does not assign any special privilege to literal meaning, but only denies there is a special *kind* of meaning that is metaphorical or symbolic. Without the assumption of such meanings we will not be led to the paradoxical result that the *same* sentence in religious texts or utterances is held to be literally false yet metaphorically or symbolically "true." But now, having ruled out recourse to this paradox, we confront the horns of another dilemma. On the one hand, if it accepts the literal meaning of its metaphorical and symbolic statements, The Theology of Symbolic Forms must face up to the way in which those sentences are "usually false." Perched on the other horn, if they emphasize the non-literal use and creative force of religious metaphors and symbols in priming people to see things in a new light, Symbolic Formists will recognize that this is largely a matter of "raids on the inarticulate" that yield at best only "hints and guesses," precluding any comprehensive theory or theology.

"Generally," according to Davidson, "it is only when a sentence is taken to be false that we accept it as metaphor and start to hunt out the hidden implication. It is probably for this reason that most metaphorical sentences are *patently* false, just as all similes are trivially true." In this light, the only semantic conclusion to take from Davidson's theory is bluntly put by historian of religions Hans Penner: "the content of religious language is *patently* false."[23]

Another conclusion to take from "What Metaphors Mean" is that Davidson has made a compelling case but an incomplete one. What about the non-propositional effects of metaphor that result in a new seeing-as? How does the transition occur from the living uses to the dead literal meanings? Most importantly, how do *new* religious uses of language happen so that eventual semantic shifts are possible over time? Since it is evident that religious folk and cognoscenti alike do not simply utilize the tools already at hand, endlessly rehashing the faith of the fathers, some

---

[23] For "usually false," see *ibid.*, 257; for "patently false," *ibid.*, 258. For Penner, see "Why Does Semantics Matter to the Study of Religion?" *Method and Theory in the Study of Religion*, 7:3, 1995: 247.

space must be afforded for the fact that old words like "God" or "moksha" get used in dramatically new sentences. Presumably, Davidsonians would relegate such questions to the desk of Wittgensteinians because they fall outside the bounds of semantic theory. Commanding both desks, Richard Rorty has sketched an original theory of cultural change in which strong poets, revolutionary scientists, and edifying philosophers toss off new metaphors that catch on, alter the environment, and, when successful, survive as literalizations.

Like Davidson, Rorty thinks that metaphors have no cognitive content or special meaning, but, unlike Davidson, he is interested in their role in effecting cultural change. Davidson's account of metaphor is useful, Rorty says, because it "lets us see metaphors on the model of unfamiliar events in the natural world – *causes* of changing beliefs and desires – rather than on the model of *representations* of unfamiliar worlds, worlds which are 'symbolic' rather than 'natural.'"[24] Metaphors, then, are not so much structures for intentional semantic change as they are leaps from one language game or vocabulary to another. "Nietzschean history of culture, and Davidsonian philosophy of language, see language as we now see evolution, as new forms of life constantly killing off old forms – not to accomplish a higher purpose, but blindly," according to Rorty.[25]

Rorty's interest in metaphor is part of his more comprehensive project of exploring the effects of metaphors as causal agents in intellectual history. Especially in "Unfamiliar Noises: Hesse and Davidson on Metaphor" and "Philosophy, as Science, as Metaphor, and as Politics," he draws on Davidson's account of metaphor to tell the story of successive cultural changes in science, philosophy, and literature. The main outlines ought to be applicable to the problem of expanding the logical space within religious traditions, too, so that large-scale conceptual change is accounted for as much in religion as in other cultural areas.

Rather than developing the literal–metaphorical contrast, Rorty prefers to contrast familiar and unfamiliar noises, or common and uncommon uses. Picturing the proper domain of semantics as "a relatively small 'cleared' area" defined by the "regular, predictable, linguistic behavior" which constitutes the literal use of language, Rorty contrasts it with the "jungle of use." Here metaphorical utterances are "mere stimuli,

[24] Richard Rorty, "Unfamiliar Noises: Hesse and Davidson on Metaphor," in *Objectivity, Relativism, and Truth* (Cambridge University Press, 1991), 163.
[25] Richard Rorty, *Contingency, Irony, and Solidarity* (Cambridge University Press, 1989), 19. Vocabularies, not propositions, are the proper unit of persuasion according to Rorty, and vocabularies, by and large, are "poetic achievements," 78, 77.

mere evocations," non-cognitive causes that do not count as intentional, rational actions. As long as they are alive, metaphors are just jungle noises which, like anomalous natural phenomena, can only be understood or interpreted by revising our antecedent theories to fit them. Rorty thinks metaphors tossed off by creative genuises may serve to expand the range of possibilities by inventing unfamiliar sentences that tempt a rising generation to try a whole new vocabulary. The living metaphors are causes, not reasons, for changes of belief. Dead metaphors no longer count as metaphors. They have become literalized.[26] Although he does not put it this way himself, one could imagine a Rortyan account of powerful new metaphors in religious contexts that result from the genius of strong poets like Buddha or Jesus or Muhammad who reinvent an existing vocabulary. Their new metaphors are not necessarily better or truer. They just happen to catch on. Saying that they catch on, however, is only the beginning of analysis. Historians of religion and others, impressed with the groundlessness and contingency of the beliefs that they study, will also want to ask about the context and conditions that provoke such beliefs.

This approach offers one way of allowing for the fact that the repertoire of religious texts and propositional attitudes over time gets creatively rewritten, either added to or abandoned, according to a process of natural selection from one historical epoch to the next. Plainly, there is something new under the semantic sun from Maimonides to Mortimer Kaplan. A Rortyan theory of religious metaphors would differ from a Davidsonian one primarily in understanding religious metaphors as "a growing point of language," one of three ways – along with perception and inference – in which a new belief can be added to the old stockpile of beliefs and desires.[27] Living religious metaphors – such as "the world is the body of God" – are an unfamiliar noise. Although their only *meaning* is literal meaning, they are useful in revising standard linguistic habits and reweaving the web of beliefs.

On a Rortyan account of religious metaphors, then, we would not *interpret* them – as though unlocking a meaning other than their literal one – but we could *explain* metaphors. We would see them as non-semantic causal triggers for changing from one familiar vocabulary or language game to another, less familiar one. The patent falsity of such

---

[26] I am prescinding for now from the problem of the imprecision of the line between living and dead metaphors and the question of whether the process of literalization of a living metaphor into a dead one should be construed as gradual or sudden. See Rorty, *Objectivity, Relativism, and Truth*, 171.

[27] Richard Rorty, *Essays on Heidegger and Others* (Cambridge University Press, 1991), 12–13.

sentences is a signal that something experimental is afoot. We are on the verge of some provocation, or groping to create a new self-image. Perhaps a whole new vocabulary is groaning into being in a time of world-historical change. According to Rorty:

Tossing a metaphor into a conversation is like suddenly breaking off the conversation long enough to make a face, or pulling a photograph out of your pocket and displaying it, or pointing at a feature of the surroundings, or slapping your interlocutor's face, or kissing him. Tossing a metaphor into a text is like using italics, or illustrations, or odd punctuation or formats. All these are ways of producing effects on your interlocutor or your reader, but not ways of conveying a message.[28]

That is, if you do not read a myth for information, neither do you use metaphors to convey messages that cannot be stated literally. Instead of thinking of metaphors as being interchangeable with a set of sentences, Rorty sees them as providing two challenges, first, to "redistribute truth-values among familiar sentences," and, second, to "invent further unfamiliar sentences."[29]

The primary impetus for this view of metaphor-as-agent-of-change is the need to have something new under the semantic sun. Rorty's view accommodates the ongoing belief revision that occurs in religious communities, and is able to construe theological revolutions as reweaving a community's web of belief, gradually assimilating and literalizing the new metaphors provided by those whose "seemingly crazy suggestions" spark conceptual revolutions and strike some people as "luminous truths."[30] It explains the reconstructive efforts of pragmatist and historicist theologians in taking the living metaphors of their traditions and killing them off so that, dying as metaphors, they might rise again as familiar and common uses. It could also explain the work of contemporary philosophers of religion who, in the tradition of Dewey, try to revamp a vocabulary about "natural piety" and "an attitude of adjustment to the whole" as metaphors intended to get us to think of "the religious" in new ways. These efforts would not then be dismissed by critics simply as "changing the subject" from religion because they happen to omit the distinguishing feature of superhuman agents.

Of principal importance in the Davidsonian approach is its parsimony in not proliferating levels of meaning and truth. By not consigning metaphor to a second, different, or hidden level of meaning in addition

---

[28] Rorty, *Contingency, Irony, and Solidarity*, 18.
[29] Rorty, *Essays on Heidegger and Others*, 14, n. 16.   [30] *Ibid.*, 15.

to literal meaning, it blocks the well-trod path taken by many religious apologists in pursuit of two levels of "truth." Of principal importance in the Rortyan approach is the non-teleological view it affords of the history of religious language and of intellectual history in general. This opens up a logical space in the jungle of uncommon uses for reinventing uses of religious language, or substitutions for it, where arresting, abnormal speech can deliver sharp critiques of selected literal meanings in the history of religion. Scholars of religion who follow through on Davidson's approach will interpret the mobile army of religious myths, metaphors, and symbols as false, thus upholding the spirit if not the letter of Nietzsche's critique. Scholars of religion who follow through on Rorty's emphasis will find that, a science of interpretation being out of the question, attention falls to the force and uses of religious metaphors, of which only a partial account is ever possible.

The metaphor-is-false approach and the metaphor-is-agent-of-change approach, though distinct emphases, are complementary avenues of analysis. The study of religion needs both as it seeks to understand the semantics and the pragmatics of religion, uncontaminated by The School of Symbolic Forms.

Taking up Davidson's argument against radically incommensurable schemes, I shall conclude by applying it, with some adaptations, to what I have been calling The Theology of Symbolic Forms. In that school, a key assumption is that the divine aseity, or the Sacred, or the Wholly Other, is utterly transcendent and ineffable. The ineffability of the religious object is the reason that symbols and metaphors and anthropomorphisms are considered the essential mode of religious discourse in the first place. In Western religious thought, the most advanced species of this school appears in the Protestant orientation toward a God who is "Wholly Other," surpassing human understanding and conceptualization, and seen only through a glass darkly. All the gilding and staining of the glass with metaphors, symbols, and anthropomorphisms, however, produces nothing by way of human knowledge. The inscrutability of the God of Luther, Calvin, Kierkegaard, Barth, and Niebuhr has much in common with the idea of an untranslatable radically alien conceptual scheme that Davidson has shown to be incoherent. Indeed, ineffability is the theological version of incommensurability.

If the criticisms in Davidson's paper "On the Very Idea of a Conceptual Scheme" work against radically other, incommensurable conceptual schemes, I suggest that they work also against the supposition of a Wholly Other who surpasses human understanding and can only be talked about symbolically. Compressed into a few key propositions, the logic of Davidson's argument moves in this way:

1 Inability to translate between two languages, in whole or in part, is a necessary condition for their possessing different conceptual schemes.
2 A second condition on there being radically different conceptual schemes is that the two languages said to contain them should recognize each other as languages.
3 The only way to know an alternative conceptual scheme exists is to describe or translate it, in which case it is shown to be not really different from the one in which the description or translation is couched.
4 Therefore, in the absence of grounds for distinguishing a conceptual scheme from an alternative conceptual scheme, the distinction collapses.
5 With that, the coherence of the very idea of a conceptual scheme collapses, and with it the coherence of most notions of truth relative to a scheme.
6 Having found no intelligible basis on which it can be said that schemes are different, we cannot intelligibly say that they are one either.[31]

The key to this many-layered argument consists in seeing the conceptual interconnections between truth and translation and belief. By showing that translation depends on general agreement, we can also show the validity of this disjunction: either there will be sufficient agreement on beliefs and meanings and we will be able to translate, or there will be insufficient agreement and we will have to doubt that we are faced with a language at all. Not even partial failure of translation is intelligible, for Davidson, simply because the agreement that is necessary in order to translate at all permeates the entire language and underwrites large-scale correctness of translation. If the Other is enough like us for us to translate, then it makes no sense to suppose there is a portion that we could *not* translate. Mistakes occur, but only against a background that must already be in place in order for anything to be recognized as missing the *correct* translation. Strangeness, we might say, presupposes familiarity.

Although I cannot do justice to it in this space, I believe that Davidson's argument demonstrates the incoherence of the idea of a Wholly Other posited in monotheism. We can either translate and thus share a common

---

[31] See Donald Davidson, "On the Very Idea of a Conceptual Scheme," in *Inquiries into Truth and Interpretation*, 183–98.

ground, in which case there is not anything Wholly Other, or we can
fail to translate, because the Other is Wholly so, and thus fail to identify
anything radically different from us. In either case, we cannot make sense
of the notion that there might be a conceptual scheme impenetrable to
our efforts to understand it. Much of the rationale for claiming that
language about the Wholly Other has symbolic meaning but no literal
application derives from the idea that there could be incommensurable
schemes with truths that ineluctably elude our grasp. But, if Davidson's
argument in "On the Very Idea of a Conceptual Scheme" is correct, it
precludes exactly this possibility.

To summarize the overall view that I have been discussing, the chief
dilemma that The Theology of Symbolic Forms confronts is this: either
a translation can be made of symbolic language, or it cannot. If it is
translatable, then it is possible to say what it "literally means" for it
has a syntax and semantics. But then it is puzzling that just such a
meaning would be coded as a symbolic message in the first place. On
the other hand, if it is not translatable, because the symbolic meaning
is supposed to exceed the literal meaning as something ineffable, then
Symbolic Formists are obligated to explain what the "extra meaning" is,
and how they are in a position to know it is different from any translation
or paraphrase. The School of Symbolic Forms has a poor record with
the second horn of this dilemma, and understandably so: in this case
we are no longer talking about *meaning* at all. On the other hand, any
success Symbolic Formists enjoy with the first horn generates an added
difficulty: once we grasp the non-symbolic meaning, that is, can perform
the translation into literal meaning, the "power" of the symbols is lost in
a way similar to the outcome of successful psychoanalysis when, seeing
through our various rationalizations, we find they no longer work.

Finally, for reasons Davidson shows, it could not be the case that
the world consists in facts that are forever beyond our ken. This does
not in itself warrant the more ambitious conclusion that there is *nothing*
Wholly Other, only that we cannot make sense of the very idea. That is a
stronger conclusion, it seems to me, than merely noting certain practical
difficulties endemic in the human predicament, or the unavoidability of
an anthropocentric view. Precisely because of that very unavoidability,
we can appreciate contingency not as a limitation that *hinders* us from
taking the God's-eye view, but as a condition that precludes there *being* a
God's-eye standpoint at all. This conclusion reinforces other findings in
the modern critique of religion, but has the value of arriving at a familiar
destination from a different starting point and without the liabilities of
empiricist assumptions.

10

Manna, mana everywhere and /∽/∽/∽

Jonathan Z. Smith

The label, historian, is the one I am most comfortable with. That the focus of my interest is the history of religious representations and the history of the academic conceptualizations of religion does not alter this basic self-identification. Historians are a funny kind of folk. Whether of the species "new," or of that sort thereby designated as "old," whether global in their reach or preoccupied with one small segment of human activity, historians share an uncommon faith in the revelatory power of a telling detail, a small item which opens up a complex whole, and which, thereby, entails a larger set of intellectual consequences. Given the anecdotal nature of their enterprise, historians are truly the descendants of Herodotus, and thereby play the role of "anthropologists" in Aristotle's sense of the term: people who delight in telling tales (*logoi*) about other folk (*anthrōpoi*), in a word, gossips (Aristotle, *Nichomachean Ethics*, 1125a5).

Let me begin with one anecdote, taken from the remote field of the textual criticism of Greek manuscripts in which a major preoccupation is the determination of the filiation of late Byzantine copies, understood as a history of errors, based on distinctive or variant readings organized into genealogical stemmata. Günther Zuntz was working on the well-known problem of the relations between two important fourteenth-century codices of Euripides – designated L and P – from the same scriptorium. Which one was the exemplum? Which one was the dependent copy? Among a number of other details, both have a misplaced punctuation mark, an erroneous rhythmical period (a colon) in Euripides, *Helen*, line 95. On June 3, 1960, Zuntz examined this reading in L at the Laurentian Library in Florence. The colon appeared to be of an odd color. After examining the paper manuscript under ultraviolet light, Zuntz asked the librarian, Anna Lenzumi, for her opinion. "She ran her finger over the place – and the 'colon' stuck to her finger. The heat of the lamp had loosened it. It was a tiny piece of straw . . . embedded in the coarse paper." It would appear that the

scribe of P, a more expensive vellum manuscript, had mistakenly copied
L's fragment of straw as a colon, thus proving that P was dependent on
L. What interests me most in this narrative is the denouement. Zuntz
writes, "the piece of straw is kept in a tiny box in the safe of the Laurentian
Library as the decisive piece of evidence."[1] As the visual root (*videns/videre*)
of the latter word, "evidence," indicates, the old Herodotean distinction
between the probity of "seeing (for oneself)" over against "hearing (from
an other)" is still in play, augmented by a characteristic positivism that
holds such evidence to be self-evident. Hence, the scrupulous preser-
vation of the little relic, the small piece of straw. As is so often the
case in historical construction, the contingent accident has proven to
be essential.

One cannot, of course, always count on the sheer presence of an object
to guarantee its interpretative force. It is not the straw's quiddity, but the
character of the argument it entails that is probative.[2]

In this chapter, I should like to examine two instances of evidence
which suggest different modes of significance and evaluation. The first
concerns an episode in biblical narrative; the second is an Oceanic
word/concept which has played a leading role in some anthropological theories of religion. All they have in common is a partial accidental

---

[1] G. Zuntz, *An Inquiry into the Transmission of the Plays of Euripides* (Cambridge, 1965), 14–15. Compare
the use of Zuntz's account in H. Don Cameron, "The Upside-Down Cladogram: Problems in
Manuscript Affiliation," in H. M. Hoenigswald and L. P. Warner (eds.), *Biological Metaphor and
Cladistic Classification: An Interdisciplinary Perspective* (Philadelphia, 1987), 232–33.

[2] As a counter-example of the inappropriate use of a "relic," one might recall the jaw-bone, navel-
string, and genitalia attributed to the Ugandan war-god, Kibuka [Kibuuka], "rescued when the
Mohammedans burned down his temple in the civil wars of 1887–1890," and now preserved
in the Ethnological Museum at Cambridge University. For James George Frazer, although only
in the third edition of *The Golden Bough*, this could be deployed as evidence for his euhemerist
theories, particularly for the origins of Osiris. If there were bodily organs, then Kibuka was
once an historical king, subsequently elevated to the rank of a god. Perhaps the same could be
said for Osiris on the basis of relics associated with the tomb of an early pharoah, excavated
by Amélineau. While stated with all due caution, the fantastic connective tissues of the relevant
paragraphs allow one to eavesdrop on Frazer's associative processes of thought. "We have seen
that at Abydos . . . the tomb of Osiris was identified with the tomb of King Khent . . . and that in
this tomb were found a woman's richly jeweled arm and a human skull lacking the lower jawbone,
which may be the head of the king himself and the arm of his queen . . . *It is possible*, although it
would be very rash to affirm, that Osiris was no other than the historical King Khent . . . that the
skull found in the tomb is the skull of Osiris himself, and that while it reposed in the grave this
missing jawbone was preserved, *like* the jawbone of a dead king in Uganda, as a holy . . . relic in
the neighboring temple. *If that were so*, we should be almost driven to conclude that the bejeweled
woman's arm found in the tomb of Osiris is the arm of Isis." J. G. Frazer, *The Golden Bough*, 3rd edn
(London, 1935), VI, 197–99, with notes (emphasis added). See further the discussion of Frazer's
analogy of the Ugandan and Egyptian materials in B. C. Ray, *Myth, Ritual, and Kingship in Buganda*
(New York–Oxford, 1991), 50–51 and Ray's discussion (pp. 184–88) of the similar treatment in
E. A. W. Budge, *Osiris and the Egyptian Resurrection* (London, 1911), esp. II, 92–96.

homophony across two unrelated language systems. *Manna* and *mana* are what translators call "false friends."

In the biblical case, the evidence's "being-there" is largely uninteresting; in the anthropological case, the evidence's not "being-there" has, for some, not diminished, in the least, the theory's interest. Such an outcome is not incongruent with Penner's taste. On the one hand, it has been difficult, over the years, to interest him in the traditional modes and issues of biblical scholarship; on the other hand, he remains persistently and creatively fascinated with the French anthropological lineage extending from Durkheim to Lévi-Strauss. In either case, this chapter is a moment in our conversations which have continued for more than thirty-five years.

MANNA

Manna, in the material medica, the concentrated juice of some vegetable, naturally exsudating from it, soluble in water, and not inflammable. (*Encyclopaedia Britannica*, 1st edn [1771])

The Jews, however, with the majority of critics, for good reasons are of the opinion that it was a totally different substance from the vegetable manna, and was specially provided by the Almighty for His people. And this is confirmed by the language of our Lord, John 6. (J. N. Brown, *Encyclopedia of Religious Knowledge* [1835])

Although immediate access to the German-born Israeli zoologist's work was made impossible by World War II, and further occluded by its initial announcements in relatively obscure publications, the conservative guild of Anglo-American biblical scholarship was electrified by Frederick Simon Bodenheimer's 1947 English-language summary of his earlier (1927) field researches in the Sinai Peninsula.[3] Manna (or, in Hebrew, *mān*)

---

[3] F. S. Bodenheimer, "The Manna of Sinai," *Biblical Archaeologist*, 10 (1947): 1–6; reprinted G. E. Wright and D. N. Freedman (eds.), *The Biblical Archaeologist Reader* (Garden City, 1961), 1, 76–80. The initial report appeared in F. S. Bodenheimer and O. Theodor, *Ergebnisse der Sinai-Expedition 1927* (Leipzig, 1929), 45–88. This was a survey undertaken when Bodenheimer, son of a distinguished Zionist leader, was Staff Entomologist at the Jewish Agency's agricultural experiment station in Tel Aviv, and published when he was Research Fellow in zoology at Hebrew University, Jerusalem. For an early notice of Bodenheimer's report, see the review by A. Kaiser, "Neue naturwissenschaftliche Forschungen auf der Sinaihalbinsel," *Zeitschrift des deutschen Palästina-Vereins*, 53 (1930), 63–75. While Bodenheimer had wide-ranging interests in biology, ethnology, and the history of zoology, he had special expertise in the *Coccidae* family of scale-insects, publishing a monograph, *The Coccidae of Palestine* (Tel Aviv, 1924), in the series, Zionist Organization Institute of Agriculture and Natural History, Agricultural Experiment Station Bulletin, 1.

It should be noted that some earlier scholars had come half-way to Bodenheimer's thesis, providing an oral rather than a rectal cause, arguing that the manna which exuded from tamarisk is neither the product of some form of Asiatic lichen (e.g., *Lecanora esculenta*) nor an exudation of the tamarisk tree (*Tamariscus gallica*, or *mannifer*), as had been previously argued.[4] It is the excretion, depending on geographic locale, of one of two species of scale-insects – *Trabutina mannipara* in the highlands, *Najacoccus serpentinus* in the lowlands – found as parasites on the stems of tamarisks. As is, perhaps, appropriate for an area of scholarly inquiry whose major publications are classified "BS" in the Library of Congress system, manna turned out to be a form of insect manure. (The latter word is, of course, another "false friend.") Notwithstanding its cloacal origins, manna was, with great relief, pronounced to be not a product of oriental imagination, but rather a fact. "On the basis of these findings, manna production is a biological phenomenon of the dry deserts and steppes."[5] The little insects and the product of their metabolism, like the "little piece of straw," can be preserved in "tiny" boxes in museums and figured in Bible dictionaries.[6]

There is, within the Hebrew Bible manna-narratives, one brief notice of this sort of conservation: "Moses said, 'This is what YHWH has commanded: "Let one omer [of the manna] be kept for future generations in order that they may see the bread with which I fed you in the wilderness when I brought you out of the land of Egypt."' And Moses said to Aaron, 'Take a jar and put an omer of manna in it and place it before YHWH, to be kept for future generations.' Aaron did as YHWH had commanded Moses, and placed it before the Testimony [i.e., the Ark] for safe keeping" (Exodus 16.32–34). Here, the Ark's confines serve as a "cabinet of curiousities," a sort of Ripley's "Believe It or Not" Museum, where strange objects are deposited like manna and, according to Numbers 17.10, Aaron's miraculously budded rod. While this way of telling the tale emphasizes presentness – "here, you can see it" (compare the iron bed of Og in Deuteronomy 3.11) – at the expense of the narrative motif of the extreme perishability of the manna, it concludes with a learned late

---

trees did so as an effect of wounds in their stems resulting from their having been pierced by scale-insects. See, among others, Th. Hardwicke, *Asiatick Researches*, 14 (1801), 182, as cited in A. Macalister, "Manna," in J. Hastings (ed.), *Dictionary of the Bible* (New York, 1900), III, 236. The puncture thesis is still offered in the 1974 printing of the 15th edn of *Encyclopaedia Britannica*, IX, 792, or appears alongside the secretion thesis in *ibid.*, VI, 571.

4 See the summary of these views by S. A. Cooke, "Manna," in T. K. Cheyne and J. S. Black (eds.), *Encyclopaedia Biblica* (New York, 1902), III, 2929–30. Note that these two explanations still recur in the botanist R. W. Schery's article, "Manna," in the 1969 printing of the 14th edn of *Encyclopaedia Britannica*, XIV, 797.

5 Bodenheimer, "The Manna of Sinai," 6. The same sentence appears, without attribution, in J. L. Mihelic, "Manna," *Interpreter's Dictionary of the Bible* (Nashville, 1962), III, 260.

6 See, for example, Bodenheimer, "Fauna," *Interpreter's Dictionary of the Bible*, II, 255, fig. 10.

scribal gloss giving voice to a sense of historical distance, "an omer is the tenth part of the ephah" (Exodus 16.36), an explanation of an obscure, possibly archaic, term of dry measure, a Hebrew word that occurs only in Exodus 16.[7]

By and large, however, it is not with matters of factuality that the biblical narratives of the manna incident are concerned. It is not what "biological phenomenon" manna denotes, but rather what it connotes. In the varying accounts and mentions of manna, in some ten books of the Bible, we find the characteristic activity of the ancient mythographers, thinking with stories.[8] Understanding this activity requires that we make use of the identification of the variety of traditions within the Hebrew Bible as identified by more than two centuries of scholarship, but that we resist the tendency to conceive of these as "sources," or to layer them chronologically. For purposes of this chapter, they may be seen as contemporaneous moments in an ongoing argument. In this case, the stimulus for the debate is a motif well known to folklorists, that of a "marvel" expressed as an "extraordinary occurrence" in terms of "magic food." Thus, Stith Thompson classifies the two chief motifs concerning manna as D 1031.0.1 and F 962.6.2 respectively.[9] As translated into more specific terminology, we read different understandings of the significance of a narrated incident that, while in the wilderness, the Israelite ancestors received an unexpected source of food. (In some versions, they received both bread and meat, both manna and quails.)

One argument is expressed in the various framings of the incident. Is the story a positive or a negative one, a miracle tale or a cautionary fable?

We have already met one specification of the positive frame. YHWH, like a father, adopted Israel as his child when he led Israel out of Egypt. Like a father, he provided food for his children. In the passage already quoted, this takes on the character of a formula, "the bread with which I [YHWH] fed you in the wilderness when I brought you out of the land of Egypt" (Exodus 16.32). It is most common in long, poetic, *dayyênû*

---

[7] Perhaps ʿōmer is simply an archaic word that has become meaningless and is being translated in terms of a fraction of the well-known measure, an ʾēpâ. Perhaps, because ʿōmer might be confused with the common dry measure, a ḥōmer, equivalent to the load an ass might carry, it is here, by means of a note that it is equivalent to a tenth of an ʾēpâ, being clarified as a much smaller amount, about two quarts.

[8] I have been much influenced by the critical remark of C. Lévi-Strauss, *The Savage Mind* (Chicago, 1966), 95, that "the mistake of Mannhardt and the Naturalist School was to think that natural phenomena are *what* myths seek to explain, when rather they are the *medium through which* myths try to explain facts which are themselves not of a natural but a logical order."

[9] S. Thompson, *Motif-Index of Folk-Literature*, rev. edn (Copenhagen and Bloomington, IN, 1955–58).

["it would have been sufficient"] – like recitations of the gracious deeds of YHWH toward Israel, such as Psalm 105.37–45:

> Then he led forth Israel with silver and gold,
> and there were none among his tribes who
> stumbled . . .
> He spread a cloud for covering,
> and fire to give light by night.
> They asked, and he brought forth quails,
> and gave them bread from the sky in abundance.
> He opened the rock, and water gushed forth,
> it flowed through the desert like a river.
> For he remembered his holy promise,
> and Abraham his servant.
> So he led forth his people with joy,
> his chosen ones with singing.
> And he gave them the lands of the nations.

This is a celebratory hymn portraying a procession through the desert with YHWH showering his family with gifts and joy. It is also an occasion for further reflection on the nature of the deity: YHWH remembers his promise to Abraham. Here, manna is but one instance in a long series of acts that form part of a divine strategy for realizing this seemingly unlikely promise.

This positive framing gains voice in one mode of telling the elaborated manna story. It also introduces a quite different set of reflections on YHWH's nature.

In Exodus 16.13–21, the picture is one of manna (and quails) covering the ground as far as one could see. As much as was gathered, there was more. Each day, yet more. That which was not collected turned rotten and bred worms. The controlling image of manna-production in this way of telling the tale is one of a celestial cotton-candy machine gone amuck, spewing forth unending quantities of the sticky white stuff. It is *de trop*. When YHWH does something, he does it big! Manna here appears as a kratophany, a lavish, profligate display of power "that you should know that I am YHWH your God" (Exodus 16.12).

A quite different, but equally positive picture is given in another mode of telling the elaborated manna story. In Exodus 16.22–30, the manna comes down in precisely measured quantities: just enough for one day and twice as much on the day before the Sabbath. Here YHWH is depicted as a law-abiding deity, one who keeps his own rules even in the midst of performing wonders. The implication is that of a "how much more so" argument. If YHWH keeps the Sabbath commandments, how much more so Israel. For this reason, the narrative includes a caution: "On the seventh day some of the people went out to gather and they found none. YHWH said to Moses, 'How long will you people refuse to keep my commands'" (Exodus 16.27–28).

This last complaint introduces the other side of the central argument as to the significance of manna. If, in the compositions just reviewed, the major frame is that of the desert wandering as an almost paradisical time of intimacy with YHWH, the performer of mighty deeds, the keeper of his law, the opposing frame, and the majority opinion within the Hebrew Bible, views the period of the wilderness-wandering as a paradigmatic time of rebellion and disobedience, expressed in the narrative theme of Israel "murmuring" against YHWH.[10] This theme dominates the penultimate framing of the manna and quail stories in both Exodus 16 and Numbers 11.

In Exodus 16, the people are hungry and they remember the good foods they ate back in Egypt (Exodus 16.3). In Numbers 11, the same complaint is better integrated into the narrative by being transposed from Israel's reproach before the appearance of manna, where manna is sent as a response to the complaint, to an effect of the provision of manna. In the Numbers version, Israel is bored with her constant manna diet: "O that we had meat to eat! We remember the fish we ate in Egypt . . . the cucumbers, the melons, the leeks, the onions, and the garlics . . . Here there is nothing but this manna to eat" (Numbers 11.5). YHWH's response turns the blessing into a curse; the positive, kratophanic superfluity is reinterpreted as negative. The profligate provision of manna and quails is to be understood as a demonstration not of divine power, but rather of divine anger. Indeed, as the people are stuffing themselves with quail, they are smitten with a great plague and the resultant dead are buried in a cursed place called the "graves of craving" (Numbers 11.33–34; cf. Psalms 78.10–24; 106.13–16; and, for a later example, 2 Esdras 1). Here, the provision of food functions as part of a narrative reversal of the Exodus. Israel wishes to go back to Egypt; the divine feeding results in a plague.

The most complex form of this understanding of manna is given in Ezra's speech as composed in Nehemiah where it takes the form of two propositions: (1) even though YHWH provided "bread from the

---

[10] On this theme, see especially G. W. Coats, *The Murmuring Motif in the Wilderness Traditions* (Washington, D.C., 1968), in the series, Catholic Biblical Quarterly Monograph Series.

sky," the people rebelled; (2) even though Israel rebelled, YHWH "did not withhold manna" (Nehemiah 9.15–17, 20). Moderating the more optimistic assimilation of the manna story to the promise to Abraham, this way of telling argues that YHWH remembers his promise even when Israel does not.

The ultimate framing of the manna incident relies on larger narrative structures in which the provision and cessation of manna serves to bracket the forty-year period of the wilderness-wandering, marking it off as a "time out of time," which begins and ends with a water crossing. As with the Eden story, which in many ways parallels the wilderness period, and which also revolves around eating, this is a segment, as we have seen, that can be assessed positively or negatively, as a time of intimacy with YHWH and promise, or as a time of rebellion against YHWH and curse. Taken as a whole, the manna narrative gives voice to both sides of this ambivalent understanding, with the positive assessment relativized by the more dominant negative evaluation. This is sequentially reenforced by redundancy: the provision of manna is itself bracketed by two incidents of water provision in which the negative interpretation prevails. Let me only outline the elements:

A *Beginning of the forty-year wilderness-wandering.*
1 Exodus 14.1–15.22. The Israelites cross the divided "sea of reeds" on "dry ground."
2 Exodus 15.22a. Israel immediately enters the "wilderness."
3 Exodus 15.22b–25. After three days, they have no water. The people "murmur." They come to a place of "bitter water." YHWH shows Moses a tree which, when thrown in the water, makes it "sweet" and potable.
4 Exodus 16. Manna (and quail).
5 Exodus 17.1–7 (cf. Numbers 20.2–13). Israel again lacks water. The people "murmur." YHWH tells Moses to strike a rock with his rod and fresh water will flow. This element is a reversal of a previous incident where striking the Nile river with the rod made the Egyptians' waters "foul" and undrinkable (Exodus 7.14–24, alluded to in Exodus 17.5b).

B *End of the forty-year wilderness-wandering.*
1 Joshua 3.7–5.2. The Israelites cross the divided river Jordan on "dry ground." They enter Canaan thereby fulfilling the promise to both Abraham and Moses.
2 Joshua 5.12. Manna ceases. The Israelites return to eating ordinary, cultivated food, "the produce of the land," and "the people of Israel had manna no more."

If these opposing views make their points by integrating the manna incident into larger narrative structures, thereby framing it, other sorts of understandings can be found which do not require thinking with story but rather thinking about story. To cite only the best-known example, a homily attributed to Moses in Deuteronomy: "And he humbled you and let you hunger and fed you with manna, which you did not know, nor did your fathers know, *in order that* he might make you learn that humankind does not live by bread alone, but that humankind lives by everything that proceeds out of the mouth of YHWH" (Deuteronomy 8.3). Here manna is transposed from the ancient wonder to a present, recurrent phenomenon; not a fact of nature, but rather a source of moral instruction. It is a symbol of every way in which YHWH every day nurtures his people – for the school of thought represented by this particular text, preeminently through the Law. Furthermore, the text by referring to manna as that "which you did not know, nor did your fathers know" alludes to the learned scribal pun which claims that the etymology of manna is to be found in Israel's question, *mān hû*, "What is it?" (Exodus 16.15). This homily suggests that one should ask this question, quite literally, of everything, and answer, "it is from YHWH."

Another constellation of manna-speech focuses on this question, "What is it?," and seeks its answer in words taken to be synonymous with manna. Drawing on the full range of biblical and immediately post-biblical materials, manna is glossed as "bread from the sky" (Exodus 16.4; Psalms 78.24 and 105.40), "bread of angels" (Psalm 78.25; Wisdom 16.20; 2 Esdras 1.19), "heavenly food" (Sibylline Oracles 3.84), or "ambrosia" (Wisdom 19.21). These can be understood in an esoteric manner which gives rise to new questions. What might it mean for human beings to eat such food? Do they become, in some way, more than human?

I offer only one example, from the late first-century (BC) Greek Jewish work, the Wisdom of Solomon, which occurs in a now familiar frame, a catalogue of the god's gracious deeds: "You did give your people the food of angels and, without their toil, you did supply them from heaven with bread ready to eat" (Wisdom 16.20). Here, manna is understood as a transfer of divine food to the human realm, perhaps to be contrasted with the attempt at an illegitimate transfer in the tree-of-life episode in Genesis 3.22. Likewise, the food is produced "without toil," perhaps in contrast to the curse of Genesis 3.17–19. An event associated with the Exodus here signals a new creation, a new beginning (an argument made explicit in Wisdom 19.6, 11).

For the purposes of this chapter, more interest attaches to the penultimate line of this text which describes manna as a "crystalline quick-melting kind of ambrosial food" (Wisdom 19.21). This interpretation of manna as ambrosial divine food is more common than it appears. It has occurred every time I have said the word "manna," with its doubled consonant, rather than the Hebrew *mān*. *Mān* is carried over, in direct Greek transliteration, only in the Septuagint for Exodus 16; all other occurrences in the Hebrew Bible are rendered, in the Septuagint and in all other Greek versions, as *manna*. In a complex instance of interlinguistic relationship, *manna* is a Greek generic term (although possibly of Semitic derivation) referring to a powder or to granules of aromatic botanical substances, most commonly frankincense, used especially in ritual and medical procedures.[11] As such, it is part of the complex Greek system of vegetative scents elucidated by Marcel Detienne.[12] This is a transfer, introducing new denotations and connotations, which occurs entirely within the linguistic realm. It is a matter of philology, not entomology.

Manna, as a Greek word, can be associated with the immortalizing powers of ambrosia (Hesychius, s.v. *ambrosia*) as well as with well-known classical traditions that the phoenix, symbol of immortality, feeds only on aromatic substances and dew.[13] The semantic field of the Greek term came to overlap the Hebraic, as may be seen in one late (first to third centuries AD) pseudepigraphical Jewish text, "And what does it [the phoenix]

---

[11] The citations in H. G. Liddell and R. Scott, *A Greek–English Lexicon*, rev. edn (Oxford, 1968), s.v. *manna*, are sufficient to give some idea of the semantic range.

In Greek Christian texts, *manna* refers to the food supplied during the Exodus, but the ambrosial connotations are further developed through typological constructions which employ the contrast between the positive and negative framings of the manna narratives. Within the New Testament, see already Paul who identifies manna as "spiritual food" yet interprets Israel's behavior as a cautionary fable (1 Corinthians 10.1–17). In John 6, this double evaluation is highly elaborated in the juxtaposition of the Mosaic manna with the Son as the "bread of life." In Revelation 2.7 and 17, the "Tree of Life" and the "hidden manna" are placed in parallel constructions as gifts given to "him who conquers." For later Christian usage, see the citations in G. W. H. Lampe, *A Patristic Greek Lexicon* (Oxford, 1961–68), s.v. *manna*. The sole exception to the biblical referent is Hippolytus, *Refutatio omnium haeresium*, 4.31, where the word refers to a vegetable gum used in a recipe for poisoning oats.

Note that a standard reference work such as the *Encyclopaedia Britannica* could have an entry on "manna" (primarily in medicine), from the first through the eighth editions, without ever mentioning the biblical materials. The ninth through the eleventh editions add a single sentence to an appendix. It is only with the fourteenth that the biblical account of *mān* begins to overshadow the Greek understanding of *manna*.

[12] M. Detienne, *The Gardens of Adonis* (Atlantic Highlands, NJ: 1977), 5–10, *et passim*.

[13] While I have here focused on *manna*/spices as the phoenix's food, recall as well their role in the construction of the phoenix's nest and funereal pyre. See, in general, J. Hubaux and M. Leroy, *Le Mythe du Phénix dans les littératures grecque et latine* (Liège–Paris, 1939). R. van den Broek, *The Myth of the Phoenix According to Classical and Early Christian Traditions* (Leiden, 1972), especially 335–56, has a rich catalogue of texts concerning the food of the phoenix. Detienne, *Gardens of Adonis*, 29–36 has a most important structuralist interpretation of the relation of the Phoenix to spices.

eat? ... The manna of heaven and the dew of earth" (3 Baruch 6.11, Greek version). The idiom of the answer is biblical, but the Greek mythic tradition is present in the question as are the Greek associations of *manna* and dew in the answer.

What has interested me in thinking about the variety of manna texts is not so much a matter of historical confirmation or corroboration but rather one of narrative articulation and ratiocination.[14] It is not unlike the "burning bush" of Exodus 3.2–4 (cf. Deuteronomy 33.16) which has been subjected to similar confirmative attempts to identify the particular species of an apparently thorny plant (*sᵉneh*) by ransacking herbaria of Sinai flora for red-leaved shrubs or for bushes whose waxy leaves are capable of reflecting sunlight.[15] It has always seemed to me that the wonder of the plant is not so much that it was afire (bushes do burn) as that it was represented as coming to speech.

MANA

Mana, power, influence. (W. Williams, *Dictionary of the New Zealand Language* (1845))

Ma-na, s. Supernatural power, such as was supposed and believed to be an attribute of the gods. (L. Andrews, *A Dictionary of the Hawaiian Language* (1865))

Mana entered European consciousness as an italicized word, one of those glossed items of exotic native terminology that flavored nineteenth-century travel accounts by missionaries, administrators, and other colonial adventurers. *Mana*, "command, authority, power" (1843);[16] "mana, or power" (1855).[17] It first achieved general significance when F. Max Müller quoted a letter to him by a British High Church missionary

---

[14] I want to acknowledge three works on these traditions that offer important examples of approaches to biblical scholarship: B. J. Malina, *The Palestinian Manna Tradition* (Leiden, 1968); B. S. Childs, *The Book of Exodus: A Critical Theological Commentary* (Philadelphia, 1974), esp. pp. 271–304; W. H. Propp, *Water in the Wilderness* (Atlanta, 1987).

[15] The identification of the bush as thorny depends on a claimed cognate to the term for the bush, *sᵉneh*, which occurs in the Hebrew Bible only in this incident in both the Exodus narrative and the briefer allusion in Deuteronomy. For a review of the various botanical identifications, see I. Löw, *Die Flora der Jüden* (Vienna–Leipzig, 1928–34), III, 175–88.

[16] E. Dieffenbach, *Travels in New Zealand* (London, 1843), II, 371–72, as cited in the *Oxford English Dictionary, Supplement*, s.v., "mana." Dieffenbach, a German geologist, was a founding member of the London Ethnological Society.

[17] R. Taylor, *Te Ika a Maui, or New Zealand and its Inhabitants*, 1st edn (London, 1855), 279, as cited in the *Oxford English Dictionary, Supplement*, s.v. "mana." Taylor, *Te Ika A Maui*, 2nd edn (London, 1870), 184, glosses the term, "mana, virtue of the god." Note that J. White, *The Ancient History of the Maori: His Mythology and Traditions* (Wellington, 1887), I, 35, 48; III, 2 *et passim*, presents native sentences containing the word "mana" rather than simply deploying the isolated word.

in Melanesia, Robert Henry Codrington, in Müller's 1878 Hibbert Lectures, *On the Origin and Growth of Religion*. Müller deployed the citation as part of his polemic against "fetichism" as a primitive stage in evolutionary theories of religion. Codrington had written, in a not altogether coherent report, that:

The religion of the Melanesians consists, as far as belief goes, in the persuasion that there is a supernatural power about belonging to the region of the unseen; and, as far as practice goes, in the use of means of getting this power turned to their own benefit. The notion of a Supreme Being is altogether foreign to them... There is a belief in a force altogether distinct from physical power, which acts in all kinds of ways for good and evil, and which it is of the greatest advantage to possess or control. This is Mana. The word is common I believe to the whole Pacific... It is a power or influence, not physical, and in a way supernatural; but it shews itself in physical force, or in any kind of power or excellence which a man possesses. This Mana is not fixed in anything, and can be conveyed in almost anything; but spirits, whether disembodied souls or supernatural beings, have it and can impart it; and it essentially belongs to personal beings to originate it, though it may act through the medium of water, or a stone, or a bone. All Melanesian religion consists, in fact, in getting this Mana for one's self, or getting it used for one's benefit – all religion that is, as far as religious practices go, prayers and sacrifices.[18]

The subsequent history of mana can be organized around six chronological points: 1891, 1902, 1904, 1912, 1915, and 1936 to the present.[19] The result has been a complex, century-long drama in which a word was transformed into an incarnate power only to be reduced to a word again.

1 In 1891, Codrington published what has been termed the "classic" account of mana in *The Melanesians: Studies in Their Anthropology and Folklore*.[20] In the same year, Edward Tregear's *Maori–Polynesian Comparative*

---

[18] R. H. Codrington, "Letter to Max Müller" (July 7, 1877), as quoted in Max Müller, *Lectures on the Origin and Growth of Religion, as Illustrated by the Religions of India*, 1st edn (London, 1878), 53–54. Müller is concerned to challenge the notion of "fetichism" as the primitive stage of religion by appealing to the ubiquity of an "apprehension of the infinite." He uses Codrington's report as showing that the Maori had this notion in a "vague and hazy form." Perhaps confusing the uncertainties of Codrington with those he attributes to the natives, Müller describes mana as "one of the early, helpless expressions of what the apprehension of the infinite would be in its incipient stages" but goes on to note "the Melanesian Mana shows ample traces both of development and corruption," (*ibid*). Codrington reproduces his letter in *The Melanesians: Studies in Their Anthropology and Folk-lore*, 1st edn (Oxford, 1891; reprinted, New York, 1972), 118–19, n. 1. On Codrington, see G. W. Stocking, Jr., *After Tylor: British Social Anthropology 1888–1951* (Madison, 1995), 34–46.

[19] I note V. Valeri's comment, *Kingship and Sacrifice: Ritual and Society in Ancient Hawaii* (Chicago, 1985), 361, n. 15, "The history of the interpretation of mana remains to be written."

[20] Codrington, *The Melanesians*, esp. pp. 118–20, 191–92.

Dictionary, dedicated to Max Müller, offered detailed illustrations of the meaning of "mana" in ten Pacific-island languages which gave confidence to the notion that it was a pan-Oceanic word/concept.[21]

2   In 1902, J. N. B. Hewitt's "Orenda and a Definition of Religion"[22] began the process of identifying a cluster of Native American terminologies subsequently held to be parallel to mana, which gave confidence to the emerging claim that mana was a universal religious concept.

3   1904 saw publications by R. R. Marett[23] and H. Hubert and M. Mauss[24] which employed mana as a generic concept for theorizing about the origins of religion or magic.

4   In 1912, along with using mana as a central theoretical concept, mana was put forth as an explanatory principle for interpreting other non-Oceanic religious traditions in E. Durkheim's *Elementary Forms of Religious Life: The Totemic System in Australia*,[25] and Jane E. Harrison's *Themis: A Study of the Social Origins of Greek Religion*.[26]

---

[21]   E. Tregear, *The Maori–Polynesian Comparative Dictionary* (Wellington, 1891; reprinted, 1969), esp. p. 203.

[22]   J. N. B. Hewitt, "Orenda and A Definition of Religion," *American Anthropologist*, n.s. 4 (1902): 33–46. While offering a wide ranging set of parallels, Hewitt does not mention mana.

[23]   R. R. Marett, "From Spell to Prayer," *Folk-Lore* 15 (1904), 132–65, reprinted in Marett, *The Threshold of Religion*, 1st edn (London, 1909), 29–72. See further, Marett, "Pre-animistic Religion," *Folk-Lore* 11 (1900), 162–82 (*Threshold*, 1–28); "The Conception of Mana," *Transactions of the 3rd International Congress of the History of Religions* (Oxford, 1908), I, 46–57 (*Threshold*, 99–121); "The Tabu-Mana Formulation as a Minimum Definition of Religion," *Archiv für Religionswissenschaft* 12 (1909): 186–94 [reprinted in J. Waardenburg, *Classical Approaches to the Study of Religion* (The Hague, 1973), I: 258–63]; "Mana," in J. Hastings (ed.), *Encyclopaedia of Religion and Ethics* (New York, 1916), VIII: 375–80; "Mana," in *Encyclopaedia Britannica*, 14th edn (1929), VII, 770–71 [in later printings of this edition, Marett's article has been revised by R. M. Firth]. See the recent treatment of Marett, with a useful bibliography, by M. Riesebrodt, "Robert Ranulph Marett," in A. Michaels (ed.), *Klassiker der Religionswissenschaft von Friedrich Schleiermacher bis Mircea Eliade* (Munich, 1997), 171–84; 383–84.

[24]   H. Hubert and M. Mauss, "Esquisse d'un théorie générale de la magie," *Année sociologique*, 7 (1904), 1–146; I cite the English translation, *A General Theory of Magic* (London, 1972), esp. pp. 108–21. In a later autobiographical essay, Mauss stresses the importance of "Esquisse," writing: "In particular, at the foundation of both magic and religion we discovered a vast common notion which we called *mana*, borrowing the term from the Melanesian–Polynesian language. The idea of mana is perhaps more general than that of the sacred," M. Mauss, "An Intellectual Self-Portrait," in Ph. Besnard (ed.), *The Sociological Domain: The Durkheimians and the Founding of French Sociology* (Cambridge, 1983), 149. Cf. Hubert, "Etude sommaire de la représentation du temps dans la religion et la magie," *Annuaire de l'Ecole Pratique des Hautes Etudes, section des sciences religieuses* (1905), esp. p. 30.

[25]   E. Durkheim, *Les Formes élémentaires de la vie religieuse: Le système totémique en Australie*, 2nd edn (Paris, 1922), esp. pp. 268–92; compare the new English translation, *The Elementary Forms of Religious Life*, trans. K. E. Fields (New York, 1995), 190–206, which I cite below, in parentheses, with occasional modification, first giving the French and then the English pagination.

[26]   J. E. Harrison, *Themis: A Study of the Social Origins of Greek Religion*, 1st edn (Cambridge, 1912); 2nd edn (Cambridge, 1927; reprint, 1962), 66–69, 84–85, 137–38 *et passim*.

5   In 1915, the first monograph, a dissertation devoted to a careful and critical comparative study of mana, was prepared by Friedrich Rudolf Lehmann.[27]

6   The period from 1936 to the present has been largely devoted to challenging the utility of mana as a generic concept through linguistic studies, either analyzing its specific meaning in particular cultures, supported by the detailed examination of mana's occurrences in a corpus of native sentences, rather than constructing a composite portrait achieved by taking the term in isolation; or by arguing, on the basis of the same sort of data, that earlier accounts misunderstood its grammatical status, that mana is most commonly not a substantive noun naming an impersonal force, as had been common in the literature since Codrington,[28] but rather most frequently functions as a transitive stative verb. This critical process began with H. Ian Hogbin (1936), A. Capell (1938), and Raymond Firth (1940), and has culminated, for the present, in the work of Roger M. Keesing (1984).[29] Finally, using a quite different sort of linguistic analysis, Claude Lévi-Strauss, in a daring proposal, re-theorized mana (1950), an undertaking recently critically examined, from quite different perspectives, by both Pascal Boyer (1990) and Maurice Godelier (1996).[30]

---

[27]   F. R. Lehmann, *Mana: Eine begriffsgeschichtliche Untersuchung auf ethnologische Grundlage* (Leipzig, 1915); 2nd edn, *Mana: Der Begriff des 'ausserordenlich Wirkungsvollen' bei Südseevölkern* (Leipzig, 1922); cf. Lehmann, "Versuche, die Bedeutung des Wortes Mana," in K. Rudolph, ed., *Festschrift Walter Baetke* (Weimar, 1966), 215–40.

[28]   Codrington, *The Melanesians*, 119, n. 1: "The word mana is both a noun substantive and . . . a transitive form of the verb."

[29]   While other work could have been mentioned, I have singled out, H. I. Hogbin, "Mana," *Oceania* 6 (1936): 241–74; A. Capell, "The Word 'Mana': A Linguistic Study," *Oceania* 9 (1938): 89–96; R. Firth, "The Analysis of Mana: An Empirical Approach," *Journal of the Polynesian Society* 49 (1940): 483–510, reprinted in Firth, *Tikopia Ritual and Belief* (Boston, 1968), 174–94 and Th. G. Harding and B. J. Wallace (eds.), *Cultures of the Pacific: Selected Readings* (New York, 1970), 316–33; R. M. Keesing, "Rethinking Mana," *Journal of Anthropological Research*, 46 (1984): 137–56. Keesing writes (p. 138), mana "is in Oceanic languages canonically a stative verb, not a noun . . . Mana is used as a transitive verb as well . . . Where mana is used as a noun, it is (usually) not a substantive but an abstract verbal noun denoting the state or quality of mana-ness (of a thing or act) or being-mana (of a person)." Note that this sort of understanding has entered the wider public domain, see *Encyclopaedia Britannica*, 15th edn, Micropaedia, s.v. "mana."
    For early examples of more general strictures on mana, see the harsh verdict of G. P. Murdock, *Our Primitive Contemporaries* (New York, 1934), p. xiii: "The author began with the intention of making full use of the concept [of mana]. In tribe after tribe, however, he found it inapplicable, the more so the more deeply he dug into the facts, and he ended without being able to use it at all . . . In science, when a theory, however plausible, parts company with the facts, there is no choice; the theory must yield"; and R. W. Williamson, *Essays in Polynesian Ethnology* (Cambridge, 1939), 264–65, who focuses on the issue of generalizability: "The beliefs, customs and usage connected with the Polynesian terms *mana* and *tapu* are so widely diverse that if we were to attempt to formulate definitions which would cover all of them, such formulations would be of such a general character that they might be attributed to any human culture."

[30]   C. Lévi-Strauss, "Introduction à l'œuvre de Marcel Mauss," in M. Mauss, *Sociologie et Anthropologie* (Paris, 1950), esp. pp. xli–lii; compare the English translation, Lévi-Strauss, *Introduction to the Work*

For the purpose of this chapter, we may focus on one segment of this history, the movement from Durkheim, who risked his argument on a mana that was not there, to Lévi-Strauss, who proposed mana as a category for objects that had no "where."

As is well known, Durkheim was able to present much of his theoretical understanding of religion in works prior to the 1912 *Elementary Forms*, most particularly in the 1898–1900 course of lectures at the University of Bordeaux, "The Physics (*physique*) of Morals and of Rights" in connection with an analysis of the origins and logic of private property.[31] Early on, in these pre-1912 writings, he links the sacred with the Oceanic word/concept, *tabu*.[32] It is only with the *Elementary Forms* that he first invokes mana and couples it with the sacred, even though he had certainly read, by 1899, Codrington's 1877 letter on mana, as published in Müller.[33] Doubtless, the theoretical use of mana by Hubert and Mauss, as well as by Marett, provoked Durkheim's subsequent interest in the term.[34]

I take Durkheim, especially in the *Elementary Forms*, to be one of the great crafters of argument in the history of the study of religion. From the translation of "religion" by "society" in the very first sentence, his

of Marcel Mauss (London, 1987), 50–66; P. Boyer, *Tradition as Truth and Communication: A Cognitive Description of Traditional Discourse* (Cambridge, 1990), esp. pp. 27–30; M. Godelier, *L'Enigme du don* (Paris, 1996), I cite the English translation, Godelier, *The Enigma of the Gift* (Chicago, 1999), 18–29, *et passim*. The point of entry of Godelier's critique was to some extent anticipated in an essay first published in 1966 by J. Derrida; see Derrida, *Writing and Difference* (Chicago, 1978), 289–92. The proposal by Lévi-Strauss is prematurely dismissed by J. MacClancy, "Mana: An Anthropological Metaphor," *Oceania* 57 (1986): 148. I have discussed, with appreciation, the relationship of Lévi-Strauss to Durkheim at this point in J. Z. Smith, *To Take Place: Toward Theory in Ritual* (Chicago, 1987), 106–08. I draw on this discussion below.

    Because I have chosen to focus on the Durkheim/Lévi-Strauss trajectory, I omit discussion of the major monograph by Laura Makarius, *Le Sacré et la violation des interdits* (Paris, 1974) which constitutes a sustained and innovative reworking of the classical anthropological topoi associated with mana.

[31] E. Durkheim, *Leçons de sociologie: Physique des moeurs et du droit* (Paris, 1950); English translation, *Professional Ethics and Civic Morals* (London, 1957, reprinted, 1992), esp. pp. 133–75. See also, for important anticipations of central themes in *Elementary Forms*, Durkheim, *De la Division du travail social: Etude sur l'organisation des sociétés supérieures* (Paris, 1893); I cite the English translation, *The Division of Labor in Society* (New York, 1933), esp. pp. 168–69; Durkheim, "De la Définition des phénomènes religieux," *Année sociologique*, 2 (1899): 1–28; I cite the English translation, "Concerning the Definition of Religious Phenomena," in W. S. F. Pickering, ed., *Durkheim on Religion* (Atlanta, 1994), 74–99.

[32] The notion of tabu is central in Durkheim, "La Prohibition de l'inceste et ses origines," *Année sociologique* 1 (1898): 1–70; Durkheim, "Préface," *Année sociologique* 2 (1899): i–iv; as well as in Durkheim, *Leçons de sociologie*.

[33] Durkheim cites Müller's *Lectures on the Origin and Growth of Religion* (see above, n. 18) in "Definition," 76 and 98, n. 3.

[34] See above, notes 23 and 24. See also Durkheim's discussion of both Marett and Hubert and Mauss in *Elementary Forms* (287–89/203–04).

work has a rhetorical and intellectual momentum from which it is almost impossible to disengage. For this reason, it is striking when he violates the terms of his own agendum, and introduces as a central concept the notion of mana which cannot be found within his chosen ethnographic exemplum. There is no evidence for the presence of a term fully analogous to mana among the Australian aborigines.[35]

Durkheim deploys several compositional stratagems in facing this difficulty. For example, as is quite typical in *Elementary Forms*, there is the anticipatory mention. Codrington, on the Melanesians, is first cited, early on, as part of Durkheim's discussion of a definition of magic, "in Australia as well as in Melanesia . . . the souls, bones, and hair of the dead figure among the tools most often used by the magician" (58–59/40). Codrington is next cited in the midst of a set of Australian exempla, as part of Durkheim's argument against animistic theories of religion (83/56, cf. 95/64). Four pages later, continuing the same discussion, Codrington on mana is directly quoted with the promise that Durkheim will "later make plain what the word expresses" (87–88/59). This "later" explanation will be deferred for eighty-nine pages (277/196), preceded, immediately, by another teaser, in the course of an argument with Andrew Lang. "As we will see in the next chapter, the words *wakan* and *mana* imply the idea of *sacred* itself (the first word is taken from the language of the Sioux, the second from that of the Melanesian peoples)" (265/188).

This last citation, as well as the phrase already quoted, "in Australia as well as in Melanesia," gives voice to Durkheim's more ambitious stratagem: Australian data are comparable to Native American data; Native American data are comparable to Oceanic data; therefore, Oceanic data are comparable to Australian data. For Durkheim, it is the first proposition in this problematic syllogism that requires demonstration.

As you will recall, Durkheim begins *Elementary Forms* by setting forth as his overarching question the nature of the "simplest and most primitive religion" (1/1). Characteristically, he defers identifying that religion for

---

35 Note that through either a mistranslation or a misprint, mana does appear in Australia in Fields's translation of Durkheim! In his chapter on positive rituals, Durkheim summarizes the account, in B. Spencer and F. J. Gillen, *The Native Tribes of Central Australia* (London, 1899; reprint, New York, 1968): 185–86, concerning the *intichiuma* ceremony of "the *Ilpirla* or manna totem." Spencer and Gillen had written that "*Ilpirla* is a form of 'manna' very similar to the well-known sugar-manna of gum trees but peculiar to the mulga tree (*Acacia aneura*)." Fields translates as follows: "In the clan of the Ilpirla (a sort of manna [*sorte de manne*]) . . . the group meets [in front of two groups of rocks] . . . Both represent accumulations of manna [*des masses de manne*]. The Altjuna digs in the ground at the foot of these rocks and brings forth a churinga . . . that itself is like the quintessence of mana [*sic! comme de la quintessence de manne*]" (470/333).

four chapters, where it is finally argued that totemism is the simplest and most primitive genus of religion (124/85); Australian totemism, the simplest and most primitive species presently observable (132/90). In the course of this identification, Durkheim offers a brief history of scholarship. As the derivation of the word indicates, *totem* is a Native American term first brought to European awareness in the late eighteenth century. "For nearly half a century, totemism was known exclusively as an American institution. It was only in 1841 that Grey...drew attention to the existence of similar practices in Australia. From then on, scholars began to realize that they were in the presence of a system that has a certain generality...McLennan was the first [1869–70] to try to connect totemism with general human history" (124–25/85). The history of ethnographic literature thereby justifies both the parallelism of Australian and Native American socio-religious terminology as well as the use of a native word as a generic, academic term of art.

Durkheim's second argument is more strictly sociological. He rejects the world-wide comparative use of "totemism," as, for example, employed by Frazer, inasmuch as this mixes "societies whose kind and degree of cultural development are quite disparate" (132/90–91). The relationship of the Native Americans to the Australians must be put with greater precision. With respect to social development, the Australians are "simpler," the Native Americans are more "complex." Thus he will focus on Australian data, and will "supplement" it with American materials "only when it appears well suited to helping us understand the Australian data better" (132–38, esp. 138/91–93, esp. 93). In the bulk of *Elementary Forms*, Durkheim strictly follows the consequences of this placement: the Australian data are given first, then, if relevant, the Native American (e.g. 156, 159, 191–92, 205, 223, 254–55, 370, 373–74/109, 111, 135, 145, 158, 180–81, 261, 264). This procedural rule is broken only with the introduction of mana. Here, the presence of Native American mana-like terminology allows Durkheim to infer a mana-like concept among the Australian aborigines. I am tempted to suggest that Durkheim's entire proposal to "supplement" Australian data with Native American was made so that this one inference could be legitimized, thereby enabling Durkheim to "depart" from his precisely stipulated domain, the "circle of facts" (138, n. 3/95, n. 1) limited to Australia as his primary resource, with America as his secondary support, and to import the Oceanic word/concept, mana, as the chief guarantor of his interpretation of his central second-order category, the sacred.

As might have been anticipated, Durkheim first makes this move in Book Two, chapter six, which is subtitled, "The Notion of the Totemic

Principle, or Mana, and the Idea of Force" (268–92/190–206). Durkheim begins by deducing from his previous conclusions concerning totemism, the presence of "a common principle," a "kind of anonymous and impersonal force . . . diffused in a numberless multitude of things," independent of, and yet imagined by, the native as taking particular forms, for example, as totems (269/191).

Durkheim's initial question is whether his deduction conforms to ethnographic fact; but his formulation already begins to shift attention from the putative focus on Australia. He asks, "whether in societies akin to the Australian tribes or in those very tribes, we find – and in explicit form – conceptions that differ only in degree and nuance" from his deduction of the totemic principle? His first example is Oceanic, from Samoa. As Durkheim explains, it exhibits already a development beyond his deduction. Samoa has only "survivals" of totemism, hence the data exhibits "a totemic principle that the imagination has developed in somewhat personal forms" (273 and n. 1/193–94 and 193, n. 5).

His second set of examples from Native American traditions, has been prepared for. Here they are placed, uncharacteristically but strategically, before the Australian materials. "In many American tribes, especially in those belonging to the great family of the Sioux . . . [elements of totemic systems] are still identifiable in them. Among these peoples, there is a preeminent power above all the particular gods men worship, which they call *wakan* . . . It is Power in the absolute" (274–75/194–95). Likewise the Iroquois, "whose social organization is still more markedly totemic. The word *orenda* . . . is exactly equivalent to the wakan of the Sioux" (276/195). "The same idea [with different names] is found among the Shoshone," the Algonquins, the Kwakiutl, the Tlingit, and the Haida (277/196). Parenthetically, it should be noted that this catalogue is, in part, dependent on that in Hubert and Mauss's essay on magic, as demonstrated by a mistake in bibliographic citation in the latter being repeated in Durkheim.[36]

---

[36] Hubert and Mauss, *General Theory of Magic*, pp. 113–15. In connection with the Algonquin–Objibwa, *manitou*, Hubert and Mauss (*ibid.*, p. 114) cite the unpublished dictionary of Father Thavenet as quoted in "Tesa, *Studi del Thavenet*, Pisa, 1881, p. 17." In Durkheim (277, n. 1/196, n. 21), the reference is given in even shorter form, "Tesa, *Studi del Thavenet*, p. 17," even though it had not been previously cited. The name of the author has been misspelled (it should be Teza, not Tesa), and it is a serial rather than a monographic publication. The correct full reference should be: E. Teza, *Intorno agli studi del Thavenet sulla lingua algonchina: Osservazioni di E. Teza* (Pisa, 1880), 17 in the series, Annali delle Università Toscane, 18, as cited in A. M. di Nola, "Religione degli Algonchini centrali," in A. M. di Nola (ed.), *Enciclopedia delle religioni* (Florence, 1970), I, 172–73. The reference in Hubert and Mauss is largely corrected in a translator's note by F. Baker to her translation of C. Lévi-Strauss, *Introduction to the Work of Marcel Mauss* (London, 1987), p. 71, n. 13. Emilio Teza was a stunningly polylingual philologian whose work includes not

Having established the presence of the "notion of impersonal religious force" in Native American traditions, Durkheim makes the comparison. "It is not peculiar to the Indians of America; it was first studied in Melanesia. On certain islands, it is true, the social organization is no longer based on totemism, but totemism is still visible on all of them... We find among these peoples, under the name 'mana,' a notion that is exactly equivalent to the wakan of the Sioux and the orenda of the Iroquois" (277/196). Rather than a detailed exposition, he quotes a long extract from Codrington's 1877 letter to Müller, which, in Durkheim's French translation, as well as in his selectivity, highlights the element of impersonality (277–78/196–97).[37]

With this comparison in place, Durkheim rushes to his conclusion. Given the Native American and Melanesian materials, an analogous notion must be present in Australia. "We can legitimately infer the nature of each from that of the other" (283/200). "Is this [mana] not the same notion of a diffuse and anonymous force whose seed in Australian totemism we were uncovering a moment ago?" (278/201). It is a justifiable question to ask "whether a concept analogous to wakan or mana is altogether lacking in Australia" (283, n. 4/200, n. 41). It is "by no means reckless to impute" a similar force to the Australians (278/201). The absence of the same "degree of abstraction and generality" in the

only translations from many European languages, but an interest in Native American languages. See, among other publications, Teza, *Saggi inediti de lingua Americana: Appunti bibliografici* (Pisa, 1868).

[37] Durkheim as translator is an insufficiently studied topic. I focus attention, here, only on Durkheim's translation of the pages in Codrington's *Melanesians* devoted to mana. Karen E. Fields, in her translation of *Elementary Forms*, 59, n. 26; 327, n. 102, has provided two brief notes on this topic. The first is mistaken. She claims that Durkheim's citation of Codrington, p. 125, is incorrect, "the quotation does not appear there." In my judgment, Durkheim's translation, "*des riens après comme avant la mort*" (88) is a reasonable translation of Codrington's, "nobodies alike before and after death." The second observes correctly that Durkheim has provided two slightly different renderings of the same sentence in Codrington, p. 119, n. 1, cont'd: "This Mana is not fixed in anything, and can be conveyed in almost anything." Durkheim first translates, "*Le mana n'est point fixé sur un object déterminé; il peut être amené sur toute espèce de choses...*" (277), and later translates it, with added italics, as: mana is a force which "*n'est point fixée sur un object matériel, mais qui peut être amenée sur presque toute espèce d'objet*" (461). Both translations are reasonable; though Durkheim, for his own purpose, makes Codrington's vaguer "anything" into a more definite "*objet*." More disturbing about Durkheim's quotation of Codrington, in the first instance, are the ellipsis points indicating an omission; it is a full stop in the second instance. Durkheim is using this quotation, among other reasons, to support his view of impersonality. He, therefore, halts the quote at the point that Codrington continues, "...and can be conveyed in almost anything; but spirits, whether disembodied souls or supernatural beings, have it and can impart it; and it essentially belongs to personal beings to originate it, though it may act through the medium of water, or a stone, or a bone." I must agree with E. J. Sharpe, that the notion that mana-like concepts have reference to impersonal forces "comes not from Marett but from Durkheim" (Sharpe, "Preanimism," in M. Eliade [ed.], *Encyclopedia of Religion* [New York, 1987], XI, 503).

Australian instance, when compared to the Native American, is a difference in "social milieu" (280/198), a difference in their respective totemic organizations which he had called attention to when he first suggested "supplementing" the Australian data with the Native American (132–38/91–93).[38]

To quote the old tag, "wishing does not make it so." Unlike Lévi-Strauss – recall the sloth in *The Jealous Potter* (1985, chs. 6–8) – Durkheim has no conceptual means of converting a logical and systemic requirement into an existent reality. There is nothing like the "little piece of straw," nor some vial of insect excretions to display. The Australian materials do not suggest the presence of a mana-like word or concept, setting aside the question as to whether mana and the presumed Native American cognates have been correctly understood, or what translation rule justifies the judgment that each term is "*l'équivalent exact*" (276–77/195–96) of the other.[39]

Durkheim's interest in establishing the facticity of the "totemic principle" in Australia was high. The notion of an "impersonal force" accomplished a set of important objectives. Impersonality insured a collective, social understanding of sacrality. It blocked, as well, any deistic definition of religion. Above all, social force, conceived as a parallel to force as conceptualized in the physical sciences, guaranteed facticity by providing an "objective correlative" – a goal persistently reiterated throughout Durkheim's career-long project of establishing the social

[38] In their *General Theory of Magic*, 115, Hubert and Mauss follow their presentation of the Oceanic and Native American materials with a brief paragraph on "a concept of a similar kind" in Australia, noting that "here it is clearly restricted to magic activities, and more particularly to black magic." As would be anticipated, Durkheim, *Elementary Forms*, reexamines this data at greater length (280–83/198–200). He offers two general arguments to explain this difference, and, by implication, to give reasons for why he cannot find an unambiguous cognate for mana in Australia. His first argument is one of "social milieu," that clan autonomy, and the distinction of each totemic group from the other, mitigates against a notion "that these heterogeneous worlds were only different manifestations of one and the same fundamental force." For this reason, a true mana-like concept among the Australian aborigines would be unlikely. Second, in Australia, unlike clan-based totemism, magic is "not attached to any definite social division." Therefore, it is plausible that, there, a mana-like concept would be more likely to be associated with magic.

[39] Because Irving Goldman is one of the few anthropologists to write important monographs on both Polynesian and Kwakiutl societies, I call attention to his brief comparison between the Oceanic term, *mana*, and the Kwakiutl term, *nawalak*, held to be its synonym in Hubert and Mauss and Durkheim. See Goldman, *The Mouth of Heaven: An Introduction to Kwakiutl Religious Thought* (New York, 1975), 2–3, 179–82; compare his discussion of Polynesian mana in Goldman, *Ancient Polynesian Society* (Chicago, 1970), 10–13, *et passim*. Note that, throughout this latter work, Goldman takes great pain to characterize the specific understanding of "sanctity" (Goldman's general term for mana) in each society he discusses.

sciences.[40] "When I speak of these [mana-like] principles as forces, I do not use the word in a metaphorical sense; they behave like real forces. In a sense they are even physical forces that bring about physical effects mechanically... The totemic principle is at once a physical force and a moral power" (270–71/192). "Religious forces are real, no matter how imperfect the symbols with whose help they were conceived" (292/206).

The last appearance of mana in the *Elementary Forms* is in relation to the "negative cult" and the connection of the sacred to "contagion." For the purpose of this chapter, this is not the element on which I wish to dwell, rather it is Durkheim's return to a previously enunciated argument that religious forces, being "transfigured collective forces," are in no way inherent in the "outward and physical forms in which they are imagined." Religious forces are "superadded," "they do not have a place of their own anywhere" (461–62/327; cf. 327–28/230, 603–604/424). As an illustration, Durkheim cites Codrington on mana, italicizing the quote, mana "*is a force that is by no means fixed on a material object, but that can be carried on almost any sort of object*" (461/327 [see above, n. 37]). However, Durkheim's most persuasive example of this understanding of sacrality does not require an appeal to mana, but occurs quite early on in his interpretation of the Australian data in the context of thinking about the *tjurunga* and its "superadded" markings.

As I have argued elsewhere,[41] the linchpin of Durkheim's argument is the observation that "in themselves, the tjurunga are merely objects of wood and stone like so many others; they are distinguished from profane things of the same kind by only one particularity: the totemic mark is drawn or engraved upon them. That mark, and only that mark confers sacredness on them" (172/121). It is the nature of these "marks" that interests Durkheim and provides him with his key argument. The marks are non-representational, they do not represent natural "things." Hence,

[40] For an early statement, see Durkheim, *Le suicide: Etude de sociologie* (Paris, 1897); English translation (New York, 1951), 309–10: "Collective tendencies have an existence of their own; they are forces as real as cosmic forces, though of a different sort; they, likewise, affect the individual from without, though through other channels. The proof that the reality of collective tendencies is no less than that of cosmic forces is that this reality is demonstrated in the same way, by the uniformity of effects... Whatever they are called, the important thing is to recognize their reality and conceive of them as a totality of forces which cause us to act from without, like the physico-chemical forces to which we react. So truly are they things *sui generis* and not mere verbal entities that they may be measured... as is done with the intensity of electric currents or luminous foci. Thus, the basic proposition that social facts are objective... Of course it offends common sense. But science has encountered incredulity whenever it has revealed to men the existence of a force that has been overlooked."

[41] J. Z. Smith, *To Take Place: Toward Theory in Ritual* (Chicago, 1987), esp. pp. 106–8, and the notes on pp. 174–75. I have drawn on these pages, above.

they are to be derived from social rather than from sensory experience. While the argumentative move, not natural and therefore social, is a hallmark throughout Durkheim's work, here he develops a linguistic analogy. Although the Australians are fully capable of depicting natural phenomena with reasonable accuracy (e.g. in their rock or bark paintings), they do not do so when marking their tjurungas. Those marks "consist chiefly of geometric designs... having and only capable of having a conventional meaning. The relation between the sign and the things signified [*entre la figure et la chose figurée*] is so remote and indirect that the uninformed cannot see it. Only clan members can say what meaning they attach to this or that combination of lines... The meanings of these drawings are indeed so arbitrary that the same drawing can have two different meanings for the people of two totems" (178–79/126).

Durkheim does not develop this linguistic analogy further. It remained for Claude Lévi-Strauss, in 1950, to propose a linguistic–taxonomic understanding of mana.

Lévi-Strauss takes up the Durkheimian agendum in the context of writing on Hubert and Mauss's *General Theory of Magic*. "Conceptions of the mana type are so frequent and so widespread that we should ask ourselves if we are not in the presence of a universal and permanent form of thought which, far from being characteristic of only certain civilizations or alleged 'stages' of thought... will function in a certain situation of the mind in the face of things, one which must appear each time that this situation is given."[42] To elucidate this "situation," Lévi-Strauss calls attention to the "exceedingly profound remark" of Father Thavenet, quoted by Hubert and Mauss, and, from them, by Durkheim, with respect to Algonquin, that *manitou* "particularly refers to all beings which still have no common name, which are not familiar."[43] After giving a set of ethnographic examples, Lévi-Strauss draws the striking conclusion:

[42] C. Lévi-Strauss, "Introduction à l'œuvre de Marcel Mauss," ix–lii. Passage cited, p. xliii; cf. Baker's English translation, *Introduction to the Work of Marcel Mauss*, 53, which I have not quoted but have cited in parentheses below. Note Lévi-Strauss's quite different argument in *Totemism* (Boston, 1963), 31–32, where he argues on grounds of ethnographic accuracy against the Durkheimian confusion, resulting from the "totemic illusion," between totem, mana, and tabu.

[43] Lévi-Strauss, "Introduction," xliii (54). On Thavenet, see above, note 36. The original Italian reads: "*Quando si tratta di un essere animato che non ha alcun nome di specie, o del quale non si conosce il nome, lo si distingue con il nome generico di manito.*" Note, however, that this citation is immediately preceded by a more conventional understanding of the term, "*Credo che questa parola Manito è il nome generico nel quale sono compresi tutti gli esseri animati, di qualsiasi specie...*" (Teza, *Thavenet sulla lingua algonchina*, 17). To Lévi-Strauss's understanding of this quotation and the ethnographic illustrations he adduces can be added others such as W. K. Power, *Oglala Religion* (Lincoln, 1977), 47, who offers a short list of compound names employing the element *wakan* "which were applied to items newly obtained from other Indians or the white man."

Always and everywhere, notions of this [mana-]type intervene, somewhat as algebraic symbols, to represent a value of indeterminate signification, in itself empty of meaning and therefore susceptible to the reception of any meaning whatsoever. Thus [mana's] unique function is to make good a discrepancy between the signifier and the signified, or more precisely, to signal the fact that in this circumstance, on this occasion, or in this one of its manifestations, a relationship of inadequacy is established between the signified and the signifier to the detriment of the anterior relation of complimentarity.[44]

For Lévi-Strauss, the notion of mana does not pertain to the realm of an all but physical "reality," but rather to that of thought. Mana is not a substantive category, it is a linguistic one. Mana has a "semantic function." Mana marks discontinuity rather than continuity by representing, with precision, floating or undecided signification. "It is the function of notions of the mana-type to oppose themselves to the absence of signification without allowing, by themselves, any particular signification."[45] He clarifies this function with three analogies: the phonological zero, as adumbrated by Jakobson; algebraic symbols; and the use of nominal "place holders" (Boyer provides the English example of "stuff") for objects not yet encompassed by native taxonomy or nomenclature. By such placement, thought can continue despite such occasions of discontinuity.[46] Rather than the popular, "hot" analogy of electricity to mana, Lévi-Strauss has provided one of temporary cold storage. It is as if to the Israelites' question concerning manna, *mān hû*, "what is it?," the Maori and other Oceanic peoples would answer, "*mana*." It has been named as that whose name and taxon must be deferred.

This linguistic understanding drives Lévi-Strauss to the witty conclusion that, "in one case at least the notion of mana does present those characteristics of a secret power, a mysterious force, which Durkheim and Mauss attribute to it – that [singular case] is the role which it plays in their own system. There, truly, mana is mana!"[47]

As Hans Penner has persistently reminded his colleagues, "religion is constituted, or encompassed, by language. Language, in other words, is a necessary condition for the existence of religion: no language, no religion."[48] In this chapter, we have been concerned with two

---

[44] Lévi-Strauss, "Introduction," xliv (54).   [45] *Ibid.*, 1, n. 1 (omitted in Baker's translation).

[46] *Ibid.*, xlvii–l (59–64); cf. Boyer, *Tradition as Truth and Communication*, 27. Lévi-Strauss cites, in a footnote ("Introduction," 1, n. 1 [72, n. 18]), R. Jakobson and J. Lotz, "Notes on the French Phonemic Pattern," *Word* 5 (1949), reprinted in Jakobson, *Selected Writings* (The Hague, 1962), 1, 426–34, for the notion of a "*phonème zéro.*"

[47] Lévi-Strauss, "Introduction," xlv (57).

[48] H. Penner, "Holistic Analysis: Conjectures and Refutations," *Journal of the American Academy of Religion* 62 (1994): 989.

primary, serial, sense-making modes of linguistic activity: narrative and argument.

In the case of the biblical manna-narratives, too much scholarly energy has been expended on getting "behind" the word to some natural phenomenon as if that endeavor guaranteed its being of interest. If nothing else, the narrative interchangeability of the provision of manna, or quail, or water; the multiple examples of framing and reframing the provision-tale in the service of larger reflective schemes; the consequences of substituting the Greek *manna*, carrying its own set of complex systemic relations, for the Hebrew *mān* – all argue against such a conclusion. In the case of the argumentative use of the Oceanic mana, too much scholarly energy has been expended on getting "beneath" the word to either some supernatural "reality," as in the lineage from Marett to Eliade, or some powerful social "reality," analogous to a physical force, as in Durkheim, as if such an endeavor guaranteed its being of interest. In the service of this project, mana, and the words claimed to be its equivalent, were stripped of their linguistic status and removed from the sentences in which they were embedded. The result may be termed the "manic illusion."

I am far from certain, however, that we ought to rest content with reproducing native lexicography, and, thereby, give in to the prevalent ethos of localism, branding every attempt at generalization a Western imposition. It is one thing to argue for attention to the semantics and pragmatics of native speech, it is another to proclaim that "mana as an invisible medium of power was an invention of Europeans, drawing on their own folk metaphors of power and the theories of nineteenth century physics."[49] Merely substitute for "invention" the term "translation," which always entails discrepancy and therefore always requires critical judgment, and the difference becomes clearer.[50] Besides, giving primacy to native terminology yields, at best, lexical definitions which, historically and statistically, tell how a word is used. But lexical definitions are almost always useless for scholarly work. To remain content with how "they" understand "mana" may yield a proper description, but little explanatory power. (I take Lévi-Strauss to have, in fact, proposed a proper explanation; one that can be challenged only on theoretical grounds.)

[49] Keesing, "Rethinking Mana," 148.
[50] See further, J. Z. Smith, "A Twice-told Tale: The History of the History of Religion's History," in *Numen* 48 (2001): 131–46. Note that Keesing has given his views on translation in "Conventional Metaphors and Anthropological Metaphysics: The Problematic of Cultural Translation," *Journal of Anthropological Research*, 41 (1985): 201–17. His most valuable caution is that he remains a "skeptic about attributing deeper salience to other people's conventional metaphors than we do to our own."

How "they" use a word cannot substitute for the systematic stipulative and precising procedures by which the academy contests and seeks to control second-order, specialized usage. This, too, Penner has helped us to understand.[51]

[51] See, already, H. H. Penner and E. A. Yonan, "Is a Science of Religion Possible?" *Journal of Religion* 52 (1972), 107–33. See also, S. I. Landau, *Dictionaries: The Art and Craft of Lexicography* (Cambridge, 1989), 20. With respect to mana, while intended critically, see the comments by R. Firth, "The Analysis of Mana," as reprinted in Harding and Wallace, *Cultures of the Pacific*, pp. 325 and 318. "To the Tikopia, *manu* I am sure has not the connotation of an isolatable principle, a force, a power, or any other metaphysical abstraction . . . The interpretation in terms of such abstraction can only be the work of the anthropologist." "Treated in this manner, the word *mana* becomes something of a technical term describing a specialized abstraction of the theoretical anthropologist and, as such, may have little in common with the same term as used in native phraseology." Rather than being abjured, this difference needs to be accepted by students of religion. See further, J. Z. Smith, "Twice-told Tale."

Select bibliography

Abrams, H. M. *The Mirror and the Lamp: Romantic Theory and the Critical Tradition.* Oxford University Press, 1953.

Arnold, M. *Literature and Dogma.* New York: Macmillan, 1902.

Asad, Talal. *Genealogies of Religion: Discipline and Reasons of Power in Christianity and Islam.* Baltimore: Johns Hopkins University Press, 1993.

Astuti, R. "Are We All Natural Dualists? A Developmental Cognitive Approach." *Journal of the Royal Anthropological Institute* n.s. 7 (2001): 429–47.

Baker, F. *Introduction to the Work of Marcel Mauss.* London, 1987.

Baker, Lynne Rudder. *Saving Belief: A Critique of Physicalism.* Princeton University Press, 1987.

Barrett, J. L. "Exploring the Natural Foundations of Religion." *Trends in Cognitive Sciences* 4:1 (2000): 29–34.

Barrett, J. L. and F. C. Keil. "Anthropomorphism and God Concepts: Conceptualizing a Non-natural Entity." *Cognitive Psychology* 3 (1996): 219–47.

Barrett, J. L. and E. T. Lawson. "Ritual Intuitions." *Journal of Cognition and Culture* 1:2 (2001).

Barth, F. *Ritual and Knowledge among the Baktaman of New Guinea.* Oslo and New Haven, CT: Universitetsforlaget and Yale University Press, 1975.

Beattie, J. "Ritual And Social Change." *Man* 1 (1966): 67–74.

Bell, C. *Ritual Theory, Ritual Practice.* New York: Oxford University Press, 1992.

Ritual Perspectives and Dimensions. New York: Oxford University Press, 1997.

"Printing and Religion in China: Some Evidence from the *Taishang ganying pian.*" *Journal of Chinese Religions* 20 (Fall 1992): 173–86.

" 'A Precious Raft to Save the World': The Interaction of Scriptural Traditions and Printing in a Chinese Morality Book." *Late Imperial China* 17:1 (June 1996): 158–200.

"Performance." In *Critical Terms in the Study of Religion*, ed. Mark C. Taylor, 205–24. University of Chicago Press, 1998.

"Sects and Exercise: One Look at the Falungong." Unpublished paper, 2000.

"Acting Ritually: Evidence from the Social Life of Chinese Rites." In *The Blackwell Companion to Sociology of Religion*, ed. Richard Fenn, 371–87. London: Blackwell, 2001.

Bellah, R. *Beyond Belief: Essays on Religion in a Post-Traditional World.* New York: Harper and Row, 1970.

Berger, Peter L. *The Sacred Canopy: Elements of A Sociology of Religion*. New York: Doubleday, 1967.

Bloch, M. *From Blessing to Violence*. Cambridge University Press, 1986.

Prey into Hunter: The Politics of Religious Experience. New York: Cambridge University Press, 1992.

How We Think They Think: Anthropological Approaches to Cognition, Memory, and Literacy. Boulder, CO: Westview, 1998.

"Symbols, Song, Dance and Features of Articulation: Or Is Religion an Extreme Form of Traditional Authority?" *Archives Européennes de Sociologie* 15 (1974): 55–81.

"Language, Anthropology and Cognitive Science." *Man* 26, no. 2 (1991): 183–98.

"What Goes without Saying: The Conceptualisation of Zafirmaniry Society." In *Conceptualising Society*, ed. A. Kuper. London: Routledge, 1992.

Bloch, M., G. Solomon, and S. Zafimaniry Carey. "Understanding of What is Passed on from Parents to Children. A Cross-cultural Approach." *Journal of Cognition and Culture* 1:1 (2001): 43–68.

Bodenheimer, F. S. *The Coccidae of Palestine*. Zionist Organization Institute of Agriculture and Natural History, Agricultural Experiment Station Bulletin, 1. Tel Aviv, 1924.

"The Manna of Sinai," *Biblical Archaeologist* 10 (1947): 1–6. Reprint, *The Biblical Archaeologist Reader*, ed. G. E. Wright and D. N. Freedman, 76–80. Garden City, NJ, 1961.

"Fauna." *Interpreter's Dictionary of the Bible*. Vol. 2. Nashville, 1962.

Bodenheimer, F. S. and O. Theodor, *Ergebnisse der Sinai-Expedition 1927*. Leipzig, 1929.

Boyer, P. *Tradition as Truth and Communication: A Cognitive Description of Traditional Discourse*. Cambridge University Press, 1990.

The Naturalness of Religious Ideas. Berkeley: University of California Press, 1994.

Religion Explained: The Evolutionary Origins of Religious Thought. New York: Basic Books, 2001.

"Cognitive Aspects of Religious Ontologies: How Brain Processes Constrain Religious Concepts." In *Theory and Method in the Study of Religion*, ed. T. Ahlback. Donner Institute, 1998.

"Evolution of a Modern Mind and the Origins of Culture: Religious Concepts as a Limiting Case." In *Evolution and the Human Mind: Modularity, Language and Meta-Cognition*, ed. P. Carruthers and A. Chamberlin. Cambridge University Press, 2000.

Boyer, P. and C. Ramble. "Cognitive Templates for Religious Concepts: Cross-Cultural Evidence for Recall of Counter-intuitive Representations." *Cognitive Science* 25 (2001): 535–64.

Brandom, R. *Making It Explicit: Reasoning, Representing, and Discursive Commitment*. Cambridge, MA: Harvard University Press, 1994.

"Heidegger's Categories in *Being and Time*." *The Monist* 66 (1983): 387–409.

Braun, W. and R. McCutcheon, eds. *Guide to the Study of Religion*. New York: Cassell, 2000.

Buckley, SJ, M. J. "The Study of Religion and the Rhetoric of Atheism: A Paradox." Unpublished manuscript, 1999.

Budge, E. A. W. *Osiris and the Egyptian Resurrection*. London: Medici Society, 1911.

Burkert, W. *Creation of the Sacred: Tracks of Biology in Early Religions*. Cambridge, MA: Harvard University Press, 1996.

Cameron, H. Don. "The Upside-Down Cladogram: Problems in Manuscript Affiliation." In *Biological Metaphor and Cladistic Classification: An Interdisciplinary Perspective*, ed. H. M. Hoenigswald and L. P. Warner. Philadelphia: University of Pennsylvania Press, 1987.

Capell, A. "The Word 'Mana': A Linguistic Study." *Oceania* 9 (1938): 89–96.

Caro, M. de, ed. *Interpretations and Causes: New Perspectives on Donald Davidson's Philosophy*. Dordrecht: Kluwer, 1999.

Cassirer, E. *The Problem of Knowledge*. New Haven, CT: Yale University Press, 1981.

Chalmers, D. J. *The Conscious Mind: In Search of a Fundamental Theory*. Oxford University Press, 1996.

Chidester, D. "Material Terms for the Study of Religion." *Journal of the American Academy of Religion* 68:2 (June 2000): 367–79.

Childs, B. S. *The Book of Exodus: A Critical Theological Commentary*. Philadelphia: Westminster Press, 1974.

Ch'ung, Wang. "Taoist Untruths." In *The Columbia Anthology of Traditional Chinese Literature*, ed. Victor Mair, 62–77. New York: Columbia University Press, 1994.

Coats, G. W. *The Murmuring Motif in the Wilderness Traditions*. Washington, D.C.: Catholic Biblical Quarterly Monograph Series, 1968.

Codrington, R. H. *The Melanesians: Studies in Their Anthropology and Folk-lore*. 1st edn. Oxford, 1891. Reprint, New York, 1972.

"Letter to Max Müller" (July 7, 1877). In Max Müller, *Lectures on the Origin and Growth of Religion, as Illustrated by the Religions of India*. 1st edn. London, 1878.

Converse, P. "The Nature of Belief Systems in Mass Publics." In *Ideology and Discontent*, ed. David Apter, 206–61. New York: Free Press, 1964.

Cooke, S. A. "Manna." *Encyclopaedia Biblica*, ed. T. K. Cheyne and J. S. Black. Vol. 3. New York: Macmillan, 1902.

Creuzer, Friedrich. *Symbolik und Mythologie der alten Völker*. Leipzig and Darmstadt: Heyer und Leske, 1810–12.

Crocker, C. "My Brother the Parrot." *Animal Myth and Metaphors in South America*, ed. G. Urton. Salt Lake City: University of Utah Press, 1985.

Davaney, S. *Pragmatic Historicism: A Theology for the Twenty-First Century*. Albany: State University of New York Press, 2000.

Davidson, D. *Inquiries into Truth and Interpretation*. Oxford: Clarendon Press, 1984.

"A Coherence Theory of Truth and Knowledge." In *Truth and Interpretation: Perspectives on the Philosophy of Donald Davidson*, ed. Ernest Lepore, 307–19. London: Blackwell, 1986.

"The Myth of the Subjective." In *Relativism: Interpretation and Confrontation*, ed. Michael Krausz. Notre Dame, IN: University of Notre Dame Press, 1989.

"The Structure and Content of Truth." *Journal of Philosophy* 87 (1990): 281–328.

"Three Varieties of Knowledge." In *A. J. Ayer: Memorial Essays*, ed. A. Phillips Griffiths, 153–66. Cambridge University Press, 1991.

"Radical Interpretation Interpreted." In *Philosophical Perspectives 8: Logic and Language*, ed. James E. Tomberlin, 121–28. Atascadero, CA: Ridgeview Publishing Co., 1994.

"Could There Be a Science of Rationality?" *International Journal of Philosophical Studies* 3 (1995): 1–16.

"The Folly of Trying to Define Truth." *Journal of Philosophy* 94 (1997): 263–78.

"Reply to Kirk Ludwig." In *Donald Davidson: Truth, Meaning and Knowledge*, ed. Ursula M. Zeglen, 46–47. New York: Routledge, 1999.

"Interpretation: Hard in Theory, Easy in Practice." In *Interpretations and Causes: New Perspectives on Donald Davidson's Philosophy*, ed. M. de Caro, 31–44. Dordrecht: Kluwer, 1999.

"Truth Rehabilitated." In *Rorty and His Critics*, ed. Robert B. Brandom. Oxford: Blackwell, 2000.

Dawkins, R. "Snake Oil and Holy Water." *Forbes ASAP*, October 4, 1999.

Deely, J. *Basics of Semiotics*. Bloomington: University of Indiana Press, 1990.

Derrida, J. *Writing and Difference*. University of Chicago Press, 1978.

Detienne, M. *The Gardens of Adonis*. Atlantic Highlands, NJ: Humanities Press, 1977.

di Nola, A. M. "Religione degli Algonchini centrali." *Enciclopedia delle religioni*, ed. A. M. di Nola. Vol. 1. Florence, 1970.

Dieffenbach, E. *Travels in New Zealand*. London: J. Murray, 1843. Cited in the *Oxford English Dictionary, Supplement*, s.v., "mana."

Dominichini, J. P. *Les Dieux au Service des Rois. Histoire Orale des Sampin'Andriana*. Paris: Editions du centre National de recherche scientifiques, 1985.

Durkheim, E. *De la Division du travail social: Etude sur l'organisation des sociétés supérieures*. Paris, 1893; English translation, *The Division of Labor in Society*. New York, 1933.

Le suicide: Etude de sociologie. Paris, 1897; English translation, New York, 1951.

Les Formes élémentaires de la vie religieuse: Le système totémique en Australie, 2nd edn. Paris, 1922. English translation, *The Elementary Forms of Religious Life*. Trans. and with an Introduction by K. E. Fields. New York: The Free Press, 1995.

Leçons de sociologie: Physique des moeurs et du droit. Paris, 1950; English translation, *Professional Ethics and Civic Morals*. London, 1957, reprint, 1992.

"La Prohibition de l'inceste et ses origines." *Année sociologique* 1 (1898): 1–70.

"De la Définition des phénomènes religieux." *Année sociologique* 2 (1899): 1–28; English translation, "Concerning the Definition of Religious Phenomena." In *Durkheim on Religion*, ed. W. S. F. Pickering. Atlanta, 1994.

"Préface." *Année sociologique* 2 (1899).

Eco, U. *Semiotics and the Philosophy of Language.* Bloomington: University of Indiana Press, 1984.

Belief or Non-Belief: A Confrontation. New York: Arcade Publishing, 2000.

Edwards, J. C. *Ethics without Philosophy: Wittgenstein and the Moral Life.* Tampa: University of South Florida, 1982.

The Authority of Language: Heidegger, Wittgenstein, and the Threat of Philosophical Nihilism. Tampa: University of South Florida, 1990.

Eliade, M. "Methodological Remarks on the Study of Religious Symbolism." In *The History of Religions: Essays in Methodology,* ed. Mircea Eliade and Joseph M. Kitagawa, with preface by Jerald C. Brauer. University of Chicago Press, 1959.

Evans-Pritchard, E. *Nuer Religion.* Oxford University Press, 1956.

Feuerbach, L. *The Essence of Christianity.* Trans. George Eliot. New York: Harper & Row, 1957.

Firth, R. "The Analysis of Mana: An Empirical Approach." *Journal of the Polynesian Society* 49 (1940): 483–510. Reprint, *Tikopia Ritual and Belief.* Boston, 1968 and Th. G. Harding and B. J. Wallace, eds., *Cultures of the Pacific: Selected Readings.* New York, 1970.

Fish, S. *Professional Correctness: Literary Studies and Political Change.* New York: Clarendon Press, 1995.

Føllesdal, Dagfinn. "Intentionality and Rationality." In *Rationality, Relativism and the Human Sciences,* ed. J. Margolis, M. Krausz and R. M. Burian. Boston: Martinus Nijhoff, 1986.

Foucault, M. *The Order of Things: An Archeology of the Human Sciences.* New York: Vintage, 1973.

Frankenberry, N. "On the Very Idea of Symbolic Meaning." In *Interpreting Neville,* ed. J. Harley Chapman and Nancy Frankenberry. Albany: State University of New York Press, 1999.

Frankenberry, N. K. and H. H. Penner. "Clifford Geertz's Long-Lasting Moods, Motivations, and Metaphysical Conceptions." *Journal of Religion* 79 (1999): 617–40.

Frankenberry, N. K. and H. H. Penner, eds. *Language, Truth, and Religious Belief: Studies in Twentieth-Century Theory and Method in Religion.* Atlanta: Scholars Press, 1999.

Frazer, J. G. *The Golden Bough.* 3rd edn. Vol. 6. London: Macmillan, 1935.

Freud, S. "Obsessive Actions and Religious Practices." *Standard Edition* IX: 122–23.

Frisina, W. "Response to J. Wesley Robbins' 'Donald Davidson and Religious Belief.'" *American journal of Theology and Philosophy* 17:2 (May 1996): 157–66.

Geertz, C. "Religion as a Cultural System." In *Anthropological Approaches to the Study of Religion,* ed. Michael Banton, 87–125. London: Tavistock, 1966. Reprint, *The Interpretation of Cultures: Selected Essays.* New York: Basic Books, 1973.

Geuss, Raymond. *The Idea of a Critical Theory: Habermas and the Frankfurt School.* New York: Cambridge University Press, 1981.

Girard, R. *La violence et le sacré*. Paris: B. Grasset, 1972.

Godelier, M. *The Enigma of the Gift*. Trans. Nora Scott. University of Chicago Press, 1999; originally published *L'Enigme du don*. Paris, 1996.

Godlove, T. *Religion, Interpretation and Diversity of Belief: The Framework Model from Kant to Durkheim to Davidson*. New York: Cambridge University Press, 1989. Reprint, Mercer University Press, 1997.

  "Interpretation, Reductionism, and Belief in God." *The Journal of Religion* 69:2 (1989): 184–98.

Goldman, I. *The Mouth of Heaven: An Introduction to Kwakiutl Religious Thought*. New York, 1975.

  Ancient Polynesian Society. University of Chicago Press, 1970.

Graf, F. W. "The German Theological Sources and Protestant Church Politics." In *Weber's Protestant Ethic: Origins, Evidence, Contexts*, ed. Hartmut Lehmann and Guenther Roth. New York: Cambridge University Press, 1993.

Graham, A. C. *Disputers of the Tao*. Chicago: Open Court, 1989.

Griffin, D. *Reenchantment Without Supernaturalism: A Process Philosophy of Religion*. Ithaca, NY: Cornell University Press, 2000.

Guthrie, S. *Faces in the Clouds: A New Theory of Religion*. Oxford University Press, 1993.

Hanson, C. *A Taoist Theory of Chinese Thought*. New York: Oxford University Press, 1992.

Harding, S. F. *The Book of Jerry Falwell: Fundamentalist Language and Politics*. Princeton University Press, 2000.

Hardwick, C. *Events of Grace: Naturalism, Existentialism, and Theology*. Cambridge University Press, 1996.

Hardwicke, T. *Asiatick Researches*, 14 (1801): 182.

Harman, G. "Meaning and Semantics." In *Reasoning, Meaning, and Mind*. Oxford University Press, 1999.

Harman, G. and J. Jarvis Thomson. *Moral Relativism and Moral Objectivity*. Cambridge: Blackwell, 1996.

Harrison, J. E. *Themis: A Study of the Social Origins of Greek Religion*. 1st edn. Cambridge, 1912; 2nd edn. Cambridge, 1927, reprint, 1962.

Hegel, G. W. F. *Phenomenology of Spirit*. Trans. A. V. Miller. Oxford: Clarendon Press, 1977.

Hewitt, J. N. B. "Orenda and A Definition of Religion." *American Anthropologist* n.s. 4 (1902): 33–46.

Hogbin, H. I. "Mana." *Oceania* 6 (1936): 241–74.

Hopkins, J. "Wittgenstein, Davidson and Radical Interpretation." In *The Philosophy of Donald Davidson*, ed. Lewis Edwin Hahn. Chicago: Open Court, 1999.

Horton, R. *Patterns of Thought in Africa and the West*. Cambridge University Press, 1993.

  "Tradition and Modernity Revisited." In *Rationality and Relativism*, ed. M. Hollis and S. Lukes, 201–60. Oxford: Blackwell, 1982.

Horwich, P. *Meaning*. New York: Oxford University Press, 1998.

Hubaux, J. and M. Leroy. *Le Mythe du Phénix dans les littératures grecque et latine.* Liège–Paris, 1939.

Hubert, H. "Etude sommaire de la représentation du temps dans la religion et la magie." *Annuaire de l'Ecole Pratique des Hautes Etudes, section des sciences religieuses* (1905): 30.

Hubert, H. and M. Mauss. "Esquisse d'un théorie générale de la magie." *Année sociologique* 7 (1904): 1–146. English translation, *A General Theory of Magic.* London, 1972.

Hume, D. *Natural History of Religion*, ed. H. E. Root. Stanford University Press, 1957.

Humphrey, C. and J. Laidlaw. *The Archetypal Actions of Ritual.* Oxford: Clarendon Press, 1994.

Hymes, R. "Truth, Falsity, and Pretense in Sung China." Unpublished paper.

Jackson, T. *Love Disconsoled.* Cambridge University Press, 1999.

Jakobson, R. and J. Lotz. "Notes on the French Phonemic Pattern." *Word* 5 (1949). Reprint, R. Jakobson, *Selected Writings.* The Hague, 1962.

James, W. *A Pluralistic Universe.* Cambridge, MA: Harvard University Press, 1977.
Essays in Philosophy. Cambridge, MA: Harvard University Press, 1978.
The Will to Believe and Other Essays in Popular Philosophy. Cambridge, MA: Harvard University Press, 1979.
The Principles of Psychology. Cambridge, MA: Harvard University Press, 1983.
Pragmatism. Cambridge, MA: Harvard University Press, 1985.
The Varieties of Religious Experience. Cambridge, MA: Harvard University Press, 1985.

Jensen, L. M. *Manufacturing Confucianism.* Durham: Duke University Press, 1997.

Johnston, M. "Objectivity Refigured: Pragmatism without Verificationism." In *Reality, Representation, and Projection*, ed. John Haldane and Crispin Wright. Oxford University Press, 1993.

Jordan, D. K. "The jiaw of Shigaang (Taiwan): An Essay in Folk Interpretation." *Asian Folklore Studies* 35:2 (1976): 81–107.

Kaiser, A. "Neue naturwissenschaftliche Forschungen auf der Sinaihalbinsel." *Zeitschrift des deutschen Palästina-Vereins* 53 (1930): 63–75.

Kaminer, W. *Sleeping with Extra-Terrestrials: The Rise of Irrationalism and the Perils of Piety.* New York: Pantheon, 1999.

Keesing, R. M. "Rethinking Mana." *Journal of Anthropological Research* 46 (1984): 137–56.
"Conventional Metaphors and Anthropological Metaphysics: The Problematic of Cultural Translation." *Journal of Anthropological Research* 41 (1985): 201–17.

Keil, F. C. *Concepts, Kinds, and Cognitive Development.* Cambridge, MA: MIT Press, 1989.

Kierkegaard, S. *Fear and Trembling/Repetition.* Trans. H. and E. Hong. Princeton University Press, 1983.
Philosophical Fragments/Johannes Climacus. Trans. H. and E. Hong. Princeton University Press, 1985.

Kittay, E. F. *Metaphor: Its Cognitive Force and Linguistic Structure*. Oxford: Clarendon Press, 1987.

Kolakowski, L. *Religion*. London: Collins/Fontana, 1982.

Kopitoff, I. "Ancestors as Elders." *Africa* 41:11 (1971): 129–42.

Kulik, J. and R. Brown. "Flashbulb Memory." In *Memory Observed: Remembering in Natural Contexts*, ed. U. Neisser. San Francisco: W. H. Freeman, 1982.

Lampe, G. W. H. *A Patristic Greek Lexicon*. Oxford: Clarendon Press, 1961–68.

Landau, S. I. *Dictionaries: The Art and Craft of Lexicography*. Cambridge University Press, 1989.

Lawson, E. T. *Bringing Ritual to Mind: Psychological Foundations of Cultural Forms*. Cambridge University Press, 2002.

"Religious Ideas and Practices." In *The MIT Encyclopedia of the Cognitive Sciences*, ed. Frank Keil and Robert Wilson. Cambridge, MA: MIT Press, 1999.

"The Psychology of Religious Agency." In *Religion in Mind*, ed. Jensine Andresen. Cambridge University Press, 2000.

"Toward a Cognitive Science of Religion." *Numen* 47 (2000): 338–49.

"Cognition." In *Guide to the Study of Religion*, ed. Willi Braun and Russell T. McCutcheon. London: Cassell, 2000.

Lawson, E. T. and R. N. McCauley. *Rethinking Religion: Connecting Cognition and Culture*. Cambridge University Press, 1990.

Leach, E. R. *Political Systems of Highland Burma*. Cambridge, MA: Harvard University Press, 1954.

Lehmann, F. R. *Mana: Eine begriffsgeschichtliche Untersuchung auf ethnologische Grundlage*. Leipzig, 1915; 2nd edn *Mana: Der Begriff des 'ausserordenlich Wirkungsvollen' bei Südseevölkern*. Leipzig: O. Spamer, 1922.

"Versuche, die Bedeutung des Wortes Mana." In *Festschrift Walter Baetke*, ed. K. Rudolph. Weimar, 1966.

Lenclud, G. "Vues de l'Esprit, Art de l'Autre." *Terrain* 14 (1990).

"Beliefs, Culture and Reflexivity." Unpublished manuscript, n.d.

Lepore, E., ed. *Truth and Interpretation: Perspectives on the Philosophy of Donald Davidson*. London: Blackwell, 1986.

Lévi-Strauss, C. *Totemism*. Boston: Beacon Press, 1963.

The Savage Mind. Trans. George Weidenfeld and Nicolson, Ltd. University of Chicago Press, 1966.

The Naked Man. New York: Harper & Row, 1981.

Introduction to the Work of Marcel Mauss. Trans. F. Baker. London: Routledge & Kegan Paul, 1987.

"Introduction à l'œuvre de Marcel Mauss." In M. Mauss, *Sociologie et Anthropologie*. Paris, 1950. English translation, Lévi-Strauss, *Introduction to the Work of Marcel Mauss*. London, 1987.

Liddell, H. G. and R. Scott. *A Greek–English Lexicon*. Rev. edn. Oxford: Clarendon Press, 1968.

Lopez, Donald S., Jr. "Belief." In *Critical Terms for Religious Studies*, ed. Mark C. Taylor, 21–35. University of Chicago, 2000.

Löw, I. *Die Flora der Jüden*. Vol. 3. Vienna–Leipzig, 1928–34.

Macalister, A. "Manna," in *Dictionary of the Bible*. Vol. 3. Ed. J. Hastings. New York, 1900.

McCauley, R. N. and E. T. Lawson. *Bringing Ritual to Mind: Psychological Foundations of Cultural Forms*. Cambridge University Press, 2002.

MacClancy, J. "Mana: An Anthropological Metaphor." *Oceania* 57 (1986): 148.

McDannell, C. *Material Christianity: Religion and Popular Culture in America*. New Haven: Yale University Press, 1995.

McDowell, J. *Philosophy and Phenomenological Research*. 67:1 (March 1997): 157.

Makarius, L. *Le Sacré et la violation des interdits*. Paris, 1974.

Malina, B. J. *The Palestinian Manna Tradition*. Leiden: E. J. Brill, 1968.

Malinowski, B. *Magic, Science and Religion*. New York: Anchor Books, 1954.

Marett, R. R. "Pre-animistic Religion." *Folk-Lore* 11 (1900): 162–82.

"From Spell to Prayer." *Folk-Lore* 15 (1904): 132–65. Reprint, Marett, *The Threshold of Religion*. 1st edn. London, 1909.

"The Conception of Mana." *Transactions of the 3rd International Congress of the History of Religions*. Oxford, 1908.

"The Tabu-Mana Formulation as a Minimum Definition of Religion." *Archiv für Religionswissenschaft* 12 (1909): 186–94. Reprint, J. Waardenburg, *Classical Approaches to the Study of Religion*, The Hague, 1973, 1: 258–63.

"Mana." In *Encyclopaedia of Religion and Ethics*, ed. J. Hastings. New York, 1916.

"Mana." In *Encyclopaedia Britannica*. 14th edn. (1929).

Mauss, M. "An Intellectual Self-Portrait." In *The Sociological Domain: The Durkheimians and the Founding of French Sociology*, ed. Ph. Besnard, 149. Cambridge University Press, 1983.

Mazuzawa, T. "From Theology to World Religions." In *Secular Theories on Religion: Current Perspectives*, ed. Tim Jensen and Mikael Rothstein, 149–66. University of Copenhagen, 2000.

Meyeroff, B. "A Death in Due Time: Construction of the Self and Culture in Ritual Drama." In *Rite, Drama, Festival, Spectacle*, ed. John J. MacAloon. Philadelphia: Institute for the Study of Human Issues, 1984.

Mihelic, J. L. "Manna." *Interpreter's Dictionary of the Bible*. Vol. 3. Nashville, 1962.

Mill, J. S. *On Liberty*. Indianapolis, IN: Hackett, 1978.

Monk, R. *Ludwig Wittgenstein: The Duty of Genius*. London: Penguin, 1990.

Mungello, D. E., ed. *The Chinese Rites Controversy: Its History and Meaning*. Nettetal: Steyler Verlag, 1994.

Murdock, G. P. *Our Primitive Contemporaries*. New York: The Macmillan Company, 1934.

Nagel, T. *The View from Nowhere*. New York: Oxford University Press, 1986.

Needham, R. *Belief, Language and Experience*. University of Chicago Press, and Oxford: Blackwell, 1972.

Neville, R. C. *The Truth of Broken Symbols*. Albany, State University of New York Press, 1996.

"Responding to My Critics." In *Interpreting Neville*, ed. J. Harley Chapman and Nancy Frankenberry. Albany: State University of New York Press, 1999.

Nietzsche, F. "The Anti-Christ." In *Twilight of the Idols/The Antichrist*. Trans. R. J. Hollingdale. New York: Penguin, 1968.
  "On Truth and Lies in an Extra-Moral Sense." In *The Portable Nietzsche*, ed. Walter Kaufman, 42. New York: Viking Press, 1954.
Pals, S. "Intellect." In *Guide to the Study of Religion*. New York: Cassell, 2000.
Paper, J. *The Spirits are Drunk: Comparative Approaches to Chinese Religion*. Albany: State University of New York Press, 1995.
Peirce, C. S. "The Fixation of Belief." In *Writings of Charles Sanders Peirce*, ed. C. J. W. Kloesel. Bloomington: Indiana University Press, 1986.
Penner, H. H. *Impasse and Resolution: A Critique of the Study of Religion*. New York: Peter Lang, 1989.
  "Holistic Analysis: Conjectures and Refutations." *Journal of the American Academy of Religion*, 62 (1994).
  "Why Does Semantics Matter to the Study of Religion?" *Method and Theory in the Study of Religion* 7:3 (1995): 221-49.
  "Interpretation." In *Guide to the Study of Religion*, ed. Willi Braun and Russell T. McCutcheon. London and New York: Cassell, 2000.
Penner, H. H., ed. *Teaching Lévi-Strauss*. Atlanta, GA: Scholars Press, 1998.
Penner, H. H. and E. A. Yonan. "Is a Science of Religion Possible?" *Journal of Religion* 52 (1972): 107-33.
Pouillon, J. "Remarques sur le verb 'croire.'" In *La Fonction Symbolique*, ed. M. Izard and P. Smith. Paris: Gallimard, 1979.
Powers, W. K. *Oglala Religion*. Lincoln: University of Nebraska Press, 1977.
Propp, W. H. *Water in the Wilderness*. Atlanta, GA: Scholars Press, 1987.
Proudfoot, W. *Religious Experience*. Berkeley: University of California Press, 1985.
  "William James on an Unseen Order." *Harvard Theological Review* 93:1 (2000): 66.
Ramberg, B. *Donald Davidson's Philosophy of Language*. Oxford: Blackwell, 1989.
Rappaport, R. "The Obvious Aspects of Ritual." In *Ecology, Meaning and Religion*. Richmond, NC: North Atlantic Books, 1979.
  Ritual and Religion in the Making of Humanity. Cambridge University Press, 1999.
Ray, B. C. *Myth, Ritual, and Kingship in Buganda*. New York: Oxford University Press, 1991.
Ricoeur, P. *Freud and Philosophy: An Essay on Interpretation*. New Haven, CT: Yale University Press, 1970.
Riesebrodt, M. "Robert Ranulph Marett." In *Klassiker der Religionswissenschaft von Friederich Schleiermacher bis Mircea Eliade*, ed. A. Michaels, 171-84, 383-84. Munich, 1997.
Robbins, J. W. "Donald Davidson and Religious Belief." *American Journal of Theology and Philosophy* 17:2 (May 1996): 141-56.
Rorty, R. *Philosophy and the Mirror of Nature*. Princeton University Press, 1979.
  Contingency, Irony, and Solidarity. Cambridge University Press, 1989.
  Essays on Heidegger and Others. Cambridge University Press, 1991.
  Objectivity, Relativism, And Truth: Philosophical Papers. Cambridge University Press, 1991.
  Truth and Progress. New York: Cambridge University Press, 1998.

Philosophy and Social Hope. New York: Penguin, 1999.
"Pragmatism, Davidson, and Truth." *Objectivity, Relativism, and Truth*. Cambridge University Press, 1991.
"Representation, Social Practice, and Truth." *Objectivity, Relativism, and Truth*. Cambridge University Press, 1991.
"Religion as Conversation-stopper." In *Common Knowledge* 3:1 (Spring 1994): 1–6; Reprint, Rorty, *Philosophy and Social Hope*.
"Religious Faith, Intellectual Responsibility, and Romance." In *The Cambridge Companion to William James*, ed. Ruth Ann Putnam, 84–102. Cambridge University Press, 1997.
"Pragmatism as Romantic Polytheism." In *The Revival of Pragmatism: New Essays on Social Thought, Law, and Culture*, ed. Morris Dickstein, 21–36. Durham and London: Duke University Press, 1998.
Rosaldo, R. *Ilongot Headhunting 1883–1944: A Study in Society and History*. Stanford University Press, 1980.
Culture and Truth: The Remaking of Social Analysis. Boston: Beacon Press, 1989. Reprint, 1993.
"Of Headhunters and Soldiers: Separating Cultural and Ethical Relativism." *Santa Clara Magazine* 42:2 (Fall 2000): 18–21.
Ross, L. D. "The Intuitive Psychologist and His Shortcomings: Distortions in the Attribution Process." *Advances in Experimental Social Psychology, Ed. L. Berkowitz* 10 (1977): 173–220.
Santurri, E. "Nihilism Revisited." *Journal of Religion* (January 1991): 67–78.
Schelling, F. W. J. von. *Werke* 6. Munich: Beck, 1924.
Schery, R. W. "Manna." In *Encyclopaedia Britannica*. Vol. 14 (1969): 797.
Schilbrack, K. "The Study of Religious Belief after Davidson." *Method and Theory in the Study of Religion* 14:2 (2002).
Schopen, G. "Relic." In *Critical Terms for Religious Studies*, ed. Mark C. Taylor, 256–68. University of Chicago Press, 2000.
Sellars, W. *Empiricism and the Philosophy of Mind*. Cambridge, MA: Harvard University Press, 1997.
Shaffer, E. S. *'Kubla Khan' and the Fall of Jerusalem*. Cambridge University Press, 1975.
Sharpe, E. J. "Preanimism." In *Encyclopedia of Religion*, ed. M. Eliade, 503. Vol. 11. New York, 1987.
Shermer, M. *Why People Believe Weird Things: Pseudoscience, Superstition and Other Confusions of Our Time*. New York: W. H. Freeman and Company, 1997.
How We Believe: The Search For God in an Age of Science. New York: W. H. Freeman and Company, 2000.
Shweder, R. A. "Anthropology's Romantic Rebellion Against the Enlightenment, or There's More to Thinking than Reason and Evidence." In *Culture Theory: Essays on Mind, Self, and Emotion*, ed. Richard A. Shweder and Robert A. LeVine, 27–66. Cambridge University Press, 1984.
"Post-Nietzschian Anthropology: The Idea of Multiple Objective Worlds." In *Relativism: Interpretation and Confrontation*, ed. Michael Krauz, 99–139. Notre Dame University Press, 1989.

Skrupskelis, I. and E. Berkeley, eds. *The Correspondence of William James*. Vol. 5. Charlottesville, VA: University of Virginia Press, 1992.

Smith, B. H. *Belief and Resistance: Dynamics of Contemporary Intellectual Controversy*. Cambridge, MA: Harvard University Press, 1997.

Smith, H. *The World's Religions* (formerly *Religions of the World*, 1958) San Francisco: HarperCollins, 1991.

Smith, J. Z. "I am a Parrot (Red)." In *Map Is Not Territory: Studies in the History of Religions*. Leiden: E. J. Brill, 1978. Reprint 1993.

Imagining Religion: From Babylon to Jonestown. University of Chicago Press, 1982.

To Take Place: Toward Theory in Ritual. University of Chicago Press, 1987.

Drudgery Divine: On the Comparison of Early Christianities and the Religions of Late Antiquity. University of Chicago Press, 1990.

"Religion, Religions, Religious." *Critical Terms for Religious Studies*, ed. Mark C. Taylor. University of Chicago Press, 2000.

"A Twice-told Tale: The History of the History of Religion's History." *Numen* 48 (2001): 131–46.

Smith, W. C. *Belief and History*. Cambridge, MA: Harvard University Press, 1997.

"Belief: A Reply to Response," *Numen* 27:2 (1980): 147–255.

Spence, J. D. *The Memory Palace of Matteo Ricci*. New York: Viking, 1984.

The Search for Modern China. New York: Norton, 1990.

Spencer, B. and F. J. Gillen. *The Native Tribes of Central Australia*. London, 1899. Reprint, New York, 1968.

Sperber, D. *On Anthropological Knowledge*. Cambridge University Press, 1983.

Rethinking Symbolism. Cambridge University Press, 1994.

Explaining Culture: A Naturalistic Approach. London: Blackwell, 1996.

"Apparently Irrational Beliefs." In *Rationality and Relativism*, ed. M. Hollis and S. Lukes. Oxford: Blackwell, 1982.

"Intuitive and Reflexive Beliefs." *Mind and Language* 12:1: 67–83.

Spiro, M. "Religion: Some Problems of Definition and Explanation." In *Anthropological Approaches to the Study of Religion*, ed. M. Banton. London: Tavistock, 1966.

Stark, R. "Rationality." In *Guide to the Study of Religion*, ed. W. Braun and R. T. McCutcheon. New York: Cassell, 2000.

Stocking, Jr., G. W. *After Tylor: British Social Anthropology 1888–1951*. Madison: University of Wisconsin Press, 1995.

Strenski, I. *Four Theories of Myth in Twentieth-Century History*. University of Iowa Press, 1987.

Stromberg, P. "Consensus and Variation in the Interpretation of Religious Symbolism: A Swedish Example." *American Ethnologist* 8 (1981): 544–59.

Stout, J. *The Flight From Authority*. University of Notre Dame Press, 1981.

Ethics After Babel. Boston: Beacon Press, 1988, 2001.

Tambiah, S. *Culture, Thought And Social Action*. Cambridge, MA: Harvard University Press, 1975.

"A Performative Approach to Ritual." In *Culture, Thought, and Social Action*. Cambridge, MA: Harvard University Press, 1985.

Taylor, M. C., ed. *Critical Terms for Religious Studies*. University of Chicago Press, 2000.

Taylor, R. *Te Ika a Maui, or New Zealand and its Inhabitants*. 1st edn. London: Wertheim and Macintosh, 1855, as cited in the *Oxford English Dictionary, Supplement*, s.v. "mana."

Te Ika A Maui. 2nd edn. London, 1870.

Teza, E. *Saggi inediti de lingua Americana: Appunti bibliografici*. Pisa, 1868.

Intorno agli studi del Thavenet sulla lingua algonchina: Osservazioni di E. Teza. Pisa, 1880.

Thompson, S. *Motif-Index of Folk-Literatur*. Rev. edn. Copenhagen and Bloomington: Indiana University Press, 1955–58.

Thourangeau, R. and R. Sternberg. "Aptness in Metaphor." *Cognitive Psychology* 13 (1981): 27–55.

Tomberlin, J. E. *Philosophical Perspectives 8: Logic and Language*. Atascadero, CA: Ridgeview Publishing Co., 1994.

Tregear, E. *The Maori–Polynesian Comparative Dictionary*. Christchurch: Whitcome and Tombs, 1891. Reprint, 1969.

Turner, V. *The Forest Of Symbols*. Ithaca, NY: Cornell University Press, 1967.

Tylor, E. B. *Primitive Culture*. 2 vols. London: J. Murray, 1871.

Tzu, Mo. "On Ghosts." In *The Columbia Anthology of Traditional Chinese Literature*, ed. Victor Mair, 31–39. New York: Columbia University Press, 1994.

Valeri, V. *Kingship and Sacrifice: Ritual and Society in Ancient Hawaii*. University of Chicago Press, 1985.

van den Broek, R. *The Myth of the Phoenix According to Classical and Early Christian Traditions*. Leiden: E. J. Brill, 1972.

White, J. *The Ancient History of the Maori: His Mythology and Traditions*. Wellington: G. Didsbury, 1887–90.

Whitehouse, H. *Inside the Cult*. Oxford: Clarendon Press, 1995.

Arguments and Icons. Oxford University Press, 2000.

Wiebe, D. "On the Transformation of 'Belief' and the Domestication of 'Faith' in the Academic Study of Religion." *Method and Theory in the Study of Religion* 4:1–2 (1992): 47–67; reprised in "The Role of 'Belief' in the Study of Religion." *Numen* 26:2 (1979): 234–49.

Williams, M. "Meaning and Deflationary Truth." *Journal of Philosophy* 96:11 (1999): 545–64.

Williamson, R. W. *Essays in Polynesian Ethnology*. Cambridge University Press, 1939.

Wittgenstein, L. *Philosophical Investigations*. Oxford: Blackwell, 1953.

Remarks on Frazer's Golden Bough, ed. Rush Rhees, trans. A. C. Miles, revised by Rush Rhees. Atlantic Highlands, NJ: Humanities Press, Inc., 1979.

"Lectures on Religious Belief." In *L. Wittgenstein: Lectures and Conversations on Aesthetics, Psychology and Religious Belief*, edited and trans. Cyril Barrett, 54–72. Berkeley: University of California, 1967.

"Religious Belief." In *Language, Truth and Religious Belief: Studies in Twentieth-Century Theory and Method in Religion*, ed. Nancy K. Frankenberry and Hans H. Penner, 311–28. Atlanta, GA: Scholars Press, 1999.

Wolf, A. P. "Gods, Ghosts, and Ancestors." In *Religion and Ritual in Chinese Society*. Stanford University Press, 1974.

Wolf, M. "The Woman Who Didn't Become a Shaman." In *A Thrice Told Tale*. Stanford University Press, 1992.

Wong, D. B. *Moral Relativity*. Berkeley: University of California Press, 1984.

Xiaotong, Fei. "The World Without Ghosts." In *Land Without Ghosts*, ed. R. David Arkush and Leo O. Lee, 175–81. Berkeley: University of California, 1989.

Yü, Han. "Memorial on the Bone of the Buddha." In *Sources of Chinese Tradition*. Vol. 1, ed. William Theodore de Bary, Wing-Tsit Chan, and Burton Watson, 372–74. New York: Columbia University Press, 1960.

Zeglen, U. M., ed. *Donald Davidson: Truth, Meaning and Knowledge*. New York: Routledge, 1999.

Zuntz, G. *An Inquiry into the Transmission of the Plays of Euripides*. Cambridge University Press, 1965.

Index